THE DYNAMICS OF RELIGIOUS ORGANIZATIONS

Other Books by the Author

The Campus Clergyman (1966)

Religion in Social Context: Tradition and Transition (with N. J. Demerath III, 1968)

The School Prayer Decisions: From Court Policy to Local Practice (with K. M. Dolbeare, 1971)

The Structure of Human Society (with others, 1975)

Varieties of Civil Religion (with R. N. Bellah, 1980)

The Role of Ideology in Church Participation (1980)

The Protestant Presence in Twentieth-Century America: Religion and Political Culture (1992)

Religion and Personal Autonomy: The Third Disestablishment in America (1992)

With Liberty for All: Freedom of Religion in the United States (1998)

Soka Gakkai in America: Accommodation and Conversion (with D. W. Machacek, 1999)

Books edited by the author

Sociologists at Work: The Craft of Social Research (1964)

American Mosaic: Social Patterns of Religion in the United States (with B. Johnson, 1970)

Beyond the Classics? Essays in the Scientific Study of Religion (with C. Y. Glock, 1974)

The Sacred in a Secular Age: Toward Revision in the Scientific Study of Religion (1985)

The Future of New Religious Movements (with D. G. Bromley, 1987)

The Dynamics of Religious Organizations

The Extravasation of the Sacred and Other Essays

PHILLIP E. HAMMOND

OXFORD
UNIVERSITY PRESS

OXFORD

UNIVERSITY PRESS

Great Clarendon Street, Oxford OX2 6DP

Oxford University Press is a department of the University of Oxford.
It furthers the University's objective of excellence in research, scholarship,
and education by publishing worldwide in

Oxford New York

Athens Auckland Bangkok Bogotá Buenos Aires Calcutta
Cape Town Chennai Dar es Salaam Delhi Florence Hong Kong Istanbul
Karachi Kuala Lumpur Madrid Melbourne Mexico City Mumbai
Nairobi Paris São Paulo Singapore Taipei Tokyo Toronto Warsaw

and associated companies in Berlin Ibadan

Oxford is a registered trade mark of Oxford University Press
in the UK and in certain other countries

Published in the United States
by Oxford University Press Inc., New York

British Library Cataloguing in Publication Data

Data available

Library of Congress Cataloging in Publication Data

Data available

ISBN 0–19–829762–9

1 3 5 7 9 10 8 6 4 2

Typeset by Hope Services (Abingdon) Ltd.
Printed in Great Britain
on acid-free paper by
Biddles Ltd.,
Guildford & King's Lynn

*To the graduate students who, for four decades,
gave me the privilege of working with them.*

FOREWORD

David W. Machacek

In 1999 the *Los Angeles Times* reported that abstinence-only programs are gaining support both from educators concerned about problems of teen pregnancy and from the federal government, which now offers matching grant incentives to states incorporating abstinence education into their sex education programs.[1]

The debate over what gets taught about sex in public schools necessarily raises issues of religious values and morality. Thus that debate highlights, importantly to the essays in this book, the dilemma now facing American society as a result of the reality of religious pluralism. As Americans become more and more religiously plural, the vestiges of a one-time Protestant Christian consensus increasingly disappears from public institutions. For churches, this means a certain loss of influence over public affairs. As churches lose some of the functions they once served in defining American culture, other institutions step in. In teaching abstinence, for instance, the public schools have, in a sense, adopted a function that has traditionally been the job of religious organizations—teaching morality. We have here an excellent example of what Hammond describes in the first essay as the 'extravasation' of the sacred. The taking-over of moral education by public schools illustrates a certain loss of sovereignty by religious organizations; while secular institutions of education gain some of the sovereignty over public morality that the churches lose. The sacred does not simply disappear, therefore, but seeps out of one vessel into another. Each of the essays in Part I of this book addresses the significance of this process for religious organizations in America.

We need not look far to find where the sacred seeped: in the present example it is found in school board meetings and congressional debates. Although some opponents of the abstinence legislation accuse conservatives of passing stealth legislation, it is notable that the abstinence-only education funding was approved as part of a welfare reform bill. This points to the issue raised in Part II of this book: that religious conviction—the sacred—can and does have a place in American public life, but it must be advanced in terms that are not specific to particular religious viewpoints. It must be promoted, in

[1] Smith, L., 'Chastity makes a comeback', *LA Times* (10 August 1999), A1, 14.

other words, in terms on which all—whatever their religious viewpoint—can agree.

Many churches may applaud the abstinence-only funding as a victory over what they regard as value-neutral, 'Secular Humanism' (upper case), but in truth, the language and logic used by both schools and government to promote sexual morality *is* that of secular humanism (lower case), and, Hammond argues, so it must be. In other words, the schools are not promoting abstinence *because* churches define sex outside of marriage as immoral and thus demand that public institutions of education conform sex education classes to their standards of morality. Rather, schools promote abstinence as an effective means of stemming the tide of social, psychological, and physical health problems associated with sexual promiscuity—problems that, in principle, all citizens recognize. To put the issue another way, to promote abstinence as a response to rising sexual immorality would be an unconstitutional establishment of a sectarian position, but to promote abstinence as an effective means of responding to problems of unwanted pregnancy, sexually transmitted diseases, and the sexual abuse of minors is not an unconstitutional establishment, even if the people calling for such legislation are motivated by their religious convictions. What the reader will understand much better after reading Part II of this book is that religious convictions can inform public policy in a secular society, but the logic of such policies must be framed in terms of the general public welfare, and the language used to debate the merits of public policy must be a language transcending the particularities of any sectarian viewpoint.

The essays in this volume, then, provide a way to understand the changing place and function of religion in American social life. True to Phillip Hammond's form, they are written with a clarity that makes complex insights accessible to a broad audience. As one of those who collaborated on two of these essays with Professor Hammond, a more personal note is in order. As is evident in the essays that follow, many of us began our research and writing careers as graduate students working with Hammond on collaborative projects. In addition to culminating in co-authored publications, these collaborative efforts often laid the groundwork for further inquiry. More than a few careers have been built by pursuing the implications and questions emerging from Hammond's tutelage.

Every great teacher has had a great teacher, and those readers versed in the classics in the sociology of religion will recognize the influence on Hammond's thought of such scholars as Talcott Parsons, Emile Durkheim, and Max Weber. By connecting his own work with those who inspired him, and by training graduate students in the context of collaborative research projects, Hammond has not only passed on a scholarly tradition but has also helped map a way into the future of the social scientific study of religion.

The essays in this volume cannot offer a definitive solution to the entire puzzle of religion's place in a secular society, but they do specify dimensions of the problem in a way that invites hypothesis, empirical analysis, and refinement. And this, after all, is how social science is properly done.

PREFACE

Recently I was asked to contribute to a collection of essays in which authors were to discuss why they chose the research topics they did, how they went about conducting their research, how they responded to unanticipated problems, etc.[1] In carrying out that task, I discovered something quite unanticipated: my scholarly life has had more coherence—or at least continuity—than I felt as I lived it.

Assembling the essays of this book led to a similar experience. In the process of deciding what to include and how selections should be ordered, I found an organizing theme that is not found in any one essay but around which all fourteen essays more or less cohere. This theme is best seen as emanating from the condition known in the United States as the separation of church and state, though something comparable is found in every society since religion and politics are inexorably related. However, the United States has, in Rodney Stark's terms, a relatively unregulated religious economy; with government interfering little in church—and vice versa—the dynamics of religious organizations, both internal and external, are quite volatile.

In the United States, the constitutional decision to keep religion out of politics and politics out of religion, in so far as possible, had inevitable consequences for religious institutions as well as inevitable consequences for non-religious institutions. For religious institutions it meant a loss of cultural power and authority, and for other institutions it meant absorption of some of what religious institutions lost. Religious institutions retained a kind of *de facto* establishment status well into the nineteenth century, but that status has been chipped away bit by bit as the implications of the Establishment Clause have become clearer. Non-religious institutions—some governmental, some private—have taken on some of the functions that churches once performed.

The essays of Part I—especially the first three, but all seven to some degree—look at the first set of consequences, the dynamics internal to religious organizations by which the loss occurs. The essays of Part II—especially the final three, but all seven to some degree—look at the second set of consequences, how 'secular' institutions are influenced by what religious institutions have lost.

---

[1] Hammond, P., 'Of churches, courts, and moral order', in J. R. Stone (ed.), *The Craft of Religious Studies* (New York, NY: St. Martin's Press, 1998).

The evidential base of these essays is unavoidably American, since that is the scene I know best. I would hope, however, that many of the ideas—theories—expressed here are applicable to other societies. After all, whatever arrangement a nation chooses in relating 'church' and 'state' will reverberate in both the religious and non-religious realms.

All of these essays have been revised—some more than others—and a few have been substantially updated. Written over a period of little more than a decade, they have common references, invoke many of the same authorities, and therefore approach similar problems from different angles. I have edited out as much of this duplication as was possible, but the reader will notice some avoidable repetition.

When I began graduate work, I imagined that, when finished, I would return as a teacher to a small liberal arts campus such as the one I had so enjoyed as an undergraduate. That was not to be. My first appointment was at Yale, and subsequent appointments have been at other research universities with graduate programs. As this book's dedication indicates, however, this unexpected academic journey turned out to be a blessing, for it gave me the opportunity to work with many wonderful graduate students. Most of the essays here were written in response to a request for a contribution to someone's projected volume. As I undertook that request, I would sometimes suggest collaboration with a graduate student. These occasions always turned out well and provided great pleasure as well as intellectual stimulation. While I acknowledge such co-authors at the appropriate places in this book, I want here to thank Michael Burdick, David Machacek, Eric Mazur, Mark Shibley, Peter Solow, and Kee Warner for being great colleagues. David Machacek deserves special thanks for his assistance in preparing these essays for publication in book form.

ACKNOWLEDGEMENTS

The following essays are printed here with the following permissions:

Essay 1 from *Liberal Protestantism* by R. Michaelsen, and W. C. Roof (eds.), © 1986. Reprinted by permission of The Pilgrim Press.

Essays 2 and 13 from the *Journal for the Scientific Study of Religion*, 27/1 (1988), and 36/4 (1997). © Society for the Scientific Study of Religion.

Essay 4 from *Religion, Mobilization, and Social Action* by A. Shupe and B. Misztal (eds.), © 1998. Reprinted by permission of Greenwood publishing.

Essay 5 from *The Handbook on Cults and Sects in America*, D. Bromley and J. Hadden (eds.), Volume 3 of *Religion and the Social Order*, © 1993. Reprinted by permission of JAI Press.

Essay 6 from *American Buddhism* by D. R. Williams and C. S. Queen (eds.), © 1999. Reprinted by permission of Curzon Press.

Essay 7 from New Religions and the New Europe, R. Towler (ed.), © 1995. Reprinted by permission of Aarhus University Press.

Essay 8 is reprinted from *World Order and Religion* by W. C. Roof (ed.), by permission of the State University of New York Press. © 1991, State University of New York. All rights reserved.

Essay 9 from *The Future of New Religious Movements* by D. Bromley and P. Hammond (eds.), © 1987. Reprinted by permission of Mercer University Press.

Essay 10 from *Annals of the American Academy of Political and Social Science*, Volume 527, © 1993 by American Academy of Political and Social Science. Reprinted by permission from Sage Publications, Inc.

Essay 11 from *Sociology of Religion*, Volume 55/3 (1994), © Association for the Sociology of Religion, Inc.

Essay 12 from *Journal of Church and State*, Volume 37/3 (1995), © J. M. Dawson Institute of Church-State Studies.

Essay 14 from *The Power of Religious Publics* by W. Swatos and J. Wellman (eds.), © 1999 by Praeger. Reproduced with permission of Greenwood Publishing Group, Inc., Westport, CT.

CONTENTS

LIST OF FIGURES AND TABLES

PART I

Internal Dynamics

ONE

The Extravasation of the Sacred and the
Crisis in Liberal Protestantism

Extravasate: Df. To pass by infiltration or effusion from a channel (such as a blood vessel) into surrounding tissue.

Although secularization is a major term in the social scientific study of religion—and has been from the beginning—knowledge of just how it occurs is less certain than the belief that it does occur. After all, people do not believe they create the sacred but encounter it; likewise, it seems, we can more readily encounter the result of secularization than control the process itself. How holy things escape from their 'proper vessels' is puzzling indeed; the extravasation of the sacred is not easy to understand. Yet understand it we must if the current crisis in liberal Protestantism is, in turn, to be understood. At least that is the operative assumption here. The puzzle I address is this: how did the great denominations of the American past, the churches that once dominated American culture, lose their custodial position? How was it, so to speak, that the sacred was let out of its once 'proper' vessels?

The ultimate answer is to be found in Protestant theology itself, denying as it does that the church is a necessary, that is, proper, vessel for all that is holy. Salvation, Protestantism asserts, is a matter between people and God, requiring no sacrament, no priest, and thus no church. At most the church can be a gathering of like believers, but one of those shared beliefs is the conviction that persons come together to glorify God, not to conform to ecclesiastical demands. To varying degrees therefore, Protestants have been suspicious of ritual, authority, pomp, and costume. The church may, therefore, be a *tool* of the sacred, but it is not ultimately the *vessel* of the sacred.

Such Protestant conviction is at least the theoretical explanation for the extravasation of the sacred; Protestants, in principle, have been reluctant to exalt their churches. In actuality, however, Protestant churches, no less than Catholic, have enjoyed a sanctified status. Their leaders have often been charismatic; their spaces regarded as holy; their rules believed to be God-ordained. Put briefly, membership in a Protestant church has oftentimes been seen to carry the same sacred obligation as membership in the Roman Catholic Church. Protestants never went so far as to *say* that outside the church there is no salvation, but many Protestants certainly behaved as if they believed as much. Protestant churches have thus claimed informal establishment status as eagerly as formal establishment status has been eschewed.

Informal establishment status is precisely what a number of Protestant denominations—those we now call liberal—enjoyed in America, at least until late in the nineteenth century. Even after that time, after the experience Robert T. Handy calls 'the second disestablishment',[1] certain Protestant denominations continued their custodial relationship with American culture, and thus came to be regarded as 'mainstream' or 'mainline' churches. Well into the twentieth century, for example, most public school teachers were presumed to be members of one or another of these denominations. Higher education modeled itself after a few universities historically tied to these denominations. William Bowen, for instance, who assumed the presidency of Princeton University in 1970, was the first Princeton president who was neither a Presbyterian clergyman nor the son of one. And all three branches of the federal government were disproportionately in the hands of persons who claimed affiliation with these denominations.

Talcott Parsons had special insight into this subtly maintained custodial relationship. The family, he allowed, was a key to understanding how, despite decreasing formal status, liberal Protestantism diffused outward and remained influential. Families played a critical role in the transmission of these values, because it was 'taken for granted that the overwhelming majority will accept the religious affiliations of their parents. . . . [Even] if some should shift to another denomination it is not to be taken too tragically since the new affiliation will in most cases be included in the deeper moral community'.[2] Only in the event of a radical reorganization of society would churches generally—and liberal Protestant churches specifically—relinquish their custodial relationship with the central Protestant values, Parsons believed. As long as these values were spreading throughout the social structure, so to speak, and as long as each generation continued to 'inherit' the religious affiliations of the parents, then church membership would be a major way by which Americans identified with their society, and liberal Protestantism would continue to have special custody of America's central values.

It was in the nature of these values that their holders would welcome the 'liberal protestantization' of Judaism and Catholicism, and it was Will Herberg's view—obviously shared by Parsons—that being Protestant,

---

[1] Handy, R. T., *A Christian America*, 2nd edn. (New York, NY: Oxford University Press, 1984).

[2] Parsons, T., 'Christianity and modern industrial society', in E. A. Tiryakian (ed.), *Sociology Theory, Values, and Sociological Change* (New York, NY: The Free Press, 1963), 61.

Catholic, or Jew in America was merely a set of alternative ways to be 'American', of declaring one's attachment to society's core values.[3]

Toward the end of this essay I shall return to this relationship of church-family-values. It is enough for now to say that, while the theological warrant for a greatly reduced role for churches can be traced to the Reformation itself, this reduction has not, until recently, been particularly visible. The extravasation of the sacred has perhaps been occurring over a long period of time, but many of the consequences of this process are only now becoming noticeable. So dramatic are these consequences now, however, that Roof and McKinney see fit to call the present a time of 'third disestablishment'[4]—a truly significant alteration in the relationship of liberal Protestantism and American culture. How are we to understand the situation?

GETTING TO THE PRESENT

During the years from approximately 1890 to 1920, the American Protestant-ism that had enjoyed near-establishment status for a century confronted the forces of modernity and responded in basically two ways. One of these responses was to attempt to hold firm—on doctrine especially perhaps, but also on ethics, church polity, worship, and the meaning of religious experi-ence. It was 'defensive', to use Peter Berger's term, in its approach to culture.[5] The other response was to accommodate to culture, especially those sectors of the culture most caught up in social change.

The first response led to conservative Protestantism, which, for all the dif-ferences to be found within it because of selective emphasis—some defend-ing biblical inerrancy, others the centrality of the Holy Spirit, yet others dispensationalism—had as a common feature a resolve not to adjust to the changing cultural standards, but to hold on to standards regarded as absolute. Evangelicals were, and are, a major component of this conservative response, so much so in fact that the labels evangelicalism and conservative Protestantism are often used interchangeably today.

The second response led to liberal Protestantism, which, for all its differ-ences, had as a common feature precisely the willingness to adapt its stand-ards of truth, value, and justice to standards drawn from beyond its own traditions.

---

[3] Herberg, W., *Protestant, Catholic, Jew* (Garden City, NY: Doubleday Anchor, 1960).

[4] Roof, W. C., and McKinney, W., *American Mainline Religion: Its Changing Shape and Future* (New Brunswick, NJ: Rutger's, 1987).

[5] Berger, P., *A Rumor of Angels: Modern Society and the Rediscovery of the Supernatural* (Garden City, NY: Doubleday, 1969), 153.

Conservative Protestantism thus elected, for the most part, not to engage the culture at large, but to ignore it where discrepancy existed, whereas liberal Protestantism became liberal primarily in order to remain in relationship with culture. Evidence now suggests that many church members remained conservative in outlook in almost all denominations, but most of the large church bodies at the turn of the century—Methodist, American Baptist, Presbyterian, Lutheran, Congregational, Episcopal, Disciples— were 'captured' by those of the liberal persuasion. Their leaders, colleges, seminaries, publications, and a great many of their clergy toed the liberal line. They accommodated by their concern for social ministry, their willingness to co-operate across denominational lines, and their openness to 'higher criticism' of the Bible. Sometimes, then, liberal Protestantism is known as Social Gospel, ecumenical, or modernist Protestantism.

Liberal Protestantism, in seeking to remain culturally engaged by responding to the forces of modernity, thus began a radically redefined relationship with American culture. Moreover, this radical redefinition may have represented—and may represent yet—the only relationship possible for any religion in a religiously plural situation if it seeks cultural engagement. If true, this means that not only will today's evangelicalism be unable to recapture the cultural role once played by Protestantism-turned-liberal, but so also will liberal Protestantism be unable to recapture its own former role. Put a second way, the hegemony gained by liberal religion over conservative religion after the turn of the century was hegemony won at the cost of greatly altering religion's place in society. Put yet another way, the second disestablishment led inexorably to the third disestablishment.

MOTIVATION VS. ADJUDICATION

Part of this story is well known and is argued most forcefully by Peter Berger: pluralization of religion leads to the privatization of all religions, which means that, however important religion might be in the private lives of individuals, the mutual interchange of persons drawn from different religions tends to downplay, if not exclude, their religions.[6] To understand how this happens, we need to distinguish religion at the motivational level from religion at the adjudicatory level, and this part of the story is not so well known.

Modernity and religious pluralism may tend, empirically, to diminish the role played by religion in the mental process of individuals, especially to the degree that they encounter and acknowledge religious claims conflicting

---

[6] Berger, P., *A Rumor of Angels: Modern Society and the Rediscovery of the Supernatural* (Garden City, NY: Doubleday, 1969), 153.

with their own. But this is not necessarily the case. Mere knowledge that others are religiously different does not automatically weaken one's own religion. People may still be powerfully motivated by their spiritual outlook, and indeed it would be surprising if, in a society as devout as America, one did not frequently run into such people. In addition, numerous insulating techniques—from isolated communities to separate schools—help to protect religion at the motivational level.

At the adjudicatory level a different picture emerges, as the implications of religious pluralism become clearer. For example, person A claims that her religious convictions not only permit, but may even dictate, abortion under some circumstances, while person B claims that her religious convictions prohibit abortion not only for herself, but for all persons. More commonly perhaps, person A makes a claim based on religious convictions, but person B—who does not hold such religious convictions—rejects the claims. For example, Hindu parents insist on vegetarian meals for their children in the American public school cafeteria, while other parents—having no religious scruples about meat—disapprove of such an adjustment. How do these persons adjudicate their differences, assuming their mutual desire to remain in the same society?

In a certain sense one side inevitably 'wins', and the other 'loses'. Abortion will or will not be allowed; vegetarian meals will or will not be served. If religious pluralism is to be maintained, the winning side will not—in winning—have its religious convictions vindicated, and the losing side will not—in losing—have its religious convictions discredited. Rather, religious convictions on both sides will, at this adjudicatory level, be held in abeyance—however important they may be at the motivational level. Not to hold religious convictions in abeyance at the adjudicatory level is to establish one religion over another, something explicitly prohibited in the US Constitution and implicitly unacceptable in all modern nations that are also religiously plural.

On what basis, then, are such cases adjudicated? The answer is on the basis of 'principles' variously labeled legal, ethical, or moral. In a functioning system, such principles must meet two distinguishing qualifications: First, the principles must be abstract—that is, applicable not just to the case at hand, but to other cases as well. People need to be able to discern from principles invoked in one case how similar cases—including those in which entirely different religious convictions may be involved—would be decided. The second qualification is that, since such principles cannot be articulated in the religious language peculiar to either contending party, they must be articulated in a language *common* to the contending parties—which, as society gains in religious pluralism, is a language increasingly devoid of religious references and, therefore, often called 'secular humanism'.

Now this set of circumstances happens to be relatively easy to perceive in the legal setting,[7] but it is no less operative in any social setting where persons of diverse religious backgrounds interact. Religion may yet be important at the motivational private level, but it inevitably recedes in importance at the adjudicatory level. The 'public square', as Richard Neuhaus says, becomes 'naked'.[8]

Social circumstances, chiefly immigration, forced 'established' Protestantism after the Civil War to recognize the fact of religious pluralism. Even if individual Protestants remained as convinced as ever of their singular hold on religious truth, they were destined—because of pluralism—to see that conviction challenged.

I am by default, however, describing chiefly the liberal Protestant view of things, not the evangelical view. To a significant degree, conservative Protestants 'withdrew' from cultural engagement, which minimized their need to recognize their altered relationship to it. Liberal Protestants, however—ever eager to maintain their embrace of that culture, even if it were religiously plural—set themselves up for the rude awakening they now experience.

WAKING UP TO THE RUDE REALITY

That account brings us to the present—and to the contrasting situations of liberal and conservative Protestantism. One is dispirited, the other optimistic, but neither is quite aware of what its future can be. In the case of evangelicalism, the ordeal of modernity, especially the full import of pluralism, has yet to be squarely faced. When it is, there is every reason to assume that a domestication process will occur not unlike the process that gave rise to liberal Protestantism. Indeed, ample evidence suggests such a process is already underway, especially among the politicized evangelicals who are sincerely trying to influence American culture; their only choice, so to speak, is to compromise at the adjudicatory level with those who share their political aims but not their religious motives. In the process, religious language recedes, as does religion in an adjudicatory sense.

But if evangelical Protestants are slow in realizing that their religious motives are not coin of the realm at the adjudicatory level, liberal Protestants have yet to realize the full meaning for them of the pluralistic game they have been playing for decades. Unlike their conservative brethren—whose loss to

---

[7] See Hammond, P., 'The courts and secular humanism: How to misinterpret church/state issues', *Society*, 21/4 (1984) for illustration.

[8] Neuhaus, R., *The Naked Public Square* (Grand Rapids, MI: William B. Eerdmans, 1984).

liberals early in this century left them both culturally powerless and, until recently, culturally disengaged, and thus unconcerned about being culturally powerless—liberal Protestants have remained culturally engaged but not fully aware of their cultural powerlessness. The extravasation of the sacred has gone largely unnoticed. The reason, put simply, is that the culture toward which Protestantism is powerless has only slowly lost its Protestant appearance. That slowness camouflaged—especially perhaps for liberal Protestants themselves—the altered relationship they had had with culture since the turn of the century; American culture remained 'Protestant' far longer than the American population.

THREE EXAMPLES

Three examples of the rude awakening Protestantism now experiences can be cited, all three deserving fuller treatment than can be given here. Although drawn from quite different sectors of church life, each exemplifies the process of extravasation—the seeping out of the sacred from the vessel of the church.

Foreign Missions

Even after the second disestablishment, mainline Protestant churches continued their foreign missions designed to 'Christianize' diverse peoples. Granted, in accommodating to external standards of what constitutes worthy mission work, Bible reading, hymn-singing, and personal witnessing diminished as concern for education, public health, and crop yield increased. But the motivation of missionaries was not called into question—by themselves or others—by this transition; they were still Christians doing Christian deeds. When, therefore, alternate means of doing foreign missions came into existence through such structures as Crossroads Africa or the American Friends Service, Christian ideals were not being forsaken, but the close links between church and Christian motivation were. These programs were able to recruit people inspired by the goal of insect control or clean water. As long as expertise, enthusiasm, and physical stamina were present, what did spiritual maturity and wisdom—let alone doctrinal orthodoxy—matter?

Even so, the loss of the sacred from foreign mission-sponsoring churches did not get starkly revealed until the Peace Corps, modeled after Crossroads Africa, became the major channel for youthful expertise, enthusiasm, and stamina. The church, it could now be seen, had lost control of the 'sacred' in foreign missions. The link may still have been there in some volunteers' motives, but it was not there at the adjudicatory level; the church chose

neither these missions nor these missionaries, for example. Extravasation of
the sacred had taken place in foreign missions.

Social Services

A similar process occurred in the curing of souls. Part of the accommodation
made during the second disestablishment was the adjustment from 'curate'
to welfare worker and pastoral counselor. Recognizing that agencies other
than churches were delivering mental health care and social services, more
and more denominations added social welfare and counseling techniques to
their seminary training. But just as, say, the Methodists who built a hospital
had to recognize that there is no such thing as a Christian (let alone
Methodist) appendectomy, so did churches offering free meals or psychological advice come to realize that the 'Christian' curing of souls was an elusive
concept indeed. That personnel may be motivated by Christian charity
might still be true, but who was to care? And how would they know? The
models of practice were now imported from non-Christian contexts, as were
the standards for judging the success of those models.

As long as churches nonetheless remained major vehicles by which such
services were delivered, the loss of the sacred in the curing of souls was not
widely noticed. As competing government and 'private' agencies grew popular, however, not only was the line separating church-delivered services
from secular services growing increasingly hazy, but so also did it make
decreasing difference whether the practitioner was Christianly motivated,
and therefore even Christian. Extravasation of the sacred had taken place in
the cure of souls.

Higher Education

A third example is found in the Protestant ministry to higher education.
Before the second disestablishment, of course, higher education generally
was part of the Protestant establishment. Even the first of the great public
universities were disproportionately administered and staffed by clergy or
the sons of clergy. And the private colleges, most of which were founded by
mainline Protestant denominations, regarded moral philosophy, frequent
chapel, and religious study, as natural parts of their undertaking.

The nearly automatic link between higher education and Protestantism
was broken by the turn of the century, and chapel services diminished,
became voluntary, or disappeared altogether. No longer did the school day
begin with a moral exhortation from the clergyman-president. Many more
subjects were added to the curriculum, as preparation for the ministry, for
example, became only a minor goal of colleges and universities.

By no means did Protestantism's custodial relationship with higher education disappear, however. For one thing, until after World War II and the rapid expansion of higher education, church-related colleges continued to play a dominant leadership role. For another, 'the church followed its students', to use the title of an influential book chronicling these events.[9] If the campus was no longer a surrogate parish, then the parish would move to the campus. As a result, the extravasation of the sacred in higher education—occurring as public sponsorship replaced church sponsorship—was hardly noticed. By offering social activities, counseling, opportunities for witness and discussion, as well as worship and fellowship, Protestantism continued to play a vital role in college and university.

In due time, however, many of the functions initiated by the Protestant ministry to higher education were taken over by higher education itself: counseling, off-campus housing service, social and political forum, etc. Because of the second disestablishment, so to speak, Protestantism could do nothing about such a takeover, even if it had wanted to. But the realization that such takeover had occurred came as part of the third disestablishment, and campus pastors were largely left to invent programs, few of which could be advertised as compulsory, compelling, or sacred; that aspect of campus ministry had already escaped.[10]

THE LINK IS BROKEN

Not only do liberal Protestant college students stay away in droves from campus ministerial programs; many also see no reason even to identify themselves by religious preference, thus preventing 'their' church from following them by way of the campus ministry. Increasing numbers, moreover, have no church preference to declare because their parents have no church affiliation. In other words, the assumption that Talcott Parsons could make nearly four decades ago—'it is to be taken for granted that the overwhelming majority will accept the religious affiliations of their parents'[11]—is now a dubious assumption indeed. Tables 1.1 and 1.2 present the evidence.

Several observations are worth making in Table 1.1. First, among Protestants in the twentieth century, deviation by children from parental religious affiliation has routinely been high—roughly a third. Second, Catholics and Jews, although experiencing lower rates of intergenerational differences

---

[9] Shedd, C. P., *The Church Follows its Students* (New Haven. CT: Yale University Press, 1938).

[10] See Hammond, P., *The Campus Clergyman* (New York: Basic Books, 1966).

[11] Parsons, J., 'Christianity and modern industrial society', 61.

Table 1.1. *Protestants, Catholics, and Jews (age 18+) who do not share their parents' religious affiliation, by year of birth (%)*

	Year of birth		
	1931 or earlier	1932–1946	1947 and since
Protestant	35 (2,361)	37 (1,239)	33 (1,090)
Catholic	13 (1,122)	17 (764)	22 (827)
Jewish	10 (135)	16 (56)	25 (57)

Note: The number of cases on which the percentages are based are in parentheses.
Source: These data are from the 1973–80 General Social Surveys conducted by the National Opinion Research Center of the University of Chicago.

in religious affiliation than do Protestants, are none the less seeing significant increases through time.

The third observation is, properly speaking, only speculation in Table 1.1, but it finds convincing confirmation in Table 1.2. It is that, while the higher Protestant rates in Table 1.1 have been owing, as Parsons assumed, to the fact of denominational switching within Protestantism, this is decreasingly true. Rather, difference between generations in religious affiliations is coming to mean not denominational switching, but defection altogether. Moreover, such defection—not uncommon among Catholics and Jews throughout this century—is becoming common indeed among liberal Protestants.

Table 1.1 shows that a third of the Protestants deviate from parental denomination, but Table 1.2 shows that, while at an earlier time only 6 per cent of these dropped out altogether, more recently the percentage is 34. Moreover, this pattern obtains in all the liberal denominations for which sufficient data are available. Catholics and Jews who deviate from parental reli-

Table 1.2. *Those who, having defected from parental religion, have departed religious affiliation altogether, by year of birth and parental affiliation*

	Year of birth		
	1931 or earlier	1932–1946	1947 and since
Protestant (all denominations)	6 (1,138)	21 (500)	34 (400)
Methodist	6 (301)	10 (127)	30 (123)
Lutheran	7 (125)	23 (66)	41 (59)
Presbyterian	7 (107)	15 (79)	35 (20)
Episcopal	13 (39)	13 (153)	31 (104)
White Baptist	8 (253)	26 (46)	38 (40)
Black Baptist	12 (60)	26 (46)	38 (40)
Catholic	26 (146)	44 (130)	55 (182)
Jewish	50 (14)	67 (9)	64 (4)

Source: See Table 1.1.

gion are even more likely than Protestants to defect altogether, but the proportion that deviates to begin with is smaller.

The point made forcefully by Will Herberg, and analyzed by Parsons—that church affiliation is a common way to identify oneself as an American, and is thus a common expression of commitment to core values that in America are institutionalized in liberal Protestant churches—must now be questioned. At the very least it can be said that churches are decreasingly the means of expressing membership in the national community; core values have so eroded or changed that they no longer resemble 'liberal Protestant' values, and thus liberal Protestant churches no longer embody them.

The consequence, of course, is the loss by liberal Protestant churches of their custodianship of American culture—a process, I have been arguing, set in motion by the turn of the century, but its products came as a clear shock only after defection rates skyrocketed after the 1960s. One message is obvious: increasing numbers of Americans find their identities and maintain their communities without church affiliation generally, and without liberal Protestant affiliation specifically.

CONCLUSION

Does this loss of custodianship represent a crisis for liberal Protestantism? It most certainly does if liberal Protestant churches continue in the assumption that they automatically create, maintain, and express the national community—and thereby are the chief purveyors of the sacred in America. If that possibility once were true, it is decreasingly so today. Protestantism's very tolerance in accepting the conditions of religious pluralism meant that its link to the national community, and thus its grip on the sacred, was loosening.

But optimism might be in order to the degree that other kinds of 'community' can be developed in and around churches. If community no longer depends on theological conviction, it is still the case that conviction emerges out of community. Emile Durkheim was right on this particular point—religion grows out of experience with the sacred, which in turn grows out of intimate relationships with others.[12]

Modernity brought about considerable discontinuity in intimate relationships, not just between generations, but between populations divided along all kinds of lines. Moreover, awareness of this discontinuity has itself become

[12] Durkheim, E., *The Elementary Forms of Religious Life* (New York, NY: The Free Press, 1995).

a mark of modernity, so that different experiences of the sacred not only exist, but also are widely known to exist. Churches, then, as embodiments of religion expressing the sacred, find their task increasingly problematic. The sacred has extravasated; being discovered instead in institutional settings sometimes far removed from churches.

Discovering alternative communities and building on them thus becomes the key to liberal Protestantism's continued presence. This is the lesson, for example, of the 'homogeneous unit' line of reasoning now appearing in the church growth literature. But the larger question is whether and how all manner of such communities can be discovered, absorbed, and served—a question addressed in many of the essays of this volume.

TWO

Religion and the Persistence of Identity

While the malaise discussed in the foregoing essay may be greater in liberal Protestantism, it is not confined there. The role played by religion in the identities of many people is undergoing change—a mark of secularization to be sure, but one that reverberates differentially in various regions of America and among the various religious traditions. This essay explores these themes.

During a summer weekend every year in Santa Barbara, a Greek Festival is held in one of the city parks. The booths selling souvlaki and dolmas are operated by, and for the benefit of, the Greek Orthodox parish in town. And this sponsorship is prominently displayed by a sign on each booth, about which I noted something interesting. Carefully and beautifully printed, they announced the sponsor as 'The Greek Church of Santa Barbara'. Then inscribed in longhand, between the words 'Greek' and 'Church', someone had added 'Orthodox'. Whoever first prepared the signs, in other words, had failed to mention the part of the label that, in substance, is of greatest importance. What church is sponsoring this booth? The Greek *Orthodox* Church!

Of course nobody was misled or in doubt. Perhaps only a perverse sociologist of religion would even notice. But *I did* notice, and I was struck by the implication of the original omission. The sign-maker, while acknowledging by his choice of words that there could be Greek sponsorship that is not the church, was also implying that church-going Greeks in Santa Barbara go to *one church* only.

How characteristic of a disappearing past, I thought to myself, to have one's church more or less dictated by one's primary group allegiances. And not just dictated by, but expressive of, those allegiances. Under these circumstances, the church is surely a vital part of people's identity. Indeed, as I ruminated further, I recalled how William Swatos argued that the American style of denominationalism, and the consequent 'religiousness' of the American people, grew out of exactly this capacity of churches to 'fit people into the local community'.[1] They could organize 'communal relationships relating to

---

[1] Swatos, W., 'Beyond denominationalism', *Journal for the Scientific Study of Religion*, 20 (1981), 223.

the transcendent realm in a pluralistic socio-cultural system'.[2] The church was one of the ways people knew who they were.

But this social function was strongest in the nineteenth century, as Swatos suggests; in the twentieth century, especially after World War II, the church decreasingly played this 'collective-expressive' role, even if exceptions may be found, as the Santa Barbara Greek Festival would suggest. After all, fewer and fewer of us are embedded in primary groups, and, what may be more important, the few primary group ties we still have are not overlapping. Instead, as the classic sociological formulation has it, we are chiefly involved in a series of segmented relationships.

For many, therefore, especially those not embedded in primary groups, the church is simply one of these segmented relationships. Far from expressing collective ties, the church is one of the ways by which individuals, often joined by other members of their nuclear families, cope with this segmented life. Very much a voluntary association, the religious organization represents for such people not an inherited relationship but a relationship that can be entered and exited with little or no impact on their other relationships. Church, for them, is not simultaneously a gathering of kin, neighbors, fellow-workers, and leisure-time friends, but rather a separate activity, expressing another meaning. This pattern is seen in study after study showing that the persons most involved in churches are the same persons most involved in other organizations as well.

Does this mean that religion, under these circumstances, has little to do with people's identity? And if, as is frequently said and is probably true, this individual-expressive pattern is replacing the collective-expressive pattern, does this mean that religion is decreasingly involved in people's identity? Such questions are what I explore here.

ON THE CONCEPT OF IDENTITY

Hans Mol has reminded us that we use the concept of identity in two very different ways in the social sciences.[3] The first way of looking at identity suggests the immutable, or at least the slowly changing core of personality that shows up in all of a person's encounters, irrespective of differing role-partners. The second way suggests the transient and changeable self as persons move from one social encounter to another, offering a somewhat different

[2] Swatos, W., 'Beyond denominationalism', *Journal for the Scientific Study of Religion*, 20 (1981), 222.

[3] Mol, H. (ed.), *Identity and Religion* (Beverly Hills, CA: Sage Publications, 1978).

identity, as it were, in each place. The first notion of identity suggests that it is involuntarily held; the second, that it can be put on and off. The first is nourished in primary groups, probably early in life; the second exists precisely because much of life is lived in arenas outside of primary groups.

About these two notions of identity, the following observations might be made:

1. Both notions can be appropriate and therefore useful.
2. Some institutional spheres, most notably the family, are inevitably important in the first sense, while other institutional spheres, most notably the workplace, are inevitably important in the second sense without necessarily being important in the first sense.
3. Some institutional spheres, and here I nominate religion but also ethnicity as examples, may, in modern societies, be shifting from being important in the first sense, to being important only in the second sense.

It happens that, though I think this third assertion holds true for both religion and ethnicity, it can be more clearly stated and more readily shown in the case of ethnicity. Indeed, as I will presently suggest, debates about ethnic group revival turn out to be debates about a shift in the role ethnicity plays in people's identity. Despite this apparent subject matter, however, my real focus here is not ethnicity but religion. It is their parallelism and close ties historically in America that allows ethnicity to serve as a sort of surrogate for religion in my discussion.

RELIGION AND ETHNICITY

Little doubt exists about the intimate link between religion and ethnicity. Whether the latter is conceived objectively or subjectively, and whether it is measured along the lines of acculturation or of assimilation, involvement in the religion characteristic of one's ethnic group is always judged to be powerfully correlated with the strength of one's ethnic identity.[4] A variant of this

---

[4] See, e.g., Price, C. A., *Southern Europeans in Australia* (Melbourne: Oxford University Press, 1963); Gordon, M., *Assimilation in American Life* (New York, NY: Oxford University Press, 1964); Lieberson, S., *Language and Ethnic Relations in Canada* (New York, NY: Wiley, 1970); Marty, M., 'Ethnicity: The skeleton of religion in America', *Church History*, 41 (1972), 5–21; Sandberg, N. C., *Ethnic Identity and Assimilation: The Polish American Community* (New York, NY: Praeger, 1974); Stout, H., 'Ethnicity: The vital center of religion in America', *Ethnicity*, 2 (1975), 204–24; Miller, R. M., and Marzik, T. D. (eds.), *Immigrants and Religion in Urban America* (Philadelphia, PA: Temple University Press, 1977); Moskos, C. C. Jr., *Greek Americans* (Englewood Cliffs, NJ: Prentice-Hall, 1980); Padgett, D., 'Symbolic ethnicity and patterns of ethnic identity assertion in American-born Serbs', *Ethnic Groups*, 3 (1980), 55–77; Reitz, J., *The Survival of Ethnic Groups* (Toronto: McGraw-Hill Ryerson, 1980).

perspective is the research showing how different ethnic groups practice a single religion differently.[5]

Despite the undeniability of this relationship, however, a sense of ambiguity about it is readily detected. Timothy Smith has argued that the religions of immigrant groups in America were not simply additional luggage from the old country, kept as nostalgic reminders and thus defenses against assimilation.[6] Instead, religion played a dynamic role in the very formation of ethnicity, as migrants created community where no sense of ethnic identity may have existed before. Abramson struggles with the same issue. It is clear, he says, that in some instances, such as the Amish, Hutterites, Mormons, and Jews, ethnicity *equals* religion.[7] That is to say, were it not for religion, the ethnic group would not even exist. In other instances, such as the Greek Orthodox or Dutch Reformed, religion is a powerful foundation of ethnicity but shares this foundational character with a unique territorial origin and very often a distinctive language as well. In yet other instances, such as Irish, Italian, German, Polish, and French Catholicism, the link between ethnicity and religion is real, but religion is not a definitive, only an empirically probable, component of ethnic identity.

What is at issue here is not simply the recognition that ethnic and religious identity can vary in *strength,* but that ethnicity and religion can differ in *meaning* as well, and thus in the kind of identity they might provide. Here is where the debate over the authenticity of ethnic 'revival' is relevant, as is the analogous debate over religious revival. So-called 'straight-line' theorists such as Gans or Steinberg argue against so-called 'cyclicists' such as Hansen or Novak.[8] While acknowledging that people's ethnic identity may undergo an upsurge, these straight-line theorists are insisting that such an upsurge is not a return of an earlier ethnic identity, but is instead an alteration in the meaning of ethnicity. In the extreme, they say, it is precisely because ethnicity has lost its structural importance that more and more people can indulge in ethnic leisure-time pursuits. Ethnicity is less important for identity in the first sense, in other words, which allows it to be important for identity in the second sense.

---

[5] See, e.g., Greeley, A., *Why Can't They Be Like Us?* (New York, NY: E. P. Dutton & Co., 1971), *Ethnicity in the United States* (New York, NY: John Wiley & Sons, 1974); Abramson, H., *Ethnic Diversity in Catholic America* (New York, NY: John Wiley & Sons, 1973).

[6] Smith, T., 'Religion and ethnicity in America', *American Historical Review*, 83 (1978), 1115–85.

[7] Abramson, H., 'Religion', in S. Thernstrom, *et al.* (eds.), *Harvard Encyclopedia of American Ethnic Groups* (Boston, MA: Belknap Press, 1980), 869–75.

[8] Gans, H., 'American Jewry: Present and Future', two parts, in *Commentary*, 22 (May–June 1956); Steinberg, S., *The Ethnic Myth* (New York, NY: Atheneum, 1981); Hansen, M. L., 'The problem of the third generation immigrant', *Commentary*, 14 (1962), 492–500; Novak, M., *The Rise of the Unmeltable Ethnics* (New York, NY: The MacMillan Company, 1971).

This argument, of course, parallels the one about religion—made most forcefully by Bryan Wilson—that, for example, America can appear to be the most religious nation because in reality it is the most secular.[9] Granted, this rendition goes, church-going rates are high, but only because such choices are voluntary and therefore structurally unimportant; they *mean* something different from involuntary church-going.

I submit that these arguments are best understood if, in each case, the cyclicist side is seen to be attributing a single meaning to identity as it relates to ethnicity or religion, while the straight line side is noting the shift in meanings. This second position says, granted ethnicity or religion may be (re)gaining importance, but if it is, it no longer provides the same *kind* of identity it used to provide.

THE ISSUE GETS SHARPENED

This issue is clearly observable in the literature on religious and ethnic inter-marriage. As an empirical generalization, we know that intermarriage rates tend to fluctuate inversely with the availability of homogeneous partners. Thus, Catholics in Raleigh or Little Rock marry non-Catholics at a higher rate than Catholics in El Paso or Providence, and Greek Americans in the South and West marry non-Greek Americans more frequently than do their fellow ethnics in the North and East.[10] What are we to make of a contrary finding? Koreans in Hawaii, where they are sizeable in number, out-married in the 1970s at a rate in excess of 80 per cent, while Los Angeles Koreans, also numerous, had an intermarriage rate only one-third that size.[11]

The explanation is quite simple. Koreans in Los Angeles are a closer-knit group; they exercise greater control over the activities of their children and provide more ethnic organizations for those children to attend. The fact that a higher proportion of the Los Angeles Koreans are first-generation American than one finds in Hawaii, or the fact that inter-ethnic contact has long been institutionalized in Hawaii, helps explain the greater insularity of the Los Angeles Koreans, of course, but the controlling agent is the insularity, whatever its causes. The empirical generalization regarding sheer numbers of a group and its members' proclivity to out-marry turns out to depend upon the group's meaning to its members. Whether many or few in number,

[9] Wilson, B., *Religion in Secular Society* (London: Watts, 1966).

[10] Thomas, J. L., 'The factor of religion in the selection of marriage mates', *American Sociological Review*, 16 (1951), 487–91; Moskos, *Greek Americans*.

[11] Kitano, H. H., *et al.*, 'Asian American interracial marriage', *Journal of Marriage and Family*, 46 (1984), 179–90.

if members' identities are importantly determined in the first of our two senses above—if their core personalities are shaped by their ethnicity—then we can expect lower intermarriage rates. Correlatively, if intermarriage rates are high, or if other evidence suggests that the ethnic group's insularity is not great, then we can assume that its members' ethnic identity exists chiefly in the second sense—an identity that may be more or less important, depending upon circumstances.[12]

We have already noted about the first kind of identity that it is involuntary, that it is thrust upon its possessor by so many others, in so many circumstances, for such a long time, that, even if one wanted to escape it, one could not. The phenomenon of ethnic 'passing', for example, of a Black as White, a Jew as Gentile—now no longer much noted—illustrated by its poignancy this essentially involuntary character; one chose to discard an identity of the first sort at great social risk, of course, but also at great psychic cost because this was no facade being peeled away but a pulling out of roots.

RELIGION AND IDENTITY

Now, it was Durkheim's great insight that religion is born out of the social circumstances providing those involuntary roots. People are led, he said, to represent their sense of unity in the groups of which they are members—to express that unity in ceremony and symbol, in belief and ritual. In the case of the central Australian aborigines he studied, there was no choice in the matter.[13]

Because modern society so little resembles the Australian outback, and because the religions Durkheim described so little resemble religions of our day, we may too easily dismiss this Durkheimian insight as no longer applicable. Perhaps it is true that society *in toto* no longer evokes this sense of unity, or, if it does so, only sporadically. We must recognize, however, that, even in modern society, the church may be an expression of intense primary group ties, especially if those ties are to overlapping groups. That is the possible significance here of the Greek Festival in Santa Barbara.

---

[12] An analogous situation is found among the Karen people, a population living on the border of Thailand and Burma. According to Keyes, the Karen people maintain that they are a single ethnic group even though they are religiously divided into 'traditional Karen animists, Protestant and Catholic Christians, Buddhists, and followers of a number of syncretic religions'. Assuming ethnic identity supercedes religious identity, we would expect more *interreligious* marriage among the Karen people than marriage between Karen and non-Karen. See Keyes, C. F., 'The dialectics of ethnic change', In C. F. Keyes (ed.), *Ethnic Change* (Seattle, WA: University of Washington, 1981), 8.

[13] Durkheim, E., *The Elementary Forms of Religious Life* (New York, NY: The Free Press, 1995).

At the same time, however, we must also recognize that for others the church is a secondary association, a voluntary activity that is switched on and off. Under these circumstances, the church may be very important to some people, and thus a source of identity for them, but the identity provided will be an identity of the second sort.

TWO VIEWS OF THE CHURCH

We have, then, two contrasting views of the church in contemporary society. On the one hand, there is what I earlier called the 'collective-expressive' view, in which involvement is largely involuntary because it emerges out of over-lapping primary group ties not easily avoided. On the other hand, there is the 'individual-expressive' view, in which involvement is largely voluntary and independent of other social ties. I also implied that the social conditions eroding the first view are the same conditions that permit, perhaps even encourage, the second view. For example, the parents of children in the ghetto who can think of no alternative to the parochial school—because: 'What would neighbors think? Where else do schoolmates also contend with English as a second language? Aren't they safer with their own kind?'—will, in due time, produce parents who choose the parochial school—because: 'The kids should know how they are different from the neighbors. Where else can they be taught their ancestors' language? Our people have become so spread out, only the parish brings us together.' In the first instance, the par-ents and children have little choice than to be involved in the church. In the second instance, the very forces that free them from mandatory involvement, are forces that encourage their voluntary involvement.

Nobody states this theoretical viewpoint regarding religion and identity better than Thomas Luckmann. At one extreme—the extreme at which Durkheim was theorizing— he says there is congruence among 'church, the sacred cosmos, and the hierarchy of meaning in the world view'.[14] As a result, public institutions 'significantly contribute to the formation of indi-vidual consciousness and personality'.[15] Once there occurs the 'institutional specialization of religion', however, the relationship of the individual to the sacred cosmos and social order is transformed:[16]

In view of this situation it is useful to regard church religiosity in two different per-spectives. First, we may view church religiosity as a survival of a traditional social form of religion . . . on the periphery of modern industrial societies. [that is, the

[14] Luckmann, T., *The Invisible Religion* (New York, NY: Macmillan, 1967), 79.
[15] Ibid., 97.   [16] Ibid., 80.

collective-expressive view] Second, we may view church religiosity as one of many manifestations of an emerging, institutionally nonspecialized social form of religion, the difference being that it still occupies a special place . . . because of its historical connections to the traditional . . . model. [that is, the individual-expressive view] (Luckmann, *The Invisible Religion*, 100–1.)

Indeed in the second of these situations, the individual is alone 'in choosing goods and services, friends, marriage partners, neighbors, hobbies, and . . . even 'Ultimate' meanings. . . . In a manner of speaking, he is free to construct his own personal identity'.[17]

My explication of Luckmann's theory suggests that people can be located on a grid, whose two dimensions are: involvement in overlapping primary groups; and involvement in secondary groups. Because of the dialectical and inverse relationship between these two dimensions, most persons score as High-Low or Low-High, though obviously cases are found everywhere on the grid. Church-affiliated people who are highly involved in overlapping primary groups but not in secondary groups, will tend toward collective-expressive involvement in the church, and their religious identity will tend to be of the involuntary, immutable type discussed above. By contrast, church-affiliated people who are low in primary group involvement but high in secondary group involvement, will tend toward individual-expressive involvement in the church, and their religious identity will tend to be of the transient, changeable type.[18]

The chief research task obviously involves discovering what primary and secondary group ties people have, and how strong those ties are. It also involves learning whether the strength of those ties is related to any

[17] Luckmann, T., *The Invisible Religion* (New York, NY: Macmillan, 1967), 98. A related theoretical perspective is the one often called the 'meaning-belonging' perspective, summarized neatly in McGuire, M., *Religion: The Social Context* (Belmont, CA: Wadsworth, 1987), 23–36; and exemplified so cogently in Roof, W. C., *Commitment and Community* (New York, NY: Elsevier, 1978) where 'localism', that is, ties to community, is seen to be analytically independent of, though perhaps empirically related in an inverse fashion to, general socioeconomic standing.

[18] There remain two other hypothetical types, both of considerable interest, but about which little can be said here. The first of these types includes persons who are highly involved in both primary and secondary groups; pressure on the church to move out of a paternalistic mode might be one expectation from this type—as the experience of the post-ethnic Roman Catholic Church in America seems to illustrate. Another expectation of the first type is exhibited by Black Americans, for whom the church is both the source of comfort and the source of challenge. The second hypothetical type, the social isolate involved in neither primary nor secondary groups, has long been a concern of the modern church, in part because of the church's failure to attract such people: 'All our studies indicate that those who belong to our churches are for the most part those who belong to everything. The church is not serving . . . a ministry to social isolation. Those who would profit most from the "fellowship" of the church . . . are those, then, least likely to be reached by the "respected" churches'. See Pitcher, A. W., 'The politics of mass society: Significance for the churches', in Robertson, D. B. (ed.), *Voluntary Associations* (Richmond, VA: John Knox Press, 1966) 247.

difference in the meaning that church involvement has for people, and whether this difference influences their identities. While the study of voluntary association memberships provides some precedent here in the case of secondary groups, except for the considerable literature on ethnicity and assimilation, we know very little about people's primary ties outside the nuclear family. Yet note the importance attached theoretically to 'redemptive institutions',[19] 'mediating structures',[20] and 'communities of memory'.[21] Clearly such primary groups are thought to remain important in at least some people's lives—not just through ethnicity but also extended kin groups, work-related collectivities, fraternal or 'cultural' organizations, even regional or class allegiances. 'Community', defined as a 'network of social relations marked by mutuality and emotional bonds',[22] we have to assume, has not entirely disappeared.

POSTSCRIPT

Soon after the original presentation of the above remarks in 1987, I received the funding to conduct a study testing my argument and published the results in a book, *Religion and Personal Autonomy* (1992). The major finding was that persons low in collective-expressive but high in individual-expressive identity are indeed more likely to see church involvement as a matter of personal choice—and this is true at every level of church involvement. However, certain expectations were not met: strength of ethnic identity played little or no part in the equation, and the sample of 2,600 persons showed relatively little involvement in voluntary associations, thus rendering that variable inoperative. Nonetheless, the notion that the relation between religion and identity is undergoing change in the direction predicted was upheld.

[19] Nisbet, R., *The Quest for Community* (New York. NY: Oxford University Press, 1953).
[20] Berger, P. L., and Neuhaus, R. J., *To Empower People* (Washington, DC: American Enterprise Institute, 1977).
[21] Bellah, R., *et al.*, *Habits of the Heart* (Berkeley, CA: University of California Press, 1985).
[22] Bender, T., *Community and Social Change in America* (New Brunswick, NJ: Rutger's University Press, 1978), 7.

THREE

When the Sacred Returns: An Empirical Test

The thesis of the previous essay—that the meaning of religious involvement can change even if the level of that involvement does not—finds further support in this essay. It was written as a chapter in a festschrift honoring Bryan Wilson.*

As the most articulate and prolific exponent of the secularization thesis, Bryan Wilson has been called upon to do battle with those who challenge the thesis. 'Secularization', Wilson consistently maintains, 'is that process by which religious institutions, actions, and consciousness, lose their social significance'.[1] Since, in the eyes of many, religion is still around, and in many places even vibrant, critics claim that this thesis must be in error. Thus, for example, some point to the much greater church attendance in the United States than in Great Britain, and, averring the US to be the more secular of the two societies, challenge the notion that with secularization religious institutions lose their 'social significance'. Others see in the spate of so-called new religious movements emerging world-wide after the Second World War ample evidence not of secularization but of sacralization.

Wilson has met all this disagreement with equanimity but also a fierce defense. Perhaps his combative perspective was best evoked by Daniel Bell's 'The Return of the Sacred?'[2] to which Wilson responded in the *Journal for the Scientific Study of Religion.*[3] 'Return' is not the proper concept, he argues; a social pattern that may once have existed and then disappeared does not *reappear*, however prevalent may be some of the constituent elements of that pattern. In the process of retreating, the pattern plus the elements that comprised it will have changed. For Wilson, then, the sacred does not return in any usual sense, which would imply

a re-sacralization, a return to an apprehension of the supernatural, not only widespread in society but also having a profound effect on the culture. It implies new devotions and new dedication amounting to more than merely private sentiments, more than voluntary association of the like-minded for weekly acknowledgement of

---

* Mark Shibley collaborated on this essay.

[1] Wilson, B., Religion in Secular Society (London: Watts, 1966), xiv.

[2] Bell, D., 'Return of the Sacred?' *British Journal of Sociology*, 28 (1977), 419–49.

[3] B. Wilson, 'The Return of the Sacred', *Journal for the Scientific Study of Religion*, 18 (1979), 268–80.

their shared intellectual, moral, and emotional disposition. And it suggests objective social legitimation of these apprehensions. (Wilson, 'The Return of the Sacred', 279–80.)

But in fact such a re-sacralization does not occur, Wilson insists. What happens instead is a change in meaning. Religious beliefs and practices may still obtain, but their relationship to the rest of social life will be different from the situation in the earlier pattern. New religious organizations may emerge, but they will not have the economic, political, legal, and cultural significance that their predecessor organizations may once have had. Persons committed to such organizations may feel themselves just as committed as earlier generations did—and, in fact, may *be* just as committed—but their relationship to the organization cannot help but be altered in meaning because the meaning of that organization's relationship to the wider society has been altered. Secularization, Wilson argues, is a one-way process.

THE ISSUE IS JOINED

Opponents of the secularization thesis are thus obliged to show that, in 'returning', the sacred regains what it had lost. And the proponents of the thesis are obliged to show that, despite certain outward similarities between the old and the renewed, people's religious beliefs and practices do not mean what they once meant.

Despite the greatly circumscribed nature of our research data, we have an unusual opportunity to test almost exactly this issue. We have a sample of 645 persons reared as Roman Catholics, of whom 407 have been Catholic throughout their lives. Included also are 143 who, though reared Roman Catholic, dropped out of the church for a period of at least two years but have since returned. Finally, this sample of persons reared Catholic contains 95 who not only dropped out of the Catholic Church but remain out and have not identified with any other religion.[4] We make the reasonable assumption that the act of dropping out of the Roman Catholic Church by persons raised in it is a reflection of secularization and that returning is, in some sense, a reversal of this secularization. Therefore, the group of 'returnees' is the critical population: do they resemble more the 'loyalists' who never left the Catholic church? Or do they resemble the 'dropouts' who left and never returned? That is the issue we address here.

---

[4] The data are from telephone surveys with randomly selected adults aged 24–60 in California, Massachusetts, North Carolina, and Ohio, conducted during October and November 1988. Approximately 650 interviews were conducted in each state.

ON RETURNING

As we shall now observe, returnees to the Catholic Church are, on most matters touched upon in the interview schedule, somewhere between those who never left the Church and those who left and never came back. Table 3.1 provides the evidence on an array of items, the first group reflecting what we can call 'attitudinal piety' and the second group 'behavioral piety'. Of course, evidence of the sort contained in Table 3.1 does not directly address the issue of this essay. If loyalists are red-hot and dropouts ice-cold, then returnees are lukewarm; while not surprising, these findings by themselves are therefore not very helpful in our quest. But they make the quest intriguing; what are we to make of this 'lukewarmness'?

Table 3.1. *Loyalists, returnees, and dropouts compared on piety issues (%)*

Piety	Loyalists	Returnees	Dropouts
Attitudinal—agree that:			
Most churches today have lost the real spiritual part of religion.	41	56	76
The rules about morality preached by churches are just too restrictive	34	43	62
The Bible is the actual word of God, and is to be taken literally.	33	25	9
Behavioral—report:			
Weekly attendance at church	65	47	1
Reading the Bible at home within the past year	51	46	26
Always or usually saying grace at home before meals	35	24	9
N	407	143	95

Source: See note 4.

Table 3.2 tells a different story, however, for it shows in what way returnees resemble loyalists far more than they do dropouts. The items of Table 3.2 have to do with good and evil and transcendent reward and punishment. These would seem to be areas of concern largely left behind by those who dropped out and never returned, but they are areas never really relinquished in the case of returnees. Such concerns may indeed have been a factor in the decision to return.

The first two lines of the table are easy enough to interpret. Belief in eternal life and the Devil is the dominant position among loyalists and returnees, but is a minority position for the dropouts. Something of the same message is contained in what we call the 'Morality Index', as a brief explanation will show.

Table 3.2. *Loyalists, returnees, and dropouts compared on beliefs and moral issues (%)*

	Loyalists	Returnees	Dropouts
Believe in:			
Eternal life	89	88	48
The Devil (Satan)	66	65	25
Morality Index:			
Traditional	43	30	15
In-between	22	32	18
Alternative	35	38	67
N	407	143	95

The Morality Index is the combination of people's answers to three questions: about premarital sex, homosexual relations, and abortion, to which people could respond that these things are always, usually, only sometimes, or never wrong; and a fourth question asking for agreement or disagreement with the idea that the husband ought to have the main say-so in family matters. On this fourth item we counted agreement as indicative of a traditional moral position ($+1$) and disagreement as indicative of an alternative moral position (-1). Similarly, each 'always wrong' answer to the first three items was counted as reflecting a traditional viewpoint ($+1$), each 'never wrong' as reflecting an alternative viewpoint (-1), and other answers as reflecting an in-between position (0). In Table 3.2, therefore, the category 'Traditional' includes those whose combined answers totaled $+1$, $+2$, or $+3$; the category 'Alternative' includes those whose combined answers totaled -1, -2, or -3; and the 'In-between' category includes persons who gave a mix of answers, or else consistently chose neither a $+$ nor a $-$ response and thus scored 0.

The central point is that returnees, while not as traditional in this sexual-family sphere as the loyalists, are just as infrequently found as the loyalists in the alternative camp. One can almost sense that, in dropping out, these returnees were showing some displeasure with the rigidity of their church on these moral matters. But one can just as readily sense that, in coming back, they are registering dissent from the alternative moral perspective found outside the church. Returnees therefore are far more likely to be in the in-between category. When looked at in combination with their responses to the questions regarding eternal life and the Devil, therefore, these once-lapsed Catholics do seem to resemble their never-lapsed counterparts.

If the above interpretation is correct—and proof would require time-series data we do not have—then returnees only *resemble* loyalists; they are not the *equivalents* of loyalists. Put another way, we can say that the 'lukewarm' answers given by returnees and reported in Table 3.1 are what they are because returnees share many of the beliefs and practices of the loyalists, but do not share the loyalists' *feelings* about those beliefs and practices. Those beliefs and practices mean something different to many, if not all, returnees.

Why this should be the case is the question we turn to next, where the social marginality of returnees' relationships to the church will be examined. We discover that, in terms of social marginality, returnees look more like dropouts than they look like loyalists.

BEING MARGINAL

Because our project anticipated the need for an index of primary group ties, our interview asked people to think of their very closest friends, the people with whom they felt on most intimate terms. We then asked how many of their neighbors they felt this close to. How many of their relatives outside the immediate family? How many of the people they had grown up with and gone to school with? We asked about some other categories, too—work-mates, fellow ethnics, fellow church members—but because not everybody has a job, identifies ethnically, or belongs to a church, we restricted our meas-ure of primary-group ties to the first three questions: how many of their neighbors, relatives, and school chums did they feel close to? Their combined answers became our index of primary-group ties.

For the entire sample, this measure of friendship was found to be strongly related to involvement in a church, a finding that accords with general wis-dom in the sociology of religion. Church-going is, among other things, a community matter, and the closer one is to one's community, the more likely one is to be associated with a church. This generalization held for the Catholics in our sample, but the question we now put was whether—as we would expect—such primary-group ties also served to inhibit dropping out. A related issue, for which we had no expectation, was whether primary-group ties were related also to the phenomenon of returning.

The first question is easily answered. Nearly half the persons scoring at the low end of the index had dropped out. Approximately a third of those in the middle categories had dropped out. But fewer than a quarter of those with high index scores had done so. Clearly, being socially embedded in the net-work of nearby people inhibits dropping out of the church. What was not so predictable is the fact that primary-group ties not only inhibit departure from the church but also appear to encourage, though with less force, even-tual return by those who do depart. This is to say that social network ties, the weakness of which apparently 'permits' dropping out, also help deter-mine whether dropouts will return.

Analysis showed some other characteristics that dropouts were also likely to have: males dropped out more than females, those born since the Second World War more than those born before, and the better-educated more than others. Also, those identifying ethnically with national origin groups having historic, monopolistic ties to Roman Catholicism—for example, those from Italy, Ireland, Mexico, Spain, and Poland—remained loyal more frequently than those identifying ethnically with national origin groups having historic but not monopolistic ties to Catholicism—Austria, Belgium, Canada, France, and Germany. These, in turn, were more loyal than those who identify with an ethnic group with no particular religious link, at least in America—China, India, Japan, and Yugoslavia—or those indicating no ethnic identity at all.

These four characteristics—being male, young, better-educated, and having no ethnic identification with a Catholic culture—can be conceived as demographic predispositions to drop out. Indeed, in combination, they show just this pattern, with those having none of these characteristics reporting only a 16 per cent dropout rate, but those with more of the characteristics having close to a 50 per cent rate. It is worth noting, however, that this set of demographic characteristics acts in a way analogous to the friendship index: among those with a low predisposition to drop out, the relatively few who did drop out returned at a sizeable rate of 79 per cent. As people move up this predisposition scale, not only does their dropout rate increase, but their return rate decreases to a low of 40 per cent. In other words, the forces that encourage leaving also discourage returning.

MARGINALITY AND THE MEANING OF CHURCH INVOLVEMENT

We come, then, to the critical test. Returnees are midway between dropouts and loyalists in Catholic beliefs and practices. In moral perspective they are closer to loyalists than to dropouts. Where they differ most from loyalists— and resemble most their fellow dropouts who never returned—is in their social ties to the Church. Table 3.3 provides the evidence.

The first three lines of Table 3.3 document what has already been implied. In terms of primary-group ties, returnees look more like dropouts than they do loyalists. The second line of this table is, if you please, an independent confirmation of the earlier argument: not only are returnees less embedded in a close network of friends, but the friends they have are even less likely to know *each other* than the friends of either dropouts or loyalists. The third line of Table 3.3 is simply one specific indication of this marginal position:

Table 3.3. *Loyalists, returnees, and dropouts compared on social ties to the Church* (%)

Social ties	Loyalists	Returnees	Dropouts
High in primary-group ties	40	24	23
Most of one's close friends know each other	54	43	49
Most of one's close friends are of the same ethnicity	51	40	39
Membership in one's congregation is very important	42	27	—
Feel close to many of the people known at church	26	15	10
Regards oneself as a 'strong' Catholic	62	39	39

Source: See note 4.

ethnic ties are important to returnees only to the same degree that they are important to dropouts, which is less than their importance to loyalists.

The underlying issue of this investigation, however—whether, in returning, returnees recreate the prior relationship with the Church—is best answered in the last three lines of Table 3.3. The fourth line makes the fairly obvious point that loyalists regard their congregational membership as far more important than do dropouts—who, by definition, have no congregational membership. In this context, then, for returnees to indicate a 'lukewarm' position is to recapitulate the earlier pages of this essay. It is really in the fifth and sixth lines of Table 3.3 that we see the most convincing evidence that bears on the theoretical question of the 'meaning' of returnees' return. The fifth line indicates that returnees resemble dropouts in the matter of 'feeling close' to fellow church members, while the sixth line—probably the most telling of all—shows that, in terms of self-identity as 'strong' Catholics, the returnees are no more enthusiastic than the dropouts. Both lag significantly behind the loyalists, and, perhaps more telling, the dropouts continue to regard themselves as 'Catholic' at the same rate as returnees.

CONCLUSION

Without data drawn from different times in the lives of the same people, we are handicapped in documenting causation from survey data. Obviously, returnees' and dropouts' answers to our questions are influenced by their actions, and thus they may be as much effect as cause. Nevertheless, the portrait presented here has a coherence that better fits the Wilson than the Bell image of how the 'sacred returns', if and when it does. Put succinctly, on the basis of these data on American Catholics in the late 1980s, 'returning' to the church after a significant period of non-involvement is far more a matter of assent to doctrine and resumption of pious practices than it is a resumption of social ties and thus the overlapping of one's religious identity with one's other identities. It is not, in other words, a resumption of the 'social signific- ance' of religion.

In the debate in which Bryan Wilson has been so vigorous a combatant, therefore, we have to come down on the Wilson side. Yes, indeed, church membership and doctrinal assent can fluctuate, and increase as well as decrease. But, while decreases may clearly signal secularization, increases are not exactly the reversal of that secularization. At least on the basis of the evidence here, the 'return' of the sacred is associated more with change than it is with the *status quo ante*.

FOUR

The Market Paradigm and the Future of Religious Organizations*

In a manner that is at once extraordinarily clear and eminently readable, Rodney Stark has set out in stages a compelling argument about the birth, development, and decline of religion. He has, to be sure, enjoyed the assistance of others along the way, mainly persons who began their collaborations as his students or colleagues and concluded as his co-authors. Chief among these collaborations has been *The Future of Religion* with William Sims Bainbridge[1] and *The Churching of America, 1776–1990* with Roger Finke,[2] but Stark's work since his own graduate student days, and especially since the 1970s, has exhibited a systematic development that puts him in the front ranks of sociologists of religion.

Stark's theoretical approach is best illustrated in his work with Bainbridge, suggesting that all religions are formed in high tension with their surroundings, but that they will be likely succumb to social pressures and work to decrease this tension, thereby becoming more church-like. The reduction in tension allows members to gain in respectability, but such reduction costs the organization the commitment of its membership, resulting in the dissatisfaction of traditionalists, who may defect to form new sects. This theory has been put to the test in Stark's collaboration with Finke, an analysis of sect–church tensions in the marketplace of religious competition in American religious history.

Although the Finke–Stark work is not meant to be strictly a history of religion in the United States in the manner, say, of Sydney Ahlstrom's *A Religious History of the American People*,[3] the authors apply their model of market successes and failures to aspects of American religious history to demonstrate its value. Beginning with the colonial period, they conclude

---

* Eric Mazur collaborated on this essay.

[1] Bainbridge, W. S., and Stark, R., *The Future of Religion* (Berkeley: University of California Press, 1985).

[2] Finke, R., and Stark, R., *The Churching of America, 1776–1990* (New Brunswick, NJ: Rutger's University Press, 1992).

[3] Ahlstrom, S., *A Religious History of the American People* (New Haven: Yale University Press, 1972).

that the early Puritans were not as religious as traditional historians would have us believe—their level of adherence was roughly 17 per cent compared to an adherence level of roughly 60 per cent among today's Americans. They point, ironically, to religious monopoly as the reason for this low adherence rate, noting that the more established, elitist religious institutions remained sedentary, uncompetitive, and apparently unconcerned about the participation level of their members. In those places where there was only weak, if any, religious competition coupled with strong support from the state, churches had little reason to evangelize, especially if it meant leaving comfortable surroundings for the dangers and deprivations of the wild.

It is for this reason that the Baptists and Methodists succeeded in expanding rapidly with the growth of the frontier. According to Finke and Stark, the mainline churches—Presbyterian, Congregationalist, and Episcopalians—emphasized well-educated, well-paid clergy, thereby creating an insufficient number of clergy to meet the demand.[4] This imbalance meant that available clergy could be selective about their assignments, placing poorer, more remote communities at a distinct disadvantage. By contrast, Methodist and Baptist clergy were generally neither seminary trained nor well-paid, though in abundant supply, and could therefore follow the pioneers as they moved west. Over time, however, the Baptists and especially the Methodists became more established by doing away with circuit riding, instituting seminary training, providing higher pay, and, by implication, lessening their populist tendencies. They thereby lost their ability to grow with the population, in effect, declining in their ability to compete in the marketplace, and thus began losing their market share. Later, Catholic practices matched those of the early Methodists and Baptists, and this enabled them to expand their market share early in US immigrant history. If the acts of the Second Vatican Council of 1962–65 are seen as acts to reduce Catholicism's tension with its social environment, then the general proposition is once again duplicated, as Catholic attendance rates have dropped significantly.

Finke and Stark also use their model of competition to provide an explanation for the failure of 'unification efforts', most notably the National Council of Churches and the ecumenical movement of the mid-twentieth century.[5] Noting the parallels to the religious monopolies of early colonial churches, the authors conclude that cartels, like monopolies, stifle competition, thereby providing fewer sought-after products. The economic model of religious competition, designed to provide believers with what they want, must be able to respond to their changing tastes. The more democratic or populist the institution, the more ready it is to change, and thus the more likely it is to dominate the market. Those institutions that lose their

---

[4] Finke and Stark, *The Churching of America*, 54–65. [5] Ibid., 199–229.

connection to their membership eventually lose the ability to grow, relative to the population.

Of course, no economic model is complete without an examination of why it is that people are drawn to the product. Finke and Stark conclude that people are more likely to belong to a group that requires greater sacrifice for membership, such as social stigma or other-worldliness.[6] People adhere more closely to connections for which they feel they have given up something. Thus, competition is not the only key; for an institution to compete success-fully, it must require a great deal from its membership. It is this lack of soci-etal sacrifice in mainline churches that explains their decline in market share; the easier it is to be a member, the less desirable membership is. Finke and Stark assert that groups that define the mainline will provide weak competi-tion in the marketplace when pitted against more populist, higher-tension groups, thereby explaining the successes of anti-establishment religious movements in US history.

As with all good scholarship that is both theoretically informed and empirically based, Finke and Stark's work not only instructs but also becomes the basis for elaboration. It is easy to discern exactly what Finke and Stark are arguing, but it is equally easy to perceive how their argument can be extended. It is the latter that we propose to do here.

Arguments—or theories, if you prefer, although in Finke and Stark's case 'arguments' seems more appropriate—can be extended in several ways. For some dyspeptic scholars, the only extension, it seems, is by contradicting the original argument, or, more commonly, by challenging its applicability in one or more sets of circumstances. In those instances, unless there is an effort to reconcile the contradiction or explain the inapplicability, such extensions are little more than occasions for scholars to be what the Elizabethans called 'froward'.

Other ways of extending arguments are more productive. One is by invest-igating the conditions under which a particular relationship is more and less true. Another way is to investigate a logically derivative thesis: if A leads to B, then A' must lead to B'. A third extension comes about when the thesis that A leads to B is shown to resemble the thesis that C leads to D, and E leads to F, after which A, C, and E are reduced to a common theoretical term, as are B, D, and F. In a sense, this reduction process, as it has been called, is the process of induction when induction goes beyond mere empirical gener-alization and moves into more abstract levels.

Yet another way of extending arguments is the obverse of reduction, a pro-cedure Paul Lazarsfeld has called substruction.[7] Just as a larger number of

---

[6] Finke and Stark, *The Churching of America*, 237–71.

[7] Lazarsfeld, P., *The Sociology of Empirical Social Research* (Boston, MA: Allyn and Bacon, 1972).

instances can be reduced to fewer by conceiving of them in more abstract categories, so may a few instances be seen as originating from combinations of less abstract categories. For example, the notion of 'degree of hostility' may become a more abstract way to express a continuum that includes harmony, followed by threat of force, which is then followed by actual force. In this sense, the category, 'hostility', reduces disparate acts to a single dimension from low to high. Reversing the process, one can see that the continuum 'hostility' in fact originates along two dimensions: simply put, one is the presence or absence of threat, the other the presence or absence of actual force. A three-point continuum is thereby 'substructed' and yields a four-fold classification, the added category being the use of actual force without any preceding threat. Substruction thus has something in common with such terms as 'explication', 'reconstruction', or the less elegant 'unpacking'.

WHAT DO WE SUBSTRUCT?

What follows is an exercise in substruction, the starting point of which is the Starkian assertion that in the religious marketplace, groups will succeed to the degree they make costly demands on their members, and they will fail to the degree that membership is not costly. Somewhat counter-intuitive, perhaps, this assertion is nevertheless put forward only after careful consideration.[8] In summary:

The inevitable dilemma is clear. On the one hand, a congregational structure that relies on the collective action of numerous volunteers is needed to make the religion credible and potent. On the other hand, unless these volunteers are mobilized to a high level of participation, that same congregational structure threatens to undermine the level of commitment and contributions needed to make a religion viable. Costly demands offer a solution to the dilemma. *That is, the level of stigma and sacrifice demanded by religious groups will be positively correlated with levels of member participation.* (Finke and Stark, *The Churching of America*, 252. Emphasis added.)

Although *The Churching of America, 1776–1990* is a very persuasive demonstration of this assertion, using empirical evidence from more than 200 years of American church history, the assertion remains probabilistic only. That is, stigma and sacrifice are 'correlated' with member participation; the 'cost' of membership is 'positively associated' with market share; tension with the surrounding culture, whether high or low, is 'related' to a religious organization's success, whether increasing or decreasing. One can

[8] See, especially, Finke and Stark, *The Churching of America*, 252–5.

readily imagine a continuum ranging from high-tension, successful religious organizations to low-tension, failing religious organizations, in which case one has re-created exactly the picture given by Dean Kelley in his controversial but seminal book, *Why Conservative Churches Are Growing.*[9]

Another picture is also possible—one achieved by substructing that continuum into the two dimensions that comprise it: tension and market share. Simplifying reality by imagining both dimensions as dichotomies yields a scheme that looks like Table 4.1.

Table 4.1. *Tension and religious market share*

		Sociocultural tension	
		High	Low
Market share:	gaining	2	3
	not gaining	1	4

Note: Each cell has been numbered for discussion. Numbering will become more obvious later in the argument.

The continuum generated by the Stark perspective would, in Table 4.1, encompass cell 2 and cell 4, but, substructed, this portrait can be seen to contain two other types of cases: religious organizations that are in high tension with their environment but losing, or at least not gaining, market share (cell 1), and those in low tension but nonetheless gaining market share (cell 3). Extreme examples falling into cell 1 come readily and vividly to mind, including such groups as Jim Jones's People's Temple or David Koresh's Branch Davidians. The clear moral is that all sects and cults are in a state of high tension, but not all sects and cults grow—a point to be touched upon later in this essay.

More strategic here, however, are cases that fall into cell 3: religious organizations that are in low tension, or are decreasing in tension, but none the less growing. We will presently discuss this particularly interesting category.

THE DYNAMIC OF THE SUBSTRUCTION SCHEME

To this point no great intellectual leverage can be claimed; we have replaced a two-fold with a four-fold classification. But substructing also encourages an entirely new perspective: a perspective that explains why the cells of Table 4.1 are numbered as they are. Religious organizations are subject to change,

[9] Kelley, D., *Why Conservative Churches are Growing* (New York, NY: Harper & Row, 1972).

in varying degrees to be sure, but this four-fold scheme now suggests that such change, when and if it occurs, follows a predictable sequence. The scheme is thus not merely a classification device that uncovers cases of religious organizations obscured by a single-dimension continuum; it also reveals a potentially useful dynamic by which orderly organizational change might be understood.

In cell 1 are found new sects and cults that are, by definition, in high tension with their environments and numerically precarious. If they succeed in attracting significant numbers of new members, however, they will do so, according to Stark's model, not by easing tension but precisely by finding more persons willing to pay the costs of that tension. Movement to cell 2 then occurs. Only after some success in gaining members will a high-tension religious organization begin to experience pressures to lower tension, a phenomenon attributable to the 'second-generation' problem identified by H. Richard Niebuhr[10] and splendidly expanded by Stark and Roberts.[11]

In principle, no religious organization can avoid these pressures to ease tension and reduce the costs of stigma and sacrifice, but some organizations will successfully resist these pressures and remain in cell 2, while others will succumb to these pressures, doing so without losing membership commitments, at least in the short run, thus moving to cell 3. According to Stark's work, however, in the long run, reduced tension leads to reduced commitment, so, unless religious organizations can maintain or reinstate the costs of member participation, reduced commitment will result in loss of market share, and thus reclassification in cell 4. Such, it is now widely believed, is the current status of so-called mainstream denominations, most of which were at one time small religious movements in considerable tension with their environment.

This movement from cell 1 to cell 4 via cells 2 and 3 might be seen therefore in linear fashion, as depicted below. A double line separates cell 1 from cell 2, a feature meant to highlight the fact that, as Stark and Roberts state, 'cults so often lose heart and turn inward'.[12] That is to say, many more religious groups get founded than gain enough new members to be able to move into cell 2. In this regard, a new religious group can be likened to a star in an astrological evolutionary model: its critical mass will determine its ultimate fate, whereas in the star, critical mass is determined by factors of growth over time. This comparison, though loosely made, can be used to illustrate the fate of new religious groups in the following way. The fate of a star depends

[10] Niebuhr, H. R., *The Social Sources of Denominationalism* (New York, NY: H. Holt and Company, 1929).

[11] Stark, R., and Roberts, L., 'The arithmetic of social movements', *Sociological Analysis*, 4 (1982), 53–68.

[12] Ibid., 55.

on its mass. All stars burn, but small stars that never reach a critical mass will burn out, while larger stars that do reach that critical mass will experience a distinctly different future; they will expand to the point that they will either explode or implode, respectively going nova or creating black holes.

1	2	3	4

Consider the fate of a new religious community, where critical mass is understood in terms of membership—the basic component of market share—and its growth over time. According to the market paradigm, mere raw growth is insufficient for a religious organization to compete. It must experience growth relative to its competition, that is, growth in market share. Therefore, if a new religious community cannot sustain growth relative to its competition, it is destined merely to burn and burn out. However, if it can continue to grow by attracting members in increasing numbers, its future will be much more dramatic. Its very growth will cause it either to accommodate and lower tension, thereby setting the stage for an explosion of schismatic groups, or to find new ways to stay 'costly' and maintain tension, 'circling the wagons' in a restorationist move, and thereby imploding. Either way, some people are likely to become unhappy and leave.

This dynamic is illustrated in the linear evolution of religious organizations presented previously. Small religious communities stay in cell 1; that is, they never achieve critical mass and therefore never experience the gain in market share necessary to sustain themselves successfully. In fact, their tension with society may be so high that they frighten away more people than they attract, and thus are kept from gaining market share. In terms of the adapted solar model, they are celestial flashes in the pan, stars that stay small, burn, and then burn out. The religious communities on the right side of the double line are the ones that do achieve a critical mass and will continue to grow to a certain point. However, in the process of attempting to achieve greater stability in the form of lessened tension, they are likely either to explode and 'spin off' new splinter groups, or to contract fiercely in an attempt to restore the original tensions. The ability of a religious community to avoid either going nova or becoming a black hole is thus based on its ability to maintain critical mass by balancing tension and stability, and to maintain its connection to factors, such as populism and vitality, that keep it burning.

This model is far from perfect, but it may lead to a new understanding of the relationship of one cell to another within the linear progression presented previously. It suggests that the growth and evolution of a religious community is not cyclical but spiral in nature; a beginning point is never revisited as progress continues. The evolution need not be linear, and it certainly need not be unilinear, but it does depend on other elements that explain how a religious community attains the critical mass to proceed through the burning stages of the solar model.

With this model in mind, are we in a position to predict the destinies in the next millennium of the various religious organizations that now surround us? No doubt this model yields predictions that improve upon random guesses, as we will now discuss. That discussion will reveal the model to be only partially successful, however, so we will conclude with some comments on how it might be elaborated.

ILLUSTRATIONS OF THE DYNAMIC

Perhaps the easiest part of the dynamic to illustrate is cell 1, the category of religious organizations that are in high sociocultural tension and losing, or at least not gaining, in membership. Indeed, of the more than 17,000 organizations classified in J. Gordon Melton's monumental *Encyclopedia of American Religions*,[13] probably the majority fall into cell 1. Take, for example, the case of the Evangelical Apostolic Church of North America. Tracing its episcopal lineage to the consecration of Ulric Vernon Herford as Bishop Mar Jacobus in India in 1902, the church has undergone a name change and slow growth, all the while following the orthodox theology of the Church of the East. In 1991, it reported a membership of one thousand led by sixteen clergy and three bishops.[14]

Another example is the Undenominational Church of the Lord, founded in 1918 as an independent holiness mission. At last report in the 1970s, it consisted of three parishes totaling fewer than one hundred members.[15]

A third example is the Assembly of Yahvah, a group related to, but independent of, the Assemblies of Yahweh, headquartered in Holt, Michigan. An Adventist group, the Assembly of Yahvah began in the 1940s in Fort Smith, Arkansas. In 1988, it reported fewer than two hundred members in its two congregations in Alabama.[16]

We hope that the three examples suffice to make the point that there exist numerous religious groups that never get beyond cell 1. It is not clear, of course, exactly when movement from cell 1 to cell 2 occurs. Elmer Clark's *The Small Sects in America*,[17] reveals a snapshot of numerous cell 1-type

---

[13] Melton, J. G., *Encyclopedia of American Religions*, 4th edn. (Detroit, MI: Gale Research, 1993).

[14] Ibid., 286.   [15] Ibid., 386.   [16] Ibid., 586.

[17] Clark, E., *The Small Sects in America*, Revised edition (New York. NY: Abingdon-Cokesbury Press, 1949).

organizations extant before and just after World War II. Many of them, if identifiable half a century later, may have survived through time, but they have barely been able to maintain membership, never achieving a sustained growth rate that would make them competitive with more recognizable religious organizations. Even labeling groups in cell 1 as 'losing' can be misleading because they can lose members only after experiencing at least some success at gaining members. Therefore, crossing the double line from cell 1 to cell 2 probably means reaching a condition of growth through new converts, especially births to current members sufficient to insure competitiveness through generations. Thus, a group such as Transcendental Meditation—technically, the World Plan Executive Council—that by 1984 had given basic training to more than one million Americans, had seen its initiation rates drop precipitously, all within the span of one generation. In the mid-1970s, Transcendental Meditation may have appeared to be a candidate for cell 2, but by now, having clearly dropped back into cell 1, it can be seen not to have met the criterion of continuity through generations.[18] The same might soon be said of the International Society for Krishna Consciousness. It is too soon to tell, because the picture is complicated by internal disagreements within the organization—which bodes ill—and by the increased immigrant population from India, some of whom are augmenting the membership rolls of what began as a cult recruiting American youth.[19]

Scientology and the Unification Church are two other groups founded after World War II that experienced sizable growth initially and thus appear to have crossed the double line into cell 2. These churches, however, are linked to large international networks, a feature that itself lends stability. Because the Unification Church in the United States reported a 17 per cent loss of members between 1976 and 1988,[20] this link to its counterparts in Korea and Japan is especially important. Both groups also show signs of accommodating, thus suggesting some possibility of movement toward cell 3. For example, the 'Moonies' have instituted 'home church', allowing for a part-time membership. Scientology, with claims of more than one thousand one hundred centers in more than eighty countries and eight million members, appears stable enough to be around a long time. However, despite continued legal battles—signs of high tension—Scientology groups sign up to remove highway litter, advertise in the Yellow Pages, and in other ways show signs of lowering tension.

This vulnerability—the genuine difficulty of achieving stability—allows us easily to illustrate cell 4 also. Groups in cell 4 are, by definition, those that

---

[18] Melton, *Encyclopedia of American Religions*; Stark and Bainbridge, *The Future of Religion*, 284–303.
[19] Melton, *Encyclopedia of American Religions*, 857–8.   [20] Ibid., 702–3.

gained sufficient membership to achieve continuity through generations (cell 2), felt the pressures to lower tension while still gaining members (cell 3), and then experienced decline. This path is the one Finke and Stark ascribe first to the colonial 'big three' churches, Congregational, Episcopalian, and Presbyterian; second to the upstart Methodists and Baptists by the mid-nineteenth century, and now to all mainline denominations.[21] Their findings are commensurate with those reported earlier by Kelley,[22] Roof and McKinney,[23] and others. Thus, using statistics from the 1988 *Yearbook of American and Canadian Churches* for the period 1940–1985, Finke and Stark show that, in market-share terms, the Methodist, Presbyterian, Episcopal, Congregational, and Disciples denominations have suffered an average 52 per cent loss.[24]

If, in noting this significant loss of market share by the so-called mainline churches, one asks which religious organizations are gaining, the answer more or less provides the names of many of the groups found in cell 2. Such churches as the Church of God, Nazarene, and Jehovah's Witnesses, although still relatively small numerically, have gained enormously in proportionate terms since the 1940s, and more especially since the 1960s—indeed, reports indicate that the Jehovah's Witnesses' community has grown an estimated 146 per cent from 1970 to 1990.[25] These groups have done so without any noticeable decrease in tension with the surrounding society.[26] Such groups may, in the future, feel the pressures to accommodate with that society, thereby lowering the tension and moving to cell 3, but it seems very unlikely that any of these groups, or the many more that could be listed, will fail to survive into the coming generations. Their continued survival is certain. They may explode by accommodating and experience sectarian splits, or they may find a way to implode and remain in high tension.

This leaves cell 3 to illustrate—cases of religious organization that are simultaneously continuing to grow and lowering tension with the surrounding society. Mark Shibley identifies such a case in contrasting a Vineyard parish and a Calvary Chapel, which are experiencing great growth, with local Southern Baptist and Assemblies of God parishes which are not growing. The contrasts are both cosmetic and theological. All four churches share a fairly standard evangelical outlook, but in the first two this outlook permits jeans, long-haired men, rock music, and generally informal worship, while in the second two these things border on being sinful. The morality

---

[21] Finke and Stark, *Churching of America.*

[22] Kelley, *Why Conservative Churches are Growing.*

[23] Roof, W. C., and McKinney, W., *American Mainline Religion: Its Changing Shape and Future* (New Brunswick, NJ: Rutger's University Press, 1987).

[24] Finke and Stark, *Churching of America*, 248.

[25] Melton, *Encyclopedia of American Religions*, 582.

[26] Finke and Stark, *Churching of America*, 248.

drawn from this evangelical outlook is also shared by all four churches, but unlike the two that are not growing, the high-growth parishes do not push moral conservatism as mandatory for Christians, in recognition of the right to religious liberty.[27]

The ability of a religious organization to grow in conditions of lowered tension seems to defy the Stark and Bainbridge theory of growth through higher tension.[28] However, there are a number of reasons tensions might be lowered, and a similar number of reasons why, to turn Kelley's phrase, liberal churches are growing. The most obvious reason is provided in the above example of giving the membership, or in our current terminology, the 'consumers', what they want. We shall address this aspect later. Another reason for the growth of lowered tension groups is that changing times often precipitate changes in tensions. Put bluntly, a society that no longer burns people for witchcraft can be said to be one where witchcraft is in decreased tension with society. Even institutionally, decreased tensions through changes in social sensibilities often result in healthy, lower-tension groups that sustain growth over time. Two such examples are the Universal Fellowship of Metropolitan Community Churches and Seventh-day Adventism (SDA). In the first example, a movement founded by a gay minister with Pentecostal roots has become a pan-Protestant lesbian and gay denomination reported to have over 30,000 members.[29] Although the Metropolitan Community Churches' petition for observer status to the traditional mainline National Council of Churches was rejected, the fact that the petition was supported by over 45 per cent of the voting members indicates a growing acceptance of gay and lesbian spiritual concerns that was unknown thirty years ago. In the case of SDA, changing attitudes regarding health and diet have made once ridiculed religious practices seem almost normative, and membership increased 35 per cent from 1975 to 1990.[30]

However, the Seventh-day Adventists also present the other aspect of cell 3, namely its close relation to cell 4. Malcolm Bull and Keith Lockhart, in their examination of Seventh-day Adventist society, suggest that as the community has reached maturity in the form of a third generation, it is now not only possible to be born, educated, work, and die solely in the SDA community, but it is also now increasingly unlikely that members will do so.[31] As the SDA's goals and those of American society converge, it has become possible

---

[27] Shibley, M., *Resurgent Evangelicalism in the United States: Mapping Cultural Change since 1970* (Columbia, SC: University of South Carolina Press, 1996), Chapter 5.

[28] Stark and Bainbridge, *Future of Religion*.

[29] *Christian Century*, 109/35 (1992), 1097.

[30] Kosmin, B. A., and Lachman, S. P., *One Nation under God: Religion in Contemporary American Society* (New York, NY: Harmony Books, 1993), 15.

[31] Bull, M., and Lockhart, K., *Seeking a Sanctuary: Seventh-day Adventism and the American Dream* (San Francisco, CA: Harper & Row, 1989), 256–68.

to be an Adventist well-integrated into the secular world—in other words, well-educated, well-trained members of the wider community. Such persons are precisely the ones at greatest risk of being lost to the SDA community.

SPECIAL CASES

In the process of lowering socio-cultural tension by accommodating the surrounding society, a religious organization is certain to displease some of its members even as it is pleasing others. Churches are more than people and members; they are also policies and institutional practices. Therefore, in lowering tension they are bound to find themselves in internal battles that transcend individual preference, showing church organizations themselves to be ambivalent, wavering between cells 2 and 3.

This is exactly the thesis of Armand Mauss's splendid book on the Mormons, *The Angel and the Beehive*.[32] The Angel refers to all that is unique to Mormonism and therefore sets Mormons apart. The Beehive, by contrast, refers to all of the ways Mormonism has 'borrowed nectar' from the surrounding society. The first is prophetic and revelatory, and therefore tension producing; the second is assimilative and accommodative and therefore tension reducing. Mauss writes:

It is important to emphasize that a tension—even struggle—within the church between [these] countervailing tendencies is by no means a recent development. It has been present from the beginning, although the specific issues have varied across time with internal conditions and external influences. Many observers have noted that certain polarities seem to be inherent in the Mormon tradition and might never be resolved. . . . . What also seems clear from the evidence is that in each polarity one side has grown at the expense of the other. (Mauss, *The Angel and the Beehive*, 201–2.)

It is Mauss' argument that, seen historically, the forces for assimilation and accommodation have dominated, thus in our terms pushing Mormonism toward cell 3. Since 'about 1960', however, a counter-movement, or 'retrenchment' in Mauss's terms, has been developing, thus pushing Mormonism back toward cell 2.

What, then, of the future? Mauss points out that only in North America has Mormonism lived through the successful rearing of a second and subsequent generation. In other places the Mormon Church strives to maintain its purity while, at the same time, struggling to accommodate the cultural demands of those places. In an assertion similar to the premise of ethnic

[32] Mauss, A., *The Angel and the Beehive* (Urbana: University of Illinois Press, 1994).

identity that 'what the son wishes to forget, the grandson wishes to remember', Mauss is suggesting that retrenchment is less a genuine effort to recover a past than it is a move to maintain a distinctive heritage by those already confident in their relatively tension-free relationship with the surrounding society.[33]

This move to maintain a distinctive heritage is rather typical of groups wavering between cells 2 and 3. Members of the Assemblies of God, the largest Pentecostal denomination in the United States, emerged from a history of economic disadvantage and now find themselves squarely rooted in the US middle class, experiencing a significant loss of tension. Paul Tinlin and Edith Blumhofer write:

The [Decade of Harvest evangelism] program demonstrated how far the Assemblies of God had come from its humble restorationist roots. Once it had seemed pure because it had been at odds with the culture; now its message had the ring of truth because so many believed it. Once adherents had been called to live in prophetic tension with their society; now they were typically conservative white working- and middle-class people whose lifestyles resembled those of other Americans of similar social standing.   (Tinlin and Blumhofer, 'Decade of Decline or Harvest? Dilemmas of the Assemblies of God', 685.)

As a result, the Assemblies of God 'suffers from a numerical and spiritual stagnation more typically associated with mainline Protestantism'.[34]

One of the more dramatic recent examples of a religious organization wavering between cells 2 and 3 is the Southern Baptist Convention (SBC). Beginning in the 1980s, a restorationist movement began to assert control over the institutional apparatus of the SBC, renewing a commitment to a high-tension religion. By the end of the 1980s a counter-movement, rejecting this strategy, was contemplating splitting off into a new convention, although as Nancy Ammerman and Bill Leonard describe it, structural and geographic circumstances limited this possibility. Because of the historical development of the SBC, the local churches felt a strong sense of independence from the national organization, meaning that denominational control was of little specific concern to the local church, which was thus removed from the larger theological and political debates. In addition, the new national identity of the SBC meant that restorationist motives may have been influenced by a certain defensiveness.[35] Regardless, the SBC now finds itself

---

[33] Mauss, A., *The Angel and the Beehive* (Urbana: University of Illinois Press, 1994), 210.

[34] Tinlin, P., and Blumhofer, E., 'Decade of decline or harvest? Dilemmas of the Assemblies of God', *Christian Century*, 108/21 (1991), 685.

[35] See Leonard, B., *God's Last and Only Hope: The Fragmentation of the Southern Baptist Convention* (Grand Rapids, MI: W. B. Eerdmans, 1990), 181, on the first point; Ammerman, N., *Baptist Battles: Social Change and Religious Conflict in the Southern Baptist Convention* (New Brunswick, NJ: Rutgers University Press, 1990), 69–71, on the second point.

sitting in what might be considered a precarious position by some—it can either raise tensions and solidify its position in cell 2, or it can continue to lower tensions with its surroundings and move into cell 3, and eventually, by implication, cell 4. The machinations over control of the SBC will determine its future. The study by Shibley mentioned earlier suggests that, perhaps especially outside the South, such restorationist efforts are not necessarily successful.

ENTER THE DEMAND SIDE OF THE EQUATION

Stark introduced the term 'religious economy' in an essay, 'How New Religions Succeed: A Theoretical Model',[36] although conceptions of religious organizations as firms competing in a marketplace can be found in his earlier work. After Roger Finke and Laurence R. Iannaccone introduced to the study of religion the supply-side notion from economics,[37] these two scholars made common cause and have applied their combined perspectives in several papers. This development has sparked much interest in the sociology of religion, leading even to the justifiable claim that it represents a 'paradigm shift'.[38]

Because virtually all earlier efforts to explain the rise and fall of religious organizations had looked to changes in demand arising from structural changes or changes in cultural tastes, the novelty offered by the supply-side perspective was a needed corrective. That is to say, those earlier efforts were employing—albeit largely unwittingly—a demand-side perspective and therefore ignoring variations in how 'products' were being made available in a largely unregulated religious marketplace. If it is true that free competition among many firms is more likely to satisfy demand than a more restricted competition, it is also the case that judgments are being made by the many firms as to what it is they might supply that will be demanded. The two perspectives, in other words, do not contradict but rather complement one another.

When using the supply-side model to predict the future of religious organizations, one should be able to improve accuracy by including factors that also influence demand—demographic trends, for example, or socio-political

[36] In Bromley, D. G., and Hammond, P. E. (eds.), *The Future of New Religious Movements* (Macon, GA: Mercer University Press, 1987), 19.

[37] Finke, R., and Iannaccone, L., 'Supply-side explanations for religious change', *Annals of the American Academy of Political and Social Science (Religion in the Nineties)*, 527 (May 1993), 27–39.

[38] Warner, R. S., 'Work in progress toward a new paradigm for the sociological study of religion in the United States', *American Journal of Sociology*, 98/5 (1993).

changes. Any such consideration of what potential consumers might want from a religion indicates that the supply side of the model is not the sole concern but only part of the equation.

DEMAND—GIVE THE PEOPLE WHAT THEY WANT

Sacrifice is identified by Finke and Stark as the magnet or selling point that attracts people to a religious community. However, this can, in some cases, be the tail wagging the dog, because people might join a religious community for any number of reasons and only later justify their participation through the notion of sacrifice: 'I have joined this group, which requires of me a great many sacrifices, so it must be worth it, or else I would not have joined'. For example, the Jewish community in this country grew roughly 11,370 per cent from 1790 to 1920, and sacrifice had very little to do with it. Rather, growth is explained by the low numbers of Jews in colonial America, followed by the period of tremendous immigration from the 1880s to World War I. It might be surmised that, by moving to the US, Jewish immigrants, if anything, lowered the stigma and sacrifice felt in Europe. In like fashion, tension in the form of sacrifice and stigma is also rather unconvincing when describing the attraction of the SBC to Southerners, although more convincing when describing its attraction to Californians and residents of Massachusetts.[39]

Studies have shown that some religious adherents opt for a religious tradition they are better able to integrate into the pre-existing structure of their lives rather than choose one more totalistic in its demands.[40] Even adherents to what may loosely be labeled the New Age are attracted for reasons other than sacrifice, stigma, and the resulting tension. In all of these instances, one can ask what membership in the community joined means to the joiner. If people are free to choose their religious associations, it seems rather arbitrary to assume that they, like the story of the baby Moses choosing a plate of red-hot coals over one of shining jewels, will choose that religious community requiring a sacrifice of them. If that is not what they desire most, it seems unlikely they will choose it.

[39] See Bloom, H., *The American Religion* (New York, NY: Simon and Schuster, 1992), 192, on the first point; Hammond, P. E., *The Protestant Presence in Twentieth-Century America: Religion and Political Culture* (Albany, NY: State University of New York Press, 1992), 162–4, on the second point.

[40] Davidman, L., *Tradition in a Rootless World: Women Turn to Orthodox Judaism* (Berkeley, CA: University of California Press, 1991); Heilman, S., and Cohen, S., *Cosmopolitans & Parochials: Modern Orthodox Jews in America* (Chicago, IL: University of Chicago Press, 1989).

With the qualifications indicated, however, the model we have evolved out of Stark's groundbreaking theoretical work may be helpful in imagining what is in store in decades to come. Although no crystal ball can provide certainty over the future of specific religious organizations, we have provided a framework that might help supply an educated guess:

Cell 1. Is the organization able to achieve a membership that can not only sustain itself but also grow in relation to other organizations through converts and childbirths? Has the organization the stamina, in other words, to provide for growth over time? If not, it may be mired in cell 1.

Cell 2. Does the organization have a tension level commensurate with the degree to which members are willing to sacrifice? In other words, does the consumer find the product attractive? If so, the organization may be able to maintain tension and grow, firmly establishing it in cell 2.

Cell 3. Has the lowering of tension resulted in no noticeable decline in membership? If so, and growth is maintained, the organization may be able to survive in cell 3. However, cell 3 is also marked by organizations struggling over issues of tension, like our examples of the Mormons, Assemblies of God, and the SBC. Organizations on the fence will find their futures in their ability to navigate this dilemma successfully—not necessarily by increasing tension, but by successfully determining the best balance between tension and the desires of the membership.

Cell 4. Has the lowering of tension resulted in the dissatisfaction of the membership? If so, the organization may be headed for cell 4, where it will stay until it disappears or can provide a product of more interest to the consumer.

In the end, factors of both supply and demand will determine the health and future of any religious organization. Changes in social patterns and the need to respond to the membership will require religious organizations to be attentive to the world in which they operate. The economic model provided by Stark and his colleagues and substructed above will enable observers of religious organizations to be sensitive to both sides of the equation when asking about the future of new religious organizations.

FIVE

Cults and Sects in America: Organizational Development*

The so-called cults that burst onto the American scene during the 1960s and 1970s quickly became the laboratory white mice for sociologists of religion. They seemed to emerge quickly, survive for a short or long span, then change into something else—all in the length of time that allowed single individuals to study them. Within very few years, therefore, the study of new religious movements, or NRMs as they soon became labeled, captured the attention of a sizable minority of sociologists of religion in the United States. Articles and, soon after, books about the NRMs flooded the publication channels of the profession, and now we are heirs to a significant body of literature that appears secure and growing. Inevitably perhaps, the first of these works were largely descriptive or 'ethnographic', because their subject matter was eccentric and exotic, and we needed to know simply *about* the NRMs. But in short order the empiricists were joined by the abstractionists, until now we have great quantities of both raw material and theorizing about NRMs.

The task here is to consolidate a portion of this literature. Interested more in the theorizing than the raw material, we restrict our concern even further to those aspects of NRMs dealing with their emergence and destiny—to the questions of what brought these organizations into existence, and what happened to them. Our discussion has three parts. First, we identify the key issues surrounding the questions of the emergence and development of NRMs. Second, we review the existing theories dealing with those issues, pointing out some knowledge gaps. Finally, we discuss ways by which the study of the emergence and development of NRMs contributes to the general sociological enterprise.

KEY ISSUES

In one sense, the key issues here have already been named as that of the NRMs' *emergence* and of their *development*. Each of these issues embraces

* David W. Machacek collaborated on this essay.

several sub-issues, which can rather easily be identified because they are not very removed from common sense. Thus, regarding the emergence of an NRM, we can ask about facilitating conditions, triggering events, and who is initially attracted.

Facilitating Conditions

Because an NRM is a *religious* phenomenon, it can be assumed that factors facilitating the emergence of an NRM will be found in either dissatisfaction with extant religions, or dissatisfaction with other aspects of life to which a novel religion is a response. Of course, both may be applicable. In the case of the NRMs emerging in the 1960s and 1970s, some persons found that their culture had become too materialistic and worldly, while others found that their churches and synagogues were themselves too materialistic and worldly. Whatever the source of the dissatisfaction, something about it made a religious response seem plausible.

Triggering Events

For seeds to germinate, they must fall into rich soil, but first they must be planted by one or more triggering events. As we will see, here is where many 'theories' of the 'causes' of NRMs are concentrated. For example, a particular leader appears, or a change in the immigration laws occurs, or a traumatic episode in public life takes place. In reality a dialectical relationship is likely between seed and soil, between facilitating condition and triggering event. Thus, would-be religious leaders seek out receptive audiences, and people who are receptive seek out religious leaders.

Populations Initially Attracted

The same dialectical relationship exists with respect to the third sub-issue, The soil may be ready, the seed may be planted and germinate, but growth must also occur. Thus the NRMs of the 1960s and 1970s had greatest appeal to disaffected middle-class young adults, but those same people were more actively seeking religious responses and thus making themselves available to religious leaders they encountered. For all of this empirical mixing up, however, it is clear enough that the many groups coming onto favorable conditions, triggered by similar if not identical events, experienced quite different rates of success. They *developed* in different ways.

This second issue—the development of NRMs—also embraces sub-issues: the problems of recruitment beyond the initial generation, of leadership succession, and of mobilizing both members and a realistic agenda.

Recruitment Beyond the Initial Generation

Many studies make note of the fact that the forces leading to the involvement of the first generation of recruits to an NRM are not typically replicated for subsequent generations. Most obvious, perhaps, in the case of parental pioneers and their children, this problem is nonetheless endemic to NRMs. The religious organization has no choice other than to 'solve' this problem or disappear. Not only are the children of the first generation uncertain about remaining involved as adults, but also relying on such children as the sole source of recruits dooms the organization to very slow growth.

Leadership Succession

A similar inevitability applies to the problem of leadership because all leaders die. In the case of NRMs, of course, this problem can be acute because of the strategic importance of a guru, a messiah, a prophet, or other charismatic figure. The issue of succession, therefore, is likely to result in factionalism—a fate guaranteed to retard growth, at least initially.

Mobilization

The problem of maintaining sufficient appeal to attract waves of recruits and the problem of orderly leadership is found more broadly in setting and maintaining a realistic agenda. By this is meant a credible program of action for leaders and followers, with attainable goals empirically assessable, thus providing the NRM with a distinctive purpose and enthusiastic members.

This brief outline of key issues in the study of NRMs is sufficient for our purposes here because of the existence of several noteworthy bibliographic essays,[1] bibliographic monographs,[2] or collections of analytic essays.[3] Among the virtues of these works are the extensive citations to be found in them. Our purpose here, therefore, has not been to duplicate what is so read-

[1] Robbins, T., Anthony, D., and Richardson, J. T., 'Theory and research on today's new religions', *Sociological Analysis*, 39 (1978), 95–122; Beckford, J., and Richardson, J., 'A bibliography of social scientific studies of new religious movements in the U.S. and Europe', *Social Compass*, 30 (1983), 111–35.

[2] Melton, J. G., *The Encyclopedic Handbook of Cults in America* (New York, NY: Garland Publishers, 1986); Robbins, T., *Cults, Converts and Charisma: The Sociology of New Religious Movements* (London: Sage, 1988).

[3] Barker, E. (ed.), *New Religious Movements* (Lewiston, NY: Edwin Mellen Press, 1982), also *Of Gods and Men: New Religious Movements in the West* (Macon, GA: Mercer University Press, 1983); Bromley, D., and Hammond, P. (eds.), *The Future of New Religious Movements* (Macon, GA: Mercer University Press, 1987); Wilson, B., *The Social Dimensions of Sectarianism* (Oxford: Clarendon Press, 1990); Bainbridge, W. S., *The Sociology of Religious Movements* (New York, NY: Routledge, 1997); Hexham, I., and Poewe, K., *New Religions as Global Cultures* (Denver, CO: Westview, 1997).

ily available in collections such as these cited, but to offer a modest map for guidance through the now vast literature.

EXISTING KNOWLEDGE

With little adjustment at all, the study of NRMs can be fitted into the larger, older, and much debated study of church-and-sect in the sociology of religion. Because this is the case, it is possible to argue that a huge amount of knowledge therefore exists about NRMs because of the quantity of knowledge about churches and sects. Three excellent reviews of this literature can be found in Yinger,[4] McGuire,[5] and Roberts.[6]

In 1979 Swatos, in *Into Denominationalism: The Anglican Metamorphosis,*[7] offered a systematic interpretation of the dynamics of religious organizational change. This scheme might have been applied to NRMs but, to our knowledge, has not. In the same year, however, Stark and Bainbridge suggested an alternative interpretation, first in a journal article and then, surrounded by much supporting theory and evidence, in a book, *The Future of Religion.*[8] Beyond being a simpler rendition of how sects form and may develop into churches, the Stark–Bainbridge perspective had the further virtue of adding 'cults' into its scheme and, more importantly, the virtue of systematically treating secularization as an integral feature of the theory. This inclusion is critical for the task here, because much of what is claimed as knowledge about NRMs rests on the notion of secularization. We will return to this Stark–Bainbridge perspective presently, but first we review some other interpretive schemes.

NRMS AND SECULARIZATION: FACILITATING CONDITIONS

For two major thinkers, Wilson[9] and Bell,[10] the development and dispersion of new religions in contemporary Western society are evidence of the

[4] Yinger, J., *The Scientific Study of Religion* (New York, NY: Macmillan, 1970), 251–81.

[5] McGuire, M., *Religion: The Social Context* (Belmont, CA: Wadsworth, 1987), 115–42.

[6] Roberts, K., *Religion in Sociological Perspective* (Belmont, CA: Wadsworth, 1990), 181–202.

[7] Swatos, W., *Into Denominationalism: The Anglican Metamorphosis,* Society for the Scientific Study of Religion Monograph Series, No. 2.

[8] Stark, R., and Bainbridge, W. S., 'Churches, sects, and cults: Preliminary concepts for a theory of religious movements', *Journal for the Scientific Study of Religion*, 18 (1979), 117–33; also *The Future of Religion* (Berkeley, CA: University of California Press, 1985).

[9] Wilson, B., *Religion in Sociological Perspective* (Oxford: Oxford University Press,1982).

[10] Bell, D., 'The Return of the Sacred?' *British Journal of Sociology*, 28 (1977), 419–49.

ongoing process of secularization. Novel religious beliefs and practices represent the attempt by 'irrational man' to learn to survive in 'rational society'.[11] In a rational society, family and community, which formerly provided direct interpersonal experiences, explode into a larger social system. Direct personal interaction thus becomes rare. Religion and family, no longer primary groups, become external agents that re-create the effects of real interaction for the individual. In this sense, then, the experience of the individual in a rational society is mediated by social structures alien to him. When existing structures fail to re-create, legitimate, and reinforce such experiences, the individual will seek out alternatives. When, for example, the existing dominant religions fail in this regard, the way is open for novel religions to enter into the competition. The two authors who have espoused this position, Wilson and Bell, have emphasized two different aspects of this dynamic.

For Wilson, the traditional worldview associated with social activity was tied intimately to the past. In the shift from traditional to rational society, the present and future supersede the past. Progress is more a standard of truth than is tradition or the practices and conceptions of former generations. Any claim to truth must survive a more rigorous test than the fact that it is tradition. It must be convincing—either verifiable empirically, or by logical argument. Religious truths are therefore at a disadvantage in such a situation. In the contemporary world, the expansion of education and the prestige of science as the means of attaining knowledge and material reward add another blow.[12]

The process of rationalization occurs throughout society, not merely at the level of mental labor. It transforms institutions and the relations between individuals within institutional frameworks. In the areas where religion once thrived and even dominated—family and community—rationalization eroded the authority of religion as bearer and arbiter of truth, propriety, and morality. In fact, religion's role in society has so diminished that it is now an increasingly marginal phenomenon, at least in the sense of religion as a cohesive, reassuring device.

From Wilson's perspective, the new religions fail to re-create the effects once genuinely produced by traditional religion. Like the major religious traditions, in a society where religion itself is marginal, the new religions enter into competition to meet the religious demands of individuals. The individual is free to choose among a variety of products with no great social consequences attached to the choice.

While Wilson has emphasized the marginality of religion in society and the insignificance of novel religions to social processes, Bell has focused more

---

[11] Wilson, *Religion in Sociological Perspective*, 177.   [12] Ibid., 128–9.

on the individual, and thus the potential significance of NRMs in persons' lives. The major argument is that secularization actually causes individuals to seek out new religions.

In 'The Return of the Sacred?' Bell argues that modernism is characterized by secular experimentation with alternatives to religion. 'Aestheticism', for example, is the assertion of individual expression in art, turning from the restraint identified with traditional religion. 'Political religions', likewise, are attempts to free humans from their dependence on the gods.[13]

Unlike Wilson, however, who interprets new religions as the manifestation of the last vestiges of the religious consciousness among those for whom secularization has not yet removed the supernatural from the world, Bell sees the failure of secular experiments as providing the impetus toward new religious understandings. As the failure of traditional religions to accommodate changing culture and society formerly led to experimentation with secular alternatives, so the failure of these experiments necessarily leads to a search for other possibilities. 'When religions fail, cults appear. When the institutional framework of religions begins to break up, the search for direct experience which people can feel to be "religious" facilitates the rise of cults'.[14]

As something of a rebellion against modernism, these new religions, Bell predicts, will be characterized by a 'resurrection of memory. . . . They will, contrary to previous experience, return to the past, to seek for tradition and to search for the threads which can give a person a set of ties that place him in the continuity of the dead and the living and those still to be born'.[15]

To repeat, then, Wilson and Bell both see new religions as the result of the secularization process. There is a second group of theorists for whom the surge of new religions in the 1970s is the result of a specific episode in Western society: the counterculture of the 1960s. In addition to secularization they rely on concepts of deprivation and crisis.

Stephen Tipton, for example, argues that the upsurge of new religions in the 1970s and the counterculture of the 1960s tell of the failure of Protestant Christianity to provide adequate moral guidance for life in the modern world. Young people found it impossible to resolve the gap between social life as they experienced it and the moral framework provided by traditional religions. The counterculture provided an alternative set of guidelines and meaning systems. Participants, however, found it equally difficult to reconcile the value system of the counterculture to real social life.[16] The result was a turn to novel religions through which the conflict of values could be resolved. Neither traditional nor counter-cultural value systems were

---

[13] Bell, 'Return of the Sacred?', 429–38.   [14] Ibid., 443.   [15] Ibid., 444.
[16] Tipton, S., 'The moral logic of alternative religions', in M. Douglas and S. Tipton (eds.), *Religion in America* (Boston, MA: Beacon Press, 1983), 81.

conducive to life in American society, leaving 'a vacuum of meaning [which] these other ideologies are expanding to fill'.[17]

For Bellah and his associates, the crisis evidenced by the counterculture of the 1960s was not specifically the failure of Protestant traditional religion, although this played a role. For these authors, the crisis of meaning occurred at the breakdown of civil religion. The Christian symbolism adopted in American civil religion became incompatible with the 'utilitarian individualism' that came to dominate social and economic life.[18] The development of a counterculture brought this crisis to light, but the counterculture itself was unable to resolve the problem. In Bellah's view, then, the new religious movements of the 1970s were 'survival units', which 'provided a stable social setting and coherent set of symbols for young people disoriented by the drug culture or disillusioned with radical politics'.[19] A similar argument is offered by Anthony and Robbins,[20] although the crisis in American civil religion is attributed by them to a shift from entrepreneurial capitalism to managerial capitalism.

The approach that interprets the emergence of new religions in terms of cultural crisis evidenced by the 1960s has been quite popular among sociologists; the social environment conducive to the rise of novel religions is characterized by a fault between existing practices and the dominant meaning / legitimization / guidance system. Where extant conceptual frameworks are functioning well, novel religious or ideological ideas would be neither plausible nor a particularly attractive option. When such frameworks do fail, alternative ideas become more plausible options. The experience of deprivation or crisis, because of the lack of congruence between meaning system and activity, provides the motivation for individuals to seek out such alternatives.

DEVELOPMENT OF NRMS

We have reviewed theories in which alternative systems of meaning become plausible options. The next question, then, is how such options develop? Do charismatic figures appear, whose magnetic personalities attract a following?

[17] *Religion in America* (Boston, MA: Beacon Press, 1983), 104.

[18] Bellah, R., 'New religious consciousness and the crisis in modernity', in C. Glock and R. Bellah (eds.), *The New Religious Consciousness* (Berkeley, CA: University of California Press, 1976), 333–52.

[19] Ibid., 342.

[20] Anthony, D., and Robbins, T., 'Spiritual innovation and the crisis of American civil religion', in M. Douglas and S. Tipton (eds.) *Religion in America* (Boston, MA: Beacon Press, 1983).

Do groups of individuals suffering similar experiences of deprivation come together, begin to work out answers to their problems, which answers then become a system of meaning? Do individuals, experiencing a crisis of meaning, explore some hidden but ever present religious substratum, find attractive answers there, and bring them to the surface by forming a group around the idea? Each of these questions has been answered in the affirmative in at least somebody's theory. We turn next to a review of several of those theories.

Robert Ellwood: The Diachronic Model

In addition to established religion in society, Ellwood argues, there exists an alternative tradition, invisible for the most part, but which emerges from time to time in novel religious groups. The symbolic systems espoused by these groups are not really new. They have histories, a diachronic dimension. What is new about them is the group itself, not the religious system espoused. When novel groups develop, they represent 'a fresh outcropping of a spiritual perspective always latent in American life'.[21] From such a perspective, Ellwood suggests that we exchange the term 'new religion' for 'emergent religion'.[22]

When emergent religion is brought to the surface in a novel movement, it looks new. Each new group, the 'epiphenomenon', is a historically specific event and will necessarily be influenced by the contemporary environment. However, looking deeper than the epiphenomenon, one finds 'certain common symbols and deep structures', and often 'definite historical and personal linkages to other outcroppings'.[23] New Age groups today seem clearly to exemplify this perspective.

Ellwood is arguing for a method by which to study emergent religions, not offering a theory of development. His perspective, however, suggests that how, or if, an NRM develops is partly determined by events and forces somewhat removed from the facilitating conditions that led to its emergence. The next theorist elaborates on this thought.

Roy Wallis: The Cultic Milieu and Novel Religions

Ellwood's concept of a religious substratum in American culture is similar to Wallis' idea of a 'cultic milieu'. NRMs emerge from within this milieu either spontaneously or around a charismatic figure. Depending on how the group develops, particularly on the way authority is handled, a novel religious

---

[21] Ellwood, R., 'Emergent religion in America: An historical perspective', in J. Needleman and G. Baker (eds.), *Understanding the New Religions* (New York: Seabury, 1978), 280.
[22] Ibid., 280–1.   [23] Ibid., 282–3.

group will either develop in the direction of a sect, or it will face the possibility of reabsorption into the cultic milieu.[24]

We must understand the categories of 'cult' and 'sect' in Wallis' thought.
The difference between a cult and a sect as forms of religious organization
lies primarily in the locus of authority. Wallis holds that a cult is characterized primarily by individualism; the locus of authority is the individual par-
ticipant who may select from a variety of cultic practices and beliefs
according to personal taste and desire. In the cult there is no basis for evalu-
ating heresy, because it is 'epistemologically individualistic'.[25] The sect, on
the other hand, is characterized by an established hierarchy of authority, and,
correlatively, by some means of identifying heresy.[26]

Somewhere between the cult and sect is what Wallis calls the centralized
cult. This is a group that develops around a charismatic figure but has no reference to authority beyond the founder, and therefore little possibility of
avoiding reabsorption into the cultic milieu after the death of its leader.
Wallis' theory of the development of NRMs is based on a 'cult-centralized
cult-sect' continuum. He suggests that novel religions may arise at any stage,
and may in fact develop in either direction or fluctuate on the continuum.[27]

With this continuum in mind, we can look at the process of development
of novel religion. The non-centralized cult arises spontaneously from the
cultic milieu. A group of seekers *organize themselves* around some common
interest, perhaps the ideas or revelations of an individual.[28] At this simple
stage, the cult would look something like a study group or self-help therapy.
From this point, the non-centralized cult will develop some sort of authority
beyond the individual participants, which may involve the *election* of a
leader, or possibly the emergence of a charismatic leader. Otherwise, members may 'exhaust the possibilities of a specific doctrine' and be reabsorbed
into the milieu.[29]

Novel religions may also emerge directly as centralized cults, the obvious
case in groups that *form* around a charismatic founder. Authority, however,
still resides with the individual. Therefore, because the leader provides services to followers, development in this case depends on whether clients
remain loyal and the leader continues to supply their demands.

The third group Wallis identifies—the sect—is an offshoot of an already
established religious organization and thus is not likely to be invoked in a
discussion of *new* religious movements.

[24] Wallis, R., 'Ideology, authority, and the development of cultic movements', *Social
Research*, 41 (1974), 299–327 at 306–7.
[25] Ibid., 304.   [26] Ibid., 308–9.   [27] Ibid., 324.   [28] Ibid., 306.
[29] Ibid., 306–7.

Stark and Bainbridge: 'Three Models of Cult Formation'

Stark and Bainbridge make a contribution to our understanding of religious innovation by offering a comprehensive theory of cults. Their definition of cult can serve as our starting point: 'Whether domestic or imported, the cult is something new vis-à-vis the other religious bodies of the society in question'.[30] They then offer three complementary models of cult development.

In the *psychopathology model,* novel religions are born when an individual suffering some form of crisis has an 'episode' that provides that individual with new symbolic rewards addressing the crisis. These rewards are shared with others, who, suffering similar problems, are able to structure their unease and thereby find relief. They may coalesce around the originator, providing the foundation of a cult, and the rewards become the basis of a symbolic system. If an individual psychopathology can thus find 'successful social expression', a cult will form, and the sense of crisis may be alleviated for both the founder and the individual participants.[31]

The *entrepreneurial model* of innovation, like the psychopathology model, is a comment on charisma. In this model, an individual entrepreneur sees in religion an open market with great potential rewards. The entrepreneur, thus borrowing from other traditions but adding creative elements, consciously develops a system of non-empirical rewards, then actively seeks out clients, offering those rewards in exchange for material rewards. Because the development of such a system requires experience and skill, the founder of an entrepreneurial cult may have prior experience in a successful cult. For this reason, and because of borrowing from other groups, cults have 'family resemblances'.[32]

The *subcultural evolution model* of cult development represents the most radical break from the idea of charisma. This model stresses more than any other the role of group interaction in the development of the system of meaning, the election of a leader, and the means of exchanging non-empirical rewards. Stark and Bainbridge suggest that when a small group of intimately interacting individuals forms in the pursuit of scarce or non-existent empirical rewards, failure to attain the goals motivates members to begin exchanging symbolic, non-empirical compensators. This exchange preserves the group and, as well, provides the basis of a system of meaning. If the symbolic exchange is rewarding, and the social environment allows a measure of freedom, the group may undergo a process of social implosion. In this isolation, there is the possibility of developing a novel culture.[33] Cult evolution, then, is more likely in an environment that provides minimal external constraints.

---

[30] Stark and Bainbridge, *Future of Religion*, 25.   [31] Ibid., 173–7.
[32] Ibid., 178–83.   [33] Ibid., 183–7.

Stark and Bainbridge's approach to religious innovation has several strengths. First, it accounts for the idea of charisma in the process of cult development but is not dependent on it. It accounts for the influence of conditions in the social environment that encourage or hinder the development of a novel religion without making any condition necessary. Finally, it takes into account the role of group interactive processes in the development of novel belief-systems while allowing a decisive role for individuals.

The three models fall short, however, on the issue of historical specificity raised by Ellwood. Linkages with previously existing religious systems are illustrated only in the entrepreneurial model, although such linkages are necessarily present, according to Ellwood, in any novel religion. Little also is said about the types of individuals that NRMs are likely to attract. As Wallis argues in his discussion of a cultic milieu, cults are likely to develop among those upon whom established religions have little or no hold. In Stark and Bainbridge's models of cult development, novel religions could develop in any population, although they offer convincing evidence that, just as sects thrive where established religion thrives, cults are more likely to develop where established religion is weak.

RELATED THEORETICAL CONTEXTS

As we have just seen, the study of NRMs has been accompanied by considerable theorizing—from theories about the rise of one movement, to theories of movement popularity, to theories tying NRMs to secularization and church-and-sect phenomena. Much less noted are the ways by which the study of NRMs illustrates and extends social theories having no intrinsic reference at all to religion. What the study of NRMs might mean to other theoretical endeavors has hardly been explored, the obvious exceptions being those issues just reviewed: recruitment, leadership, mobilization, and so forth. In this final section, therefore, we offer a discussion of how, by extending the horizon, thoughts generated by investigation of novel religions might reach into other theoretical domains.

Let us begin with a fairly obvious observation—that in spite of the considerable hostility directed at many, if not all NRMs, their status as religions has not been much challenged, legally or culturally. One way of interpreting this lack of challenge to the religiousness of the NRMs is to do what such observers as Bell[34] and of course the devotees themselves do, which is to accept the authenticity of these movements, to recognize their truly sacred

---

[34] Bell, 'Return of the sacred?'.

character. It should be clear that the issue of 'authenticity' in this context is not metaphysical but sociocultural; not is it real, but is it coin of the realm? That is to say, one response to a novel religion is to grant that it is unconventional perhaps, but accept it as real because its followers believe it to be real. This interpretation thus resembles what Wuthnow[35] calls the neoclassical approach—the approach, he says, of Peter Berger, Robert Bellah, and Clifford Geertz, among others.

The neoclassical approach stresses the holistic meaning of things and assumes that, because most of us experience great discomfort leading meaningless lives, we seek and discover meaning, which is then often expressed religiously. New religious movements are thus innovative means of bringing order out of chaos for those persons who accept them. Being new and bizarre, these movements may have an uphill credibility battle, but their successes are as real as the historically dominant and culturally secure religious traditions and denominations, so this approach would say. Thus the *relative ease* with which NRMs have applied for, and received, tax-exempt status in the United States and many European countries—and this in spite of much public hostility.[36]

But oddly enough, the lack of legal and cultural challenge to the religiousness—as distinct from the credibility—of the NRMs might be interpreted in an entirely contradictory way. This second interpretation, instead of saying 'You may be odd, but you are real', says 'You are not real because no religion is real'. By this account, the lack of challenge stems not from an empathic tolerance for religious pluralism, but from a disinterest in something as unimportant and ephemeral as religion. The first interpretation sees NRMs as potential energizers of religion generally; the second sees NRMs as further evidence that meaning in life is inaccessible except through constant and evanescent negotiation and communication, which involves a highly individualized process. This second interpretation thus resembles the approach Wuthnow labels poststructuralism, whose representatives include Mary Douglas, Michel Foucault, and Juergen Habermas. Religion, in this approach, 'receives almost no attention' because questions of meaning are in general de-emphasized.[37]

The differences between these two approaches have been stated here in exaggerated form no doubt, but they expose what is a very interesting aspect of the development and life cycle of NRMs, an aspect that, to our knowledge, has not been remarked before. Reference is to the fact that, during the

[35] Wuthnow, R., *Meaning and Moral Order* (Berkeley, CA: University of California Press, 1987), 36.
[36] See Wilson, B., *Social Dimensions of Sectarianism* (Oxford: Clarendon Press, 1990), 69–86 for discussion.
[37] Wuthnow, *Meaning and Moral Order*, 53.

years that the NRMs burst onto the scene, appearing as new and self-contained religious alternatives to the traditional denominations, study after study of those traditional denominations was making it abundantly clear that persons were 'piecing together' their own creeds and codes. Religion now comes *à la carte*. Denominational loyalty has declined precipitously, and one could not assume that any two members of a single church shared much at all in the way of any religion.[38]

Consider what the social revolution of the 1960s and 1970s has done generally to the so-called mainstream churches: people, including people who are highly involved in the life of some parish, have reached new levels of what might be called personal autonomy, which has the effect—even if they are highly involved in a church—of conceiving of the church, of doctrine, of moral codes, and of ritual practices almost entirely in individualistic terms. So much is this the case, and so prevalent is it in many denominations—though there is, of course, some variation both by denomination and by region—that it has been called a qualitative change.[39] The relationship between religion and the American culture has been renegotiated, in other words, and it seems inconceivable that NRMs could have emerged while this renegotiation was taking place, and not be influenced by it.

A change also took place in the national political religion, of which the emerging NRMs were, so to speak, by-products. In a broader theoretical context, this change might be seen as a decline in the 'inheritability' of religion—the notion that one's religion is largely an expression of one's ascribed group memberships, especially family but including ethnicity, social class, and so forth. This decline in 'inheritability' was accompanied by the emergence of the argument that persons not only *could* choose their own religion but *should*, a normative proposition held by at least three-quarters of American adults. The conditions that 'allowed' or 'facilitated' NRMs thus represented a severe challenge to traditional religious groups.

As has been noted in other contexts, however, such individual freedom often comes in a package deal, the other element of the package being irrelevance. And here is where we see what is common to the ready acceptance of the NRMs as genuine religions, at the same time the traditional religions were being fragmented almost beyond recognition. Both processes reflect the growing *social* irrelevance of religion.

---

[38] Bibby, R., *Fragmented Gods* (Toronto: Irwin Press, 1987); McNamara, P., *Conscience First, Tradition Second* (Albany, NY: State University of New York Press, 1991); Roof, W. C., and McKinney, W., *American Mainline Religion: Its Changing Shape and Future* (New Brunswick, NJ: Rutger's University Press, 1987).

[39] See Hammond, P., *Religion and Personal Autonomy: The Third Disestablishment* (Columbia, SC: University of South Carolina Press, 1992).

Now, it is patently clear that religion is of great importance to some people, and thus it is relevant in some sense. What we are pointing to, therefore, is really the irrelevance of religion to American political culture especially. And here is where we dissent somewhat from Anthony and Robbins's invocation of the concept of the American civil religion in their discussion of NRMs.[40] Why? Only because it may cause us to look in the wrong place to understand what has happened. What was available through most of the nineteenth century was a Protestant ideological link between religion and politics. That link underwent a severe challenge toward the end of that century, the response to which challenge led, several decades later, to a different ideological link between religion and politics. It is perhaps understandable that, by the time this second ideological link was being challenged, its shaky status led to the discovery of an American civil religion, now 'broken' and no longer functioning when Bellah called it to our attention.[41] But what was being discovered—irrespective of what it is called—was a decliningly useful way by which religion was made relevant to twentieth-century American political culture. In the 1960s and 1970s the lack of such a link became even more noticeable.[42]

We arrive at a point then at which NRMs *and* traditional religions are revealed to have characteristics in common with other nurturing institutions variously called 'redemptive institutions', 'soft structures', 'mediating structures', etc. The parallels with the family are especially acute, and we conclude with an observation from a book that, though it refers not at all to religion, could just as readily be referring to the subject of this paper.

While legal ties among family members are becoming attenuated and the legal structure of the family is being loosened, the web of relationships that bind an individual to his job (and his job to him) is becoming tighter and more highly structured. . . . [An] individual's economic security against illness and old age or family disruption by death or divorce will no longer, in principle, be provided by the family, and . . . it will, in principle, be provided through her own work and work-related benefits, with government as a back-up system. (Glendon, M., *The New Family and the New Property*, 1–2.)

Families do not disappear, of course, and neither will religion and churches. But the extreme levels of individual choice—in spouses, for example, and whether to stay married—is reflected also in options made available by the popularity of new religious movements. It is the case, however, that, as in the family, individual choice is purchased at the cost of reduced security and social relevance. The study of NRMs has helped us see that.

[40] Anthony, D., and Robbins, T., 'Spiritual innovation and the crisis of American civil religion'.

[41] Bellah, R., 'Civil religion in America', *Daedalus* (Winter, 1967), 1–21.

[42] See Hammond, P., *The Protestant Presence in 20th-Century America* (Albany, NY: State University of New York Press, 1992).

SIX

The Appeal of Buddhism in America*

The doctrine of separation of church and state allows the American religious marketplace great flexibility. New religions can move in with relative ease and compete with well-established religions as well as other new religions. One new religion that appears to have achieved organizational stability is Soka Gakkai International (SGI). Having conducted a survey of American members of SGI during 1997, we offer here a glimpse of some of our findings. They bear on the appeal Buddhism may have for Americans.

As a Buddhist sect, Soka Gakkai traces its roots to the fifth century BCE and the teachings of Siddhartha Gautama. More specifically, however, it is the teachings of Nichiren Daishonin, a thirteenth-century Japanese monk, that form the basis of Soka Gakkai beliefs and practices. Organizationally, Soka Gakkai is far younger, being the creation of two Japanese educators, Tsunesaburo Makiguchi and Josei Toda, who, in the decade before World War II, founded Soka Kyoiku Gakkai—'Value Creating Education Society'—a movement imbued with Nichiren's teachings but dedicated initially to educational reform. Both founders were imprisoned for rejecting the militarism surrounding them in the 1930s. Makiguchi died there, but Toda came out of prison in 1945 and set about rebuilding the movement. Membership expanded rapidly. By the time of Toda's death in 1958, the organization claimed a membership in excess of 750,000 households in Japan. It was at this point that Daisaku Ikeda assumed the leadership position.

By 1975, Soka Gakkai had associations in many parts of the world and thus changed its name to Soka Gakkai International (SGI). The first overseas chapter was in the United States, begun and maintained originally by Japanese wives of American servicemen. In the 1960s and 1970s recruits were sought among non-Japanese as well—to the point where Japanese-Americans are now a clear minority in SGI-USA.

---

* David W. Machacek collaborated on this essay.

HOW OUR SURVEY WAS DONE

The most comprehensive listing of 'members' of SGI-USA is found in the subscription lists of the four publications distributed through the group's headquarters in Santa Monica, California. The largest of the four publications is the weekly newspaper, *World Tribune,* but persons were eligible to be part of our sample by subscribing to any one or more of the four. Our research budget allowed us to print and mail nearly 1,200 questionnaires. With an estimated 40,000 subscribers from which to select respondents, we randomly chose 3 per cent, stratified to represent proportionately each of the geographic regions of America where subscribers are found.

This process yielded 1,185 names and addresses, of which 104 were removed from the list, either because they told us they were not members or because they could not be found at the address provided and were presumed by SGI headquarters to be no longer members. Of the remaining 1081, we heard from 401, yielding a response rate of 37 per cent. Our book goes into great detail concerning the 'representativeness' of our sample,[1] but as will be shown below, the questions of greatest interest to us can be pursued even if the sample is 'biased' in some way—if, for example, females returned questionnaires at a higher rate than males.

WHAT WE ARE LOOKING FOR

In this essay we are interested in finding out why there are Soka Gakkai Buddhists in America. If, for example, one asks why there are Jews in America, the answer is found in the history of Jewish immigration and the formation in America of Jewish families who had Jewish children. The same kind of answer applies to the Greek Orthodox and other groups in which ethnicity or national origin is tied to religious identity. We understand their presence in America by understanding the history of immigration.

In its early years, SGI, then called Nichiren Shoshu Buddhism, revealed a similar pattern in America. The first members were migrants from Japan, often married to American GIs. Indeed about one in ten persons in our sample report being born into SGI, either in Japan or in America as a child of someone already a member. But this means that nine in ten converted to SGI-USA.

---

[1] Hammond, P., and Machacek, D., *Soka Gakkai in America: Accommodation and Conversion* (Oxford: Oxford University Press, 1999).

We can be even more specific, however, because, while only one in ten were born into SGI, others, only 34 of the sample converted into SGI from some other sect of Buddhism. And, although this conversion process is interesting in its own right, the question implied in our title—the appeal of Buddhism in America—clearly invites focus on persons who convert to Buddhism in America from entirely different religious backgrounds. The assumption, then, is that this third category of members made the greatest change in converting to SGI, and the first category of members made the least change, with the second category somewhere in between.

PUSHES AND PULLS

These three categories suggest the scheme we follow in this essay and elaborate in our book—a scheme based on a supply and demand model of behavior. In this case, the behavior is religious identity as a member of SGI, but the model fits many behaviors. Take, for example, the act of voluntarily migrating to a country different from the one in which a person is born. We can see immediately that two kinds of factors may operate—those factors in the native land that make continued living there less desirable, and those in the destination land that make the prospect of living there more desirable. The first factors push, while the second factors pull.

Now consider the example at hand: membership in SGI-USA. Some people find that the religion into which they are born remains desirable, at least to the degree that they do not wish to defect. They feel no push. At the same time, neither are they aware of any alternative religion that appears more attractive than their own. They feel no pull either. We have just described our first category of SGI-USA members. There is little of theoretical interest about them when it comes to the question of *why* they are members of SGI-USA. Neither push nor pull, for them, seems to play much of a role.

How about the second category—those who have switched from one kind of Buddhism to Soka Gakkai? We might expect in these cases to find that a major factor in why they are SGI-USA members is found in the 'pull', or attraction, of SGI over whatever other Buddhism they once practised. After all, in all probability they have not been 'pushed' out of Buddhism but simply drawn to a variant of the religious perspective they had already adopted. Our theoretical interest tends to focus then on how they were 'pulled' into SGI, not 'pushed' from an earlier kind of Buddhism. They, too, will be ignored here.

It is thus our third category on which the theoretical focus is greatest, because clearly persons in that category have experienced both pushes and pulls—pushes in the sense that they found traditional American religions less than satisfactory, and pulls in the sense that they evidently found in SGI an appealing alternative.

Using again the migration analogy, we can note that persons may be subject to many factors that push them away from their native land and other factors that pull them towards another country. But persons are not equally available to act on those pushes and pulls. First, some will be held back by structural features of their existence: family ties, for instance, or occupational or community loyalties. Others will be held back by ill health or lack of financial resources. Second, certain cultural features may represent barriers to migrating: language incompetence, for instance, or lack of job skills or travel experience. Together, these structural and cultural features may be so inhibiting as to make pushes and pulls irrelevant. So it is with the 'migration' from one religious identity to another; structural and cultural features may effectively render some people unavailable to the pushes and pulls of their religious existence.

This said, then, we consider both the structural and cultural availability of these American SGI converts prior to encountering SGI. These features should help us to understand better the appeal of Soka Gakkai Buddhism in America.

SUPPLY AND DEMAND

First, let us explain what we mean by the terms, 'supply' and 'demand'. By 'supply' we mean essentially the pulls in people's social environments of which they are aware. By 'demand' we mean essentially the pushes in that environment. As many have noted, few converts come out of religious settings they find pleasing, and it should go without saying that persons never convert to a religion they have never heard of. Our category of converts who have experienced both pushes and pulls therefore offers us a chance to look closely at two major issues in the sociology of religion: Firstly, what factors altered the demand-side of these SGI-USA members that rendered them dissatisfied with their earlier religious situation, and left them open to the appeals of Buddhism? Secondly, after discovering their openness to that religious perspective, what factors in the supply-side led them to SGI-USA? The remainder of this essay answers these questions.

Let us begin by considering the religious biographies of converts in our sample. For the purpose of this essay, our analysis is limited to those who reported having been raised in one of the four major religious traditions in America—Protestant, Catholic, Jewish, and 'none'. The 82 respondents whose original religion was coded 'other' in our data were excluded from this analysis.

What can be said about the structural availability of the 325 converts to SGI-USA? One clue comes from the remarkably high number of those converts who have ever been divorced—44 per cent as compared with 23 per cent of the general American adult population.[2] Fully 69 per cent were, at the time they first encountered SGI-USA, neither married nor living with a partner. 45 per cent were not employed full-time, and 43 per cent were living outside the region where their parents and/or siblings lived. In other words, they were not greatly encumbered by work, marital, or kinship ties. While we have only the 'ever-divorced' comparison with the general population, it seems safe to say that converts were in a good position to take on new religious commitments because they were structurally free of many social ties.

How about their 'cultural' availability? At least three kinds of cultural availability can be imagined. First is the religious situation of converts prior to their conversion to SGI-USA. The survey tells us they were more likely to have been raised without a religious tradition (8 per cent) than Americans at large (5 per cent). More than eight in ten reported being spiritually unsatisfied at the time they encountered SGI-USA. Over 30 per cent reported a feeling of being 'at a turning point in my life', and slightly more (36 per cent) felt a need for 'guidance and direction'. While these are clear signs of being open to new spiritual paths, remarkably few (14 per cent) report that they were actually searching for 'something new and exciting to do with my life'. Just as pushes and pulls are not in themselves sufficient to explain conversion, neither, it seems, is mere availability sufficient. Of course, retrospective questions of the sort reported here must be viewed with caution. Perhaps, for example, it is only after one becomes spiritually satisfied with the adopted religion that one realizes the earlier dissatisfaction; the large 81 per cent who report retrospective dissatisfaction must thus be weighed against the meager 14 per cent who report they were actively seeking a new path. None the less, taken together, these data suggest a high degree of availability along the spiritual front on the part of these converts. This judgment is reinforced by the fact that 30 per cent of SGI-USA converts report that, at some time prior to their conversion, they had been involved in one or more religions other than the one in which they were raised.

[2] Because SGI-USA members are disproportionately baby-boomers, born between 1946 and 1962—57%, as compared with 39% of the American adult public—we have adjusted for the age discrepancy when reporting data from the General Social Surveys of the National Opinion Research Center. Since the 1970s, the National Opinion Research Center at the University of Chicago has annually, as a rule, surveyed a randomly drawn sample of adult Americans. Many questions are asked many times, which, when results are added, yields much larger samples than most surveys employ, thus making them excellent benchmarks for comparison purposes.

A second kind of cultural availability is found in people's openness to 'foreign' things. On this score, SGI-USA converts must be regarded as quite open. In response to the question 'Had you read much about non-Western cultures?' at the time of the first encounter with SGI-USA, a surprising 43 per cent said yes, and an even more surprising 66 per cent reported having travelled outside America. In this way, too, these SGI-USA converts appear to have been culturally available.

So far, we have looked at evidence of a more-or-less general openness to change on the part of these converts. What about their openness to Buddhism? Here, too, we see signs of availability. Prior to their conversion, 25 per cent of our sample reported being 'very interested in Eastern religion and philosophy'. Twenty-seven per cent had encountered Buddhism in some form. And 25 per cent had encountered some other form of Eastern religion.

In four different ways, then, many respondents tell us that they were available for something new. They were structurally available in the sense that, as best we can surmise, they had relatively few ties to other people and institutions. Culturally they were available, too, in that they were not very embedded religiously, they were mindful of foreign matters, and, finally, they were aware of Eastern religions. There are small correlations among the latter three kinds of cultural availability: for example, a correlation of 0.363 exists between foreign interest or travel and awareness of Eastern religions, statistically significant beyond the 0.01 level. While such relationships are not surprising, it is noteworthy that no correlation exists between our measure of structural availability and any measure of cultural availability. That is to say, these conditions are independent of each other. Yet each measures a kind of openness to the operation of pushes and pulls.

Moreover, structural availability measures some other features of human existence that have bearing on the conversion process. Structural availability, for example, is positively correlated with formal education. Fifty-nine per cent of the most available have at least a bachelor's degree, which declines steadily to 37 per cent among the least structurally available. It is often noted that education weakens certainty, but it also seems to weaken social relationships. Perhaps for this reason, structural availability is related to feelings of being isolated. Asked if, prior to their first encounter with SGI-USA, they were 'feeling lonely at that time', only 11 per cent of the least available said yes, and the percentage nearly triples to 29 per cent as structural availability increases.

We have, thus, a fairly good sense that our converts were, as they first encountered SGI-USA, available in a variety of ways to become converts. The *degree* to which this is true obviously varies, but rather than take more space here to explore the implications of that variation, let us move on to the matter of pushes, or changes in religious demand.

ON THE DEMAND SIDE

What kinds of Americans would *want* to become Buddhist? Having grown up surrounded by Protestants, Catholics, and Jews—indeed, in 92 per cent of the cases having themselves been raised in one of those traditions—who would want to become a member of SGI-USA? We can make some inferences from our knowledge of the Soka Gakkai religion itself, for it does not demand of its followers that they flee from the world, that they renounce modernity and material possessions. It has no unusual restrictions on personal behavior; it makes minimal demands on members' collective life, yet offers ready-made friends and social activities.

One way to answer our rhetorical question, therefore, is to look at how SGI-USA converts differ from the American adult public. For example, 53 per cent describe themselves as political liberals, as compared with 28 per cent of the public, and only 16 per cent regard themselves as conservative, as compared with 35 per cent of the public. Not surprisingly, more than 75 per cent of the converts voted for Bill Clinton in 1996, and, by a ratio of 6-to-1, prefer the Democratic Party over the Republican. In keeping with this 'liberal' theme, SGI-USA converts are twice as likely as Americans generally to respond 'too little attention' when asked if racial and ethnic minorities receive too much or too little attention in high school and college history classes: 54 per cent vs. 25 per cent, respectively.

Another hint at the possibly greater altruism of SGI-USA converts is found in their responses to the two statements in Table 6.1.

Table 6.1. *Altruism (%)*

Agree	SGI-USA	Public
You have to take care of yourself first, and, if you have any energy left over, then help other people.	41	53
People should be allowed to accumulate as much wealth as they can, even if some make millions while others live in poverty.	30	58

Source: Hammond and Machacek (1999).

Other insights into the mindset of people who found themselves drawn to SGI Buddhism can be seen in their leisure activities. Respondents were asked whether they had participated in each of the following activities 'during the last twelve months'. Table 6.2 presents the activities grouped according to the degree converts participated more or less than American adults generally.

Table 6.2. *Cultural activities* (%)

Activity	SGI-USA	Public
SGI-USA members participate much more:		
Visited an art museum or gallery	75	42
Went to a live ballet or dance performance	47	20
Went to a classical music performance	37	16
Taken part in a music, dance, or theatrical performance	30	10
SGI-USA members participate slightly more:		
Made art or craft objects	51	42
Went out to a movie theater	85	73
Went camping, hiking, or canoeing	51	45
Grown vegetables or flowers	64	61
Played musical instrument	29	24
SGI-USA members participate slightly less:		
Participated in any sports activity	55	61
Videotaped a TV program	56	63
Attended a sports event	47	57
SGI-USA members participate much less		
Went hunting or fishing	17	37
Went to an auto or motorcycle race	6	16

Source: Hammond and Machacek (1999).

SGI converts attach less importance to domesticity than does the public. Only 37 per cent declared that 'being married' is very important, as compared with 50 per cent of the public, and 'having children' was very important to 62 per cent of the public but to only 46 per cent of the converts. By contrast, 'having faith' was very important to 92 per cent of the SGI-USA converts but to only 76 per cent of the public at large.

Clearly, then, SGI-USA converts differ from Americans generally by tending to be socially and politically more liberal than the American average. But if, as liberals, they have moved considerably away from conservative traditions, SGI-USA converts have by no means adopted an 'anything goes' position. For example, the environment, for them, is not to be exploited, and technology is not to be embraced for its own sake. Sixty-two per cent of Americans generally regard nature as sacred, but 78 per cent of the converts hold that view. One-third of the public agree that 'people worry too much about human progress harming the environment', but only one-sixth of SGI-USA converts agree.

Such a benign viewpoint is found in the significantly greater likelihood that SGI converts, as compared with the general public, agree that: 'people try to be helpful'—68 per cent vs. 48 per cent; 'people try to be fair'—62 per cent vs. 55 per cent); and 'most people can be trusted'—52 per cent vs. 37 per cent. Likewise, converts are less cynical about life and society. While 31 per cent of them agree that 'in spite of what some people say, the lot of the average person is getting worse, not better', more than twice that number, 64 per cent, of the American public agree. To the very despairing statement 'it's hardly fair to bring a child into the world with the way things look for the future', assent is given by 12 per cent of converts, whereas 39 per cent—three times the number!—of the public assent.

Our survey asked a question about the causes of poverty, offering four possibilities, and asked respondents to rate each as Very Important, Somewhat Important, or Not Important. This question was taken from the General Social Survey conducted annually by the National Opinion Research Center, so we know how the public-at-large answered. Two of the causes find poverty the result of society's failure—inadequate schools and inadequate jobs—and the other two find individuals at fault—immorality and lack of effort by the poor themselves. It was possible for a person to claim that all four are important or that none is important, but in reality some selectivity occurs, and the resulting patterns tell us something interesting about SGI-USA members.

The classic 'conservative' response pattern is to assign little importance to society as the source of poverty but great importance to individual behavior. The classic 'liberal' response pattern is the mirror image of the conservative one; society, not the individual, fails. But there remain two other patterns, one that might be called 'fatalistic' in that neither society nor individuals are found responsible; poverty, so to speak, just is. The fourth pattern—which might be termed a 'human potential perspective'—finds society the cause of poverty, and individuals the remedy. This is the modal response by SGI converts, claimed by 35 per cent, whereas the modal response by 39 per cent of the public is fatalistic. The liberal response is second in size among SGI-USA members, at 29 per cent, with the conservative response of 15 per cent, the smallest. Among the public, the conservative response is second in size, 27 per cent, and the liberal response smallest at 19 per cent.

Here again we have evidence that SGI members are liberal, but liberal with a slant. Fortunately for us, the study of SGI in Great Britain provided us with a clue to the nature of that slant, so we were able to include diagnostic questions in our survey instrument. In the Epilogue to their book analyzing SGI members in Great Britain, Bryan Wilson and Karel Dobbelaere suggest that in moving away from conservative traditions associated with the capitalistic work ethic, SGI members at the same time tend also to reject the hedonism and materialism of the consumer society. They write:

Soka Gakkai International, whilst drawing on ancient scriptures, nonetheless has a message which claims special relevance for our own time. . . . That relevance is manifest in the convergence of the general contemporary climate of economic and social permissiveness with Soka Gakkai's relinquishment of moral codes and its espousal of general abstract ethical principles which leave adherents free to discover their own form of 'taking responsibility'.   (Wilson, B., and Dobbelaere, K., *A Time to Chant: The Soka Gakkai Buddhists in Britain*, 220.)

Because they see this stance as transcending the coarser features of materialism, Wilson and Dobbelaere refer to 'post-materialism', a stance that stresses not economic growth, fighting inflation, and maintaining order; but emphasizes instead freedom of speech, more voice to the people, and a less impersonal society. On their scale, an amazing 75 per cent of SGI-UK members score as 'pure post-materialists' and another 20 per cent as 'mixed post-materialists'. The comparable figures for the British public are 21 per cent and 30 per cent.[3]

Prompted by the British study, we included this battery of questions in our survey instrument, enabling us to make the comparison between SGI members and the American public. The three questions are:

1. What should be the aims of this country for the next ten years? Below are listed some goals to which some people give priority. Would you please say which one of these you yourself consider the most important? And which would be the second most important?
   (a) maintaining a high level of economic growth;
   (b) making sure the country has strong defense forces;
   (c) seeing that people have more say in how things are done at their jobs and in their communities;
   (d) trying to make our cities and countryside more beautiful.
2. If you had to choose, which of the things on the list below would you say is most important? Which would you consider second most important?
   (a) maintaining order in the nation;
   (b) giving people more say in important government decisions;
   (c) fighting rising prices;
   (d) protecting freedom of speech.
3. Here is another list. In your opinion, which one of these is most important? And what would be the next most important?
   (a) a stable economy;
   (b) progress towards a less impersonal and more humane society;
   (c) progress towards a society in which ideas count more than money;
   (d) the fight against crime.

Each question includes two options expressive of 'post-materialism' and two items expressive of 'materialism'. Post-materialism, we argue, is reflected in (c) and (d) in the first question, (b) and (d) in the second, and (b) and (c) in the third. By assigning a score of two if the respondent gave one of the two post-materialist responses as the first choice, a score of one if the

---

[3] See table and discussion in Wilson and Dobbelaere, *A Time to Chant*, 143–4.

respondent gave a post-materialist response as the second choice, and a score of zero otherwise, we were able to assign a score to each respondent. A 'pure' post-materialist is one who scores the maximum of nine points. The SGI-USA rate of pure post-materialists did not reach the SGI-UK rate of 75 per cent, but even so it reached 51 per cent. The American converts are obviously also to be found in the post-materialist camp, with another 25 per cent ranked as mixed post-materialist. Perhaps more telling here, among the general American public, only 17 per cent rank as pure post-materialist, one-third the rate of SGI-USA members.

To this scale of post-materialism, we added four more items to broaden the measure into an index we call Transmodernism—going 'beyond' modernity as commonly understood. These items are:

1. Agrees with the statement 'I do what is right for the environment, even when it costs more money or takes up more time'.
2. Says it would be good to see reduced emphasis on money and material things.
3. Says it would be good to see a decrease in the importance of work in our lives.
4. Says it would be bad to see more emphasis on the development of technology.

These four items are related, both conceptually and empirically to the post-materialism scale, but they add some subtlety to that scale's starkness—sacrificing on behalf of the environment, de-emphasizing money and the dominance of work, and having reservations about technology. When added to the post-materialism scale, the result is an index with seven categories from Low to High. This Transmodernism Index, we believe, measures what we earlier called a 'demand' for a spiritual orientation represented by Buddhism. It measures, if you please, a 'push' toward that perspective.

How valid is the Transmodernism index? We looked at the relationship between it and a number of other variables, many of which showed high correlations that reveal more of the meaning of transmodernism. Thus, as one looks from those scoring lowest on the index to those scoring highest as expressed in percentages, one sees:

1. A lesser likelihood of regarding financial security as 'very important': from 93 to 59.
2. The greater likelihood of regarding leisure time as 'very important': from 47 to 88.
3. An increase in the view that a job is the best way for a woman to be independent: from 11 to 60.
4. An increase in self-identity as a political liberal: from 7 to 72.

5. A decrease of confidence in the US Congress from 43 to 6; the US Supreme Court, from 57 to 24; the Executive Branch, from 53 to 22; and in major corporations, from 40 to 6.
6. An increase in the view that the 'universe is basically friendly': from 36 to 65.
7. An increase in the view that 'right and wrong are not usually a simple matter of black and white': from 14 to 56.
8. A decrease in the condemnation of homosexuality, from 67 to 6; as well as the condemnation of marijuana, from 80 to 28.

The demand side of our argument is nearly finished. We have constructed a Transmodernism Index, treating it as a measure that predisposes people to look for and adopt a spiritual orientation with Buddhist-like features. The above relationships lend credence to that argument, though of course the substance of those relationships does not reflect Buddhism as such. We conclude, therefore, with three more correlations that come pretty close to expressing the Buddhist philosophy. The higher their score on the Transmodernism Index, the more persons agree that:

1. Life, as experienced by most people, is not what it should be: from 64 to 81.
2. Happiness can only be achieved through inner, spiritual transformation: from 50 to 68.
3. Happiness cannot be achieved through things external to the self: from 21 to 71.

Might it be concluded, then, that the Transmodernism Index 'predicts' who, among those raised in a Judaic-Christian culture, are more likely to seek out Buddhism? Does it not also identify who, among these SGI members—all Buddhist by definition—are 'more' Buddhist in that they express more, and/or express more intensely, those qualities that drew these people to Buddhism in the first place? We think it can and does. As we said at the outset, however, it is not enough to experience the 'demand' for a new religious perspective, a 'push' toward a new spirituality. One must also come into contact with the new perspective, and that means that somehow there must be a supplier.

ON THE SUPPLY SIDE

The study of religious conversion was, for a long time, the province of psychologists, who understandably were interested chiefly in the cognitive and emotional processes that converting people experienced. The emphasis was thus placed on the appeal of new doctrine and new ritual, and on persons' reactions to these things. One of the most significant findings to come out of the research by sociologists, once they turned their attention to the various new religious movements that became so visible in the 1970s, was the role of social, rather than cognitive or emotional, factors in the conversion process. SGI-USA is no exception to this generalization. Fully 65 per cent of these converts told us that they first encountered SGI through a friend, colleague, or acquaintance. Another 18 per cent encountered SGI through a spouse or other family member. Only six people out of 325 indicated that it was through a concert or exhibition, or from SGI literature or other publicity. Fifteen per cent chose to mark the option 'other', and many of these also reflect the importance of the social network in acquainting a would-be convert with a new religious perspective. Thus, one woman who marked 'other' told us she encountered SGI through her boyfriend's roommate, another through her hairdresser, and yet another through the 'mother of a boy who played soccer with my son'. Indeed fewer than half of those saying 'other' indicated that they had been approached out of the blue 'by two women in a diner', or 'on a park bench', or 'people going door-to-door', for example.

This information is important because, historically, Soka Gakkai practice called for members to engage in aggressive recruitment, a practice known as *shakubuku*. Ethnographic studies of SGI-USA make clear that American members have found the act of confronting total strangers on the street, and inviting them to a chanting session, to be rather distasteful. There has been a decline, therefore, in active, aggressive *shakubuku* and an increased emphasis on a more passive, show-by-example method. When asked if they had observed this change during their SGI years, 97 per cent of converts said yes, with only eight persons saying no. When asked if they approve the change, again 97 per cent said yes, the other 3 per cent disapproving.

We asked these members how soon after their first encounter they joined SGI-USA. Just over a third reported that they joined within a month, another third joined before a year passed, the remaining third taking longer. It is not surprising to find, therefore, that when asked to describe their first reaction to their first encounter with SGI, only 24 per cent chose 'immediate enthusiasm' as a response; 21 per cent expressed 'reluctance' or 'real skepticism', meaning that the majority may have been favorable but still took some time to get involved. When asked 'Apart from the teachings, can you say what originally attracted you to SGI-USA?' almost everyone answered in the space provided, the vast majority offering a single response. The social nature of the conversion process is underscored by their answers. The most common answer, with 48 per cent, was some variation of 'attracted by the members I met', with another 11 per cent mentioning the attraction of a single person. One other answer must be discussed in detail.

The central ritual in SGI is chanting, either alone or in the company of others. Chanting follows a prescribed script and is for the purpose of achieving goals, which may range from quite abstract—for example, world peace—to quite concrete—for example, a pay raise. One important part of the recruitment process therefore consists of visitors hearing testimony about members' successes with chanting, and another is encouraging the new visitor to try chanting. The visitor is given a card with the words to chant and invited to chant for his/her own goals. Because these activities occur so early in potential converts' encounter with SGI, it is understandable that 25 per cent of these converts indicated that it was the benefits—for self or others, already received or still hoped for—that were the major attraction for them.

Much smaller numbers mentioned the attraction of the aesthetics of chanting (5 per cent), SGI's activities and goals (8 per cent), SGI's philosophy (8 per cent), a need for spiritual guidance (5 per cent), or an interest in Buddhism (3 per cent). What seems clear, therefore, is the relatively small role played by so-called doctrinal matters as people convert to SGI-USA. Indeed, when asked if the original attraction is still their main attraction, 40 per cent said no, indicating that the benefits of chanting had replaced the winsomeness of members as the major attraction. It is not that SGI-USA converts lose friends among the SGI membership—only 13 per cent report having no friends among fellow members, and 50 per cent even have relatives who are members; it is that the social network that plays such a crucial part in *pulling* new members and *supplying* them with knowledge about SGI is no longer so critical to the *maintenance* of membership.

One special way the crucial role played by social factors in the conversion process is seen, therefore, is the fact that conversion to a new religion can be disruptive of a previous social network. More than half (59 per cent) of these SGI converts told us they had experienced negative reactions from relatives or friends as a result of joining SGI-USA. Parents were most often mentioned (34 per cent) as the persons being critical, but other family members (30 per cent) were also mentioned, as were friends and co-workers (16 per cent), and even spouses (11 per cent). Under these conditions, it might even be said that the *social* attraction of a new religious movement is a necessary, if not sufficient, component of the conversion process. Why endanger existing friendships unless new friendships appear likely?

CONCLUSION

How the importance of a social attraction compares with the importance of the other two components—availability and demand—cannot be assessed, of course. In one sense, availability simply fades away as a factor once a member is securely a member. Probably, too, the social attraction diminishes in importance in individual members' lives as they resolve or learn to ignore the objections of others. That leaves the 'supply' component to gain in relative importance, which no doubt has happened to the converts studied here. At first encounter they were but proto-Buddhists, as measured by our Transmodernism scale. It is their active membership that turns them into SGI Buddhists.

Even a cursory glance at the data from our survey of SGI-USA members tells a revealing story about the appeal of at least one form of Buddhism in America. Structurally, converts to SGI are characterized by loose social ties prior to encountering SGI. They have fewer restrictions on their freedom to move about in the social world. Given that freedom, it is not surprising that the most appealing quality of SGI to newcomers is its membership, which is described by converts as friendly, sincere, and helpful. Culturally, we may infer from the rather large number of former religious 'nones' among the converts, and a pattern of religious shopping prior to encountering SGI, that SGI converts were dissatisfied with the options offered by the American religious mainstream. We discovered a pattern of values among the converts that sets them apart from both religious conservatives and religious liberals— more liberal in their attitudes about sex and the causes of poverty than religious conservatives, and more cautious about science and technology and major social institutions than religious liberals.

Taken all together, this value orientation amounts to a kind of 'proto-Buddhist' perspective, which we have shown to be related to three indicators of Buddhist philosophy. In other words, at least part of the appeal of SGI Buddhism may be understood as a function of the cultural availability of converts to non-traditional alternatives, and the affinity between Buddhist philosophy and the value orientation of converts.

SEVEN

Tocqueville's Lessons from the New World for Religion in the New Europe

'The religious atmosphere of the country was the first thing that struck me on arrival in the United States.' So wrote Alexis de Tocqueville soon after his extended visit in 1831.[1] Expecting to find in America the situation he had known in France, with 'the spirits of religion and of freedom almost always marching in opposite directions', he instead found that 'the most free and enlightened people in the world zealously perform all the external duties of religion'. After repeatedly questioning the 'faithful of all communions', Tocqueville found that the Americans themselves attributed religion's 'quiet sway over their country' to 'the complete separation of church and state'.[2] Though accepting this explanation as essentially correct, the French observer none the less investigated further; what was it about church–state separation that led to religion's increased vitality in society? 'I wondered', Tocqueville wrote, 'how it could come about that by diminishing the apparent power of religion one increased its real strength'.[3]

In a most trenchant analysis of this question, Tocqueville identified two answers:

1. *The power of public opinion.* One of these answers is seen in Tocqueville's discussion of the central role played in egalitarian America by 'public opinion'. In the absence of caste and class distinctions, ascribed authority is problematic and tends, therefore, to be replaced by what 'the people' think. Public opinion thus can reach the status of religion in its power to influence individuals' behavior, and churches are conduits of this power. 'There is an innumerable multitude of sects in the United States', Tocqueville observed: 'They are all different in the worship they offer to the Creator, but all agree concerning the duties of men to one another. Each sect worships God in its own fashion, but all preach the same morality in the name of God.'[4] Americans, he was noting, enjoy religious freedom in a great variety of ways, but all are subject to the power of public opinion.

---

[1] Tocqueville, A. de, *Democracy in America*, G. Lawrence (trans.) (Garden City, NY: Doubleday Anchor, 1969), 295.

[2] Ibid., 295.   [3] Ibid., 296.   [4] Ibid., 290.

2. *The political neutrality of religious organizations*. The second answer
Tocqueville gives to the question of how religion's influence can actually be
stronger under church–state separation is his observation, made repeatedly,
that churches take care to remain non-partisan and politically unaligned:

When a religion seeks to found its sway only on the longing for immortality equally
tormenting every human heart, it can aspire to universality; but when it comes to
uniting itself with a government, it must adopt maxims which apply only to certain
nations. Therefore, by allying itself with any political power, religion increases its
strength over some but forfeits the hope of reigning over all. . . . The American clergy
were the first to perceive this truth and to act in conformity with it. They saw that
they would have to give up religious influence if they wanted to acquire political
power, and they preferred to lose the support of authority rather than to share its
vicissitudes.   (Tocqueville, A. de, *Democracy in America*, 297–9.)

Churches, in other words, in exchange for their right to promulgate the religion they chose, agreed not to seek favored status in the eyes of the government.

These two answers, of course, are related: whatever their sectarian peculiarity, Tocqueville was saying, religious people take care not to deviate from
widely perceived opinion and thus largely escape government efforts to reg-
ulate them. But, by staying out of partisan politics, churches also are free to
cater to whatever religious niche they care to serve. Stated in the usual terms,
in the America Tocqueville investigated, there was no law 'respecting an
establishment of religion' nor was there any prohibition of the 'free exercise'
of religion. There was, as everyone told him, separation of church and state.

The place in the US Constitution containing the church–state doctrine—
the First Amendment—permits various interpretations, however, and
Tocqueville somehow saw through this ambiguity. At the time they adopted
the First Amendment as part of the Bill of Rights, the Congress was well
aware that some of the thirteen newly united states still had established
churches. Their wording, therefore—'Congress shall make no law respecting
an establishment of religion, or prohibiting the free exercise thereof'—
clearly could not have been intended to outlaw established religion. At most,
its intention may have been to prevent any *federal* or *national* established
church, but certainly also it served to protect established churches in the individual states from congressional interference. As Tocqueville saw, religion
was regarded as a beneficial force, and, in all its sectarian expressions, was
to be immune from government regulation—though not denied state sponsorship if a state so desired—and free to appeal to citizens' religious
appetites.

Just as Tocqueville's two answers merge dialectically into one, so too, by
the above account, do the two religion clauses of the US Constitution. 'No
establishment' means to leave religion alone for people to practice it as they

wish, and 'free exercise' means to recognize and allow religious behavior irrespective of the political standing of its practitioners.

In due time, the 'establishment' clause came to mean both no interference and also no sponsorship—Massachusetts, in 1833, was the last state to rid itself of officially sponsored religion. And 'free exercise' came to mean that, only if government had a compelling interest on behalf of the general welfare, could it move to restrict religious behavior. Thus has the US addressed the church–state problem by trying to protect both religious equality and religious liberty; government 'protects' the free exercise of religion by not showing favoritism toward any religion, and by allowing considerable diversity of religious expression. This was what Tocqueville perceived.

GENERALIZING FROM TOCQUEVILLE

With only a little change of wording, Tocqueville's analysis becomes generalizable to every jurisdiction, since something of a church–state situation is unavoidable and must therefore be addressed somehow by every government and its people. Understandably, perhaps, there is more convergence on the actual 'solution' adopted by various nations than their formal ideologies would suggest. After a careful analysis of this issue in a handful of otherwise divergent societies, Demerath reports:

Despite religion's prominence as a source of political legitimacy and campaign rhetoric, it is rarely a dominant factor in the affairs of state. The United States is less distinctive in this regard than many Americans suppose, and insofar as its own tradition of 'church–state separation' continues, this may owe less to legal and constitutional requirements than to a range of social and political constraints which we share with other nations. (Demerath, N. J. (III), 'Religious capital and capital religions', 38.)

Francis makes a similar observation: 'At this time, virtually every church, at least in Western Europe, has achieved a remarkable measure of autonomy in the determination of its leadership, its size, and the direction of its clergy.'[5] Caplow's assessment of the church–state situation in contemporary Europe would thus seem in need of revision. He writes:

The one element that survives unchanged from the Europe of Tocqueville, Wellington, Garibaldi, and the young Marx, is the inextricable connection of politics and religion which makes it impossible for individuals to take up a political position without reference to their religious affiliations and vice-versa. (Caplow, T., 'Contrasting Trends in European and American Religion', 106.)

---

[5] Francis, J. G., 'The evolving regulatory structure of European church–state relations', *Journal of Church and State*, 34 (1992), 778–9.

Granted, the European situation may not be identical to that of the United States, but liberalism made inroads throughout nineteenth and twentieth century Europe, one effect of which has been the loosening of ties between 'church' and 'state'. And this 'loosening' has resulted, as in the US, not in a literal separation, of course, but in changing government responses to the two issues Tocqueville so perceptively noted: what limits, if any, will be placed on free religious expression? And what help and/or recognition will be given to religious organizations? Despite a convergence in the direction of looser ties between church and state, therefore, European societies exhibit differences in how they respond to these two issues.

How might these differences be characterized? Fortunately, a growing literature in the sociology of religion provides answers. Beginning with Stark and Bainbridge's introduction in 1985 of the concept of a 'religious economy',[6] there developed—by Iannacone,[7] by Finke and Stark,[8] and by Chaves and Cann[9]—clear notions of government regulation/sponsorship of religion on the one hand, and religious heterogeneity or pluralism on the other hand. We will soon show that these two dimensions are empirically related inversely, but that they are analytically distinct, reflecting rather closely the issues addressed in the US Constitution by the terms 'no establishment' and 'free exercise'. Indeed, if Tocqueville had been familiar with this conceptual development, he might have suggested that the unexpected religious vitality he encountered in America could be attributed, first, to a largely unregulated religious economy and, second, to the many religious 'firms' competing in that economy.

In fact, that is exactly what he inadvertently observed, inasmuch as his visit came toward the end of what historians of American religion call the Second Great Awakening. Finke and Stark, for example, calculate that in 1776 only 17 per cent of the American population were adherents of a church, but 55 per cent of these adherents were connected to the three denominations enjoying some 'establishment' status: Congregational, Episcopal, and Presbyterian. By contrast, only 21 per cent adhered to the Baptist, Methodist, and Catholic denominations. By 1850, however, the percentage of Americans adhering to a church had climbed to 34 per cent, but the 'established' share had dropped from 55 to 19 per cent, while the other three denominations climbed to 69 per cent. The Methodists alone went

[6] Stark, R., and Bainbridge, W., *The Future of Religion* (Berkeley, CA: University of California Press, 1985), chapters 3 and 4.

[7] Iannaccone, L. R., 'The Consequences of Religious Market Structure', *Rationality and Society*, 3 (1991), 156–77.

[8] Finke, R., and Stark, R., *The Churching of America* (New Brunswick, NJ: Rutgers University Press, 1992).

[9] Chaves, M., and Cann, D. E., 'Regulation, pluralism, and religious market structure', *Rationality and Society*, 4 (1992), 272–90.

from less than 3 per cent in 1776 to 34 per cent in 1850, chiefly by offering services at times and places and in a variety of ways people found attractive.[10] During the latter decades of this period, too, Mormons, Millerites, and Adventists entered the religious marketplace. Clearly, by the time of Tocqueville's visit, the American religious economy was less regulated than in 1776, and competition within it had increased.

IMPLICATIONS FOR THE NEW EUROPE

As we have already remarked, relationships between churches and states in the modern period have loosened in Europe, though not everywhere to the same degree. We are now in a position to think of this differential loosening as occurring in two ways: as diminished regulation or sponsorship of religion, and as increased religious competition or pluralism. The question to be addressed, therefore, is what effect might such changes have on religious activity in the New Europe. Has religious vitality increased there with church–state separation, as Tocqueville noted about America nearly two centuries ago? The answer is No, Yes, and It Depends, but the evidence is not as confusing as that answer at first suggests.

Let us look first at the No answer. Religious vitality has not only *not* increased with church–state separation, but the very processes of declining state sponsorship and increasing religious pluralization are taken as evidence of secularization. This generalization is the received wisdom handed down since the Enlightenment, and a lot of data tend to support it *as a generalization*.[11] Thus, rates of Church attendance seem everywhere in Europe to have declined, though it is recognized that the comparison periods of high rates differ considerably from one society to another, that Catholic countries have experienced such decline differently from Protestant countries, etc. Complicating the generalization further is the fact that the influence of religion in education, giving money to the churches, and observance of religious holidays and rituals, follow yet other patterns. Still, if asked whether Europe today is more religious or less religious than yesterday, most observers will answer 'less', even as they have a multitude of meanings in mind. Thus, as Roof *et al.*[12] make clear, one indicator experienced in every European society surveyed is the low rate of church involvement among the young as compared with the old.

---

[10] Finke and Stark, *Churching of America*, chapter 3.

[11] Wilson, B., 'Secularization: The inherited model', in P. E. Hammond (ed.), *The Sacred in a Secular Age* (Berkeley, CA: University of California Press, 1985), 9–20.

[12] Roof, W. C., Carroll, J., and Roozen, D. (eds.), *The Postwar Generation and Religious Establishments* (Boulder, CO: Westview Press, 1995).

But if the generalization is in some sense correct—that with declining state regulation and sponsorship of religion and increasing religious pluralism comes not *increased,* but *decreased*, religious vitality—it is misleadingly correct if it is understood to mean that decreasing regulation and increasing pluralism *causes* that declining vitality. The facts suggest just the reverse, as Chaves and Cann[13] have shown. With data on fourteen European societies, plus the US and Canada, Australia and New Zealand, those investigators develop an index of state sponsorship/regulation based on six attributes such as state recognition of one or more denominations, state approval of church leaders, state salaries for church personnel, etc. They also employ the Herfindahl Index, a measure of religious 'concentration', and thus the obverse of pluralism. What are their findings?

First of all, a calculation—not performed by Chaves and Cann but readily done from their graphs—using data from the fourteen European societies shows a significant inverse relationship between sponsorship and pluralism. The correlation is stronger for predominantly Protestant countries (Pearson's r = −0.82) than for predominantly Catholic countries (r = −0.48), but it is obvious that *declining* religious regulation and *increasing* religious pluralism go together.

Second, they find that religious vitality, as measured by church attendance, is negatively related to state sponsorship, and, because sponsorship and religious concentration go together, religious vitality is also positively related to pluralism. Chaves and Cann demonstrate, however, that pluralism's effect is very small *independently* of the sponsorship measure. In other words, we can assume that pluralism enhances religious participation, but it does so only to the degree that it is accompanied by a diminution of state sponsorship. Thus it can be said that loosening the church–state relationship—meaning little or no state regulation of religion—does not itself lead to religious vitality, but it permits and encourages religious competition, which *does* result in religious vitality.[14] To the negative answer already given to the question of church–state separation and religious vitality in Europe, we add a second, qualified, positive answer. The overall secular trend may serve to decrease religiousness in European societies, just as it tends to loosen church–state ties, but to the degree it does the latter, it retards the former. In this special sense, one can say that, yes, church–state separation increases religious vitality.

---

[13] Chaves and Cann, 'Regulation, pluralism, and religious market structure'.

[14] Predominantly Catholic countries are higher on the concentration index than all predominantly Protestant countries except Finland and Denmark. Also, their scores on the regulation index range only from 0 to 3, not 0 to 6 as with Protestant countries. The generalization just stated is therefore more applicable to Protestant Europe, although, within their limited ranges, Catholic European countries show the same directional effects.

Which leaves the third of the answers—It Depends—to be discussed. I am not being facetious in offering this third option, nor do I mean to trivialize the generalizations we have been exploring. Rather, my intention is to point to what may be the most interesting, contemporary European application of Tocqueville's insights. With state deregulation of religion comes increased freedom for religions to compete in the marketplace. More religious needs can be met in more ways under those circumstances, and—if everything else is equal—greater religious vitality can be expected. This is what we observed in the second answer, except that everything else is not equal, but, instead, embedded in a secular trend that tends to depress religious vitality. Hence the first answer is still correct, though also qualified. Now we can add the third answer—It depends—by noting that in a highly competitive religious marketplace, the very notions of religious needs, religious values, and the religious means of meeting those needs and expressing those values, become volatile.

Sects, cults, therapies, etc., can enter the marketplace, raising questions about what religion is, and what religious involvement *means*. In the New Europe, as in early nineteenth century America, religious novelty abounds, and, in their ambiguity about what religion is, people speak also of spirituality and meditation, of being holistic or centered. They can be religious without a church, and, in carrying to the extreme the cult of individualism, may even be religious in a manner unlike anyone else. Emerson, in his essay, 'Self Reliance', written almost simultaneously with Tocqueville's writing of *Democracy in America,* stated, 'Whoso would be a man, must be a nonconformist'. Do not simply comply with the demands of some sect, Emerson advised, 'But do your work, and I shall know you'.[15]

If there is one common theme running through the essays referred to above, assessing the religious situation of post-War European generations, it is that, religiously, people are 'doing their own work'. Religion has become a 'personal collage' rather than 'received', subjective rather than objective. 'Personal spiritual benefit' is replacing 'institutional demand', even as individualism is affirmed. A 'diffused religion' increases as the 'monolithic character' of organized, orthodox religion declines.[16] But does this heightened religious individualism constitute increased religious vitality? That is where the answer becomes, It Depends. There seems no doubt that new religions have sprouted in Europe as in other parts of the world. Moreover, in keeping

[15] Emerson, R. W., *Collected Works*, Vol. 2 (Boston, MA: Houghton Mifflin, 1865), 54; 'Self Reliance' was drawn from lectures given in 1836–3. Today, people do their own 'thing'.

[16] Roof, Carroll, and Roozen, *The Postwar Generation.* Even in Russia this is true. In a special report to the *Los Angeles Times* (11 February 1993), Beth Knobel claims that, 'With Russian society in transition and the Russian people frustrated by the unpredictability of their daily lives, thousands of people from Siberia to Estonia have turned for comfort to meditation, vegetarianism, holistic health, crystals and other aspects of spiritual study.'

with the second answer offered here, the evidence suggests that Stark and Bainbridge[17] are correct in asserting that new religious movements have had greater success in those European societies they judge to be more 'secular'— for which, read, 'religiously deregulated and pluralistic'. But, as Wallis and Bruce, in a critique of several papers by Stark and Bainbridge which preceded the latter's 1985 volume, argue:

The evidence suggests that the new faiths have made negligible inroads into the mass of the unchurched, who remain indifferent to organized religion of any sort. The scale of decline in the major denominations and that of the growth of the new religious movements are simply not comparable. (Wallis, R., and Bruce, S., 'The Stark–Bainbridge Theory of Religion: A Critical Analysis and Counter Proposals', 20.)

Thus they cite figures for Britain between 1970 and 1975, showing that Protestant Churches lost over half a million members while the 'conservative churches that were growing gained about fourteen thousand new members'.[18] In other words, not even 3 per cent of the drop-outs dropped back in somewhere else; the notoriety and consequent visibility of the 'new' movements in religion can lead us to exaggerate their impact on religion's vitality.

A judicious reading of the evidence regarding the impact of loosened church–state ties on religious vitality thus requires not a single answer but a mix of answers. The inexorable nature of secularization means that whatever loosens church–state ties does not restore religious vitality to once higher levels, but, on the other hand, it creates conditions for greater competition among suppliers of religion and thus leads to some greater vitality than would otherwise be the case. At the same time, however, the very nature of religion undergoes redefinition when church–state ties loosen, with the consequence that the boundaries of the religious marketplace broaden to include potentially more persons. In this latter case, the answer to the original question becomes, It Depends—not just on whether vitality has increased but also on whether what has increased is 'religion'.

Tocqueville no doubt would be of help at this point were he around to make fresh observations in the New Europe. Even as it is, however, his powers of discernment in early nineteenth century America assist us in understanding the present situation. The relationship between churches and states is undergoing change in today's Europe just as change is taking place in the ways Europeans experience religion. It seems reasonable to assume some connection between these two changes, and Tocqueville helps us explore that connection.

[17] Stark, R., and Bainbridge, W., *The Future of Religion*, chapter 21.
[18] Wallis, R., and Bruce, S., 'The Stark–Bainbridge Theory of Religion: A Critical Analysis and Counter Proposals', *Sociological Analysis*, 45 (1984), 20.

PART II

External Influences

EIGHT

World Order and Mainline Religions[*]

While it is safe to say that world order or world system theory has had most to say about economic actions and processes, religious reverberations from world order changes have also been noted.[1] The following broad assertions would seem to summarize the current outlook with respect to this relationship:

1. A nation-state's position in the world political economy is reflected in its religious institutions

2. During shifts in the world order, ideological reformation is likely, including religious unrest and diversity.[2]

3. In nation-states experiencing ascendancy and hegemony, 'establishment' religion will gain in popularity, while during periods of decline, such religion will lose in popularity.[3]

Empirical arguments advanced in support of one or more of these theoretical assertions include explanations for: the worldwide cult explosion in the 1960s and 1970s, the renewed vigor of evangelical Protestantism in the United States, Vatican Council II and attendant changes in Roman Catholicism such as the charismatic movement, the feminist movement in religious organizations, and the *havarot* movement within Judaism.

The most focused empirical effort to date to relate world order changes to changes in religious institutions, however, is Peter Smith's endeavor to show that

---

[*] Michael A. Burdick was a collaborator on this essay.

[1] See, e.g., Wuthnow, R., 'Religious movements and the transition in world order', in J. Needleman and G. Baker (eds.), *Understanding the New Religions* (New York, NY: Seabury, 1978); 'World order and religious movements', in A. Bergesen (ed.), *Studies of the Modern World System* (New York, NY: Academic Press, 1980); 'America's legitimating myths: Continuity and crisis', in T. Boswell and A. Bergesen (eds.), *America's Changing Role in the World System* (New York, NY: Praeger, 1987); and Robertson, R., and Chirico, J., 'Humanity, globalization, and worldwide religious resurgence', *Sociological Analysis*, 46/3 (1985); Robertson, R., 'The sacred and the world system', in P. Hammond (ed.), *The Sacred in a Secular Age* (Berkeley, CA: University of California Press, 1985); 'Church–state relations and the world system', in T. Robbins and R. Robertson (eds.), *Church–State Relations* (New Brunswick, NJ: Transaction, Inc., 1987) for general theoretical statements.

[2] Wuthnow, R., 'Religious movements and the transition in world order', 72.

[3] Smith, P., 'Anglo-American religion and hegemonic change in the world system, *c.* 1870–1980', *British Journal of Sociology*, 37 (1986), 88–105.

periods of national dominance have also been periods of religious florescence for those churches which cater for the middle and upper classes. Correspondingly, one of the corollaries of loss of dominance is a decline in such socially established religiosity.   (Smith, P., 'Anglo-American religion and hegemonic change in the world system', 88.)

In a general way, Smith bases his argument on evidence that: 'Major Protestant' membership in Great Britain rose from about 1830 to about 1900, then started a decline that continues today, a process correlated with Britain's changing position in the world economy; and American church membership experienced an overall, if uneven, increase from early in the twentieth century until the mid-1960s, then a decline, especially in the 'elite' Protestant denominations, a process corresponding to America's changing position in the world economy.

The virtue of Smith's study not generally shared by other empirical studies of religion and world order, is that its proposition linking independent and dependent variables is clearly stated, and the evidence is quantitative and longitudinal. Other studies have tended toward anecdotal evidence, often for a single time period and/or have been less clear regarding just how a change in the world order has effected a change in the religious situation. Such shortcomings do not negate these other studies, of course, but they do highlight the singular character of Smith's article.

Unfortunately, Smith's article is open to serious challenge, especially its American half. The challenge comes in two ways: most palpably, it can be shown that, while American church membership peaked in the 1960s, that is true of total church membership, not establishment membership 'catering for the middle and upper classes', which—by one important standard at least—had peaked *before* the United States began its world system ascendancy. Less damaging to Smith's article, but more challenging to the world system theory from which it derives, is the fact that changes in the most international aspect of establishment religion—foreign missions—not only do not conform to the world order model but seem, indeed, to contradict it. We discuss these two challenges, and then conclude with a discussion of how they might be resolved in a manner that could leave world order theory relatively intact but sensitized to some subtleties in the religious situation.

REGARDING AMERICAN CHURCH MEMBERSHIP

Nobody would question that Anglicanism in Britain is, and has been, the establishment religion.[4] Until very recently at least, with nonconformist

---

[4] Kenneth Medhurst writes: 'The presence of its [the Anglican church's] leaders on State occasions, their membership of the House of Lords, and the survival of chapels directly under

Margaret Thatcher and her nonconformist cabinet, the Church of England was rightfully called 'the Conservative party at prayer'. Smith's tracking of the vitality of establishment religiosity in relationship to Britain's ascendancy, dominance, and then decline in the world's political economy, has a certain intuitive merit, therefore.[5]

What of American establishment religion, however? Congregationalists, Episcopalians, and Presbyterians certainly catered to the middle and upper classes during the colonial period, but, while their membership rolls grew in absolute numbers as the American population grew, their *share of* the church-belonging public peaked early in the nineteenth century! In other words, other denominations—the Baptists and Methodists especially—grew even faster. Did not those two denominations then become part *of* establishment religion? The answer is 'In due time, yes', but then the Methodists' share of the church-belonging public peaked by 1920; American Baptists, not too long after.[6]

The implication is clear: what was reached in the mid-1960s in the United States was not just the apex in sheer numbers of membership figures in churches serving middle and upper classes but also the saturation of the religion market. In relative terms, however, establishment religion had long been in decline. The continued success at penetrating this market after the 1960s by evangelical Protestantism is precisely that, therefore—the continuation of a 200-year-old process by which *non*-establishment religions have been gaining a larger and larger share of the church-belonging public. Not until the overall population growth slowed down and not until so-called mainstream Protestant denominations failed to retain their youthful generations, however, was the latter's long-term market loss exposed.

Of course, it might be argued that even if sectarian, evangelical growth rates were greater than those of establishment denominations, the latter have remained large in absolute terms and have truly dominated the Protestant religious scene. They founded and still help operate the elite colleges and

Royal jurisdiction, all witness to the persistence of time-honored links with the Crown. . . . Indeed, this legacy is reflected not least in the extent to which 'top people' in Britain still manifest a Christian adherence to an exceptional degree when compared with that of ordinary citizenry'. In Medhurst, K., and Moyer, G., *Church and Politics in a Secular Age* (Oxford: Clarendon Press, 1988), vii–viii.

[5] For reasons not clear to us, Smith tracks only other major Protestants, not Anglicans, as indicative of establishment religiosity. This correction changes the percentages but not the relationship. Using the same source material and combining Anglican and other major Protestant figures, the percentage would be 27.4 per cent (1870), peaking at 28.9 per cent (1900) and then declining. In addition, Smith does not account for the momentary increase in church membership that occurred in the 1950s and early 1960s, a phenomenon corresponding to the American experience (see Table 8.1).

[6] Finke, R., and Stark, R., 'How the upstart sects won America: 1776–1850', *Journal for the Scientific Study of Religion*, 28/1 (1989).

Table 8.1. Religious affiliation of the US population for selected years (%)

	1890	1906	1923	1940	1947	1954	1960	1965	1970	1975	1980	1985
Religiously affiliated	22	36	43	49	57	60	64	64	62	62	61	60
Christians affiliated with 'established' Protestant churches	35	35	33	31	28	25	22	25	24	22	20	17
Protestants affiliated with 'established' Protestant churches	52	58	55	49	45	41	41	43	42	37	36	30

Sources: Census, 1890, 1906; National Council of Churches of Christ (NCCC) yearbooks.

seminaries, write the religious histories, and send their members to Congress in disproportionate numbers. George Bush was the fourteenth Episcopalian to be elected president, even though Episcopalians are only about 1 percent of the American population. While this argument may be correct in its facts, it nevertheless contradicts the Peter Smith thesis—which is that establishment religion flourishes and then declines *because* it is establishment religion. If non-establishment religion flourishes even more during the period of world order ascendancy, and then continues to flourish while both nation and establishment religion decline, some revision in the thesis seems called for.

REGARDING FOREIGN MISSIONS—GREAT BRITAIN

A more telling challenge comes from a quarter not considered in the Peter Smith article—the involvement of establishment religion in foreign missionary activity. It would seem logical in the world system theoretical framework to expect that the links between a nation-state's destiny in the world's political economy and its efforts at evangelizing other parts of the world would be even closer than its links to domestic religion. As Brian Stanley has shown, a convergence existed between British missionary and free trading expectations in the mid-nineteenth century: 'the years 1857–1860 were crucial in the process whereby the evangelical understanding of empire in terms of providence, natural law, and trusteeship became the established framework of British imperial thinking'.[7] The mission field is a kind of 'market', after all, and sellers and buyers make it up. We expect the participants in this market to be especially responsive to their uneven positions in the world economy, whether they are sending or receiving missionaries.

Figures for Great Britain's Anglican missionary program can be seen as support for this perspective. From a total of 687 in 1854, missionary personnel sent to foreign lands by the Anglican church rose to 1,042 in 1890, 2,107 in 1900, 2,411 in 1905, and still maintained a figure of 2,538 in 1938, dropping to 925 in 1980. While the years of ascent and descent do not coincide closely with Britain's political-economic destiny, if we allow for the fact that adding to and then dismantling foreign mission operations probably requires a lead time longer than changes in domestic operations, these figures then add credibility to the Smith thesis.

However, there is a set of facts not anticipated by the theory, if one considers the foreign mission efforts of Britain's non-Anglican Protestants. Not only were the latter already at parity with the Anglicans in 1854, but by 1905

[7] Stanley, B., ' "Commerce and Christianity": Providence theory, the missionary movement, and the imperialism of free trade', *The Historical Journal*, 26 (1983), 94.

Table 8.2. *British foreign missionary personnel deployed by Anglican and other Protestant agencies for selected years (N)*

Agency	1854	1890	1900	1905	1925	1938	1973	1980
Anglican	687	1,043	2,103	2,411	2,186	2,538	936	925
Other Protestant	679	1,352	2,461	5,381	4,140	4,255	4,105	4,209

Sources: ATS, *Ecumenical Missionary Conference*, 2 vols. (New York, NY: American Tract Society, 1900); Beach, R. (ed.), *Foreign Missions Yearbook of North America* (New York, NY: Foreign Mission Conference of North America, 1925); Bliss, E. M. (ed.), *The Encyclopedia of Missions*, 2 vols. (New York, NY: Funk and Wagnalls, 1891); Brierly, P. W. (ed.), *UK Christian Handbook: Overseas* (London: Evangelical Missionary Alliance, 1981); Newcomb, H., *A Cyclopedia of Missions* (New York, NY: Scribners, 1854); Parker, J. I. (ed.), *Interpretive Statistical Survey of the World Mission of the Christian Church* (New York, NY: International Ministry Council, 1938); Wright, H. O. (ed.), *The Blue Book of Missions* (New York, NY: Funk and Wagnalls, 1905).

they had more than double the number of Anglican personnel, maintaining that superiority in 1925 and 1938, and as of 1980 outnumbering Anglicans by a 5:1 ratio. This pattern is not at all what system theory would predict; it is not ever-growing numbers of establishment foreign mission emissaries going out on behalf of an empire but their domestic challengers. Moreover, like the continued growth of American evangelicalism even after overall church membership growth halted, British nonconforming mission personnel appear to keep increasing. Changes in a nation-state's position in the world system may still be reflected in its religious institutions, but—if the foreign mission enterprise is the focus, and a perfectly logical focus it is— clearly more explanation is needed than simply the rise and fall of world political economic position.

REGARDING FOREIGN MISSIONS—AMERICAN

American foreign mission history more severely challenges the Peter Smith thesis, however. Arthur Schlesinger, Jr., puts the matter succinctly:

One must begin by acknowledging the autonomy of the missionary impulse. . . . Whatever links the missionary enterprise might develop along the way with traders or bankers, politicians, generals, or diplomats, however much it might express in its own ways the aggressive energies of the West, the desire to save souls remains distinct from the desire to extend power or to acquire glory or to make money or to seek adventure or to explore the unknown.   (Schlesinger Jr., A., 'The missionary enterprise and theories of imperialism', 342.)

The fact is, American foreign mission activity by establishment Protestantism did follow a pattern of growth, hegemony, and then decline, but this entire cycle occurred *before* the United States reached hegemonic position in the world's political economy. The brazen assault by America's mainline Protestant missionaries peaked in the 1920s, had clearly changed strategies by the post-World War II period, and, by the mid-1960s, had become a disappearing pattern.

The dominant aim of American Protestant missionaries throughout most of the nineteenth century was religious, not cultural, imperialism. As Rufus Anderson, secretary of the American Board of Missions, 1832–1866, insisted, the goal was to 'convert souls' not argue the superiority of American culture. A mission station, he said, was *not* to become an agency of social or political reform. Anderson sought no agricultural experts or mechanics, and he called for the Gospel to be preached not in English but in the native tongue.[8]

After the Civil War, this 'Gospel alone' mentality underwent revision. Domestically, as a response to the problems created by urbanization and industrialization, a Social Gospel theology developed, and in the foreign mission field this revisionist thinking took the form, for example, in China, of missionary attacks on concubinage, foot-binding, opium, and natura-pathic medicine. In China and elsewhere, mission energy thus shifted to social, medical, educational, and agricultural efforts. Just as the newly articulated post-millennialism led domestically to church resolve to bring in the kingdom *before* Christ's return, so in foreign missions the emphasis shifted away from the salvation of individual souls and toward the salvation of entire societies by use of American technology.

Pre-millennialists—those who thought individual souls must be converted as quickly as possible before Christ's return and the eventual end of history—were still represented in foreign missions, though decreasingly among the cadres associated with mainline Protestant churches. The latter had shifted mission strategy to one that—not unlike that of their Peace Corps counterparts—harbored feelings of Western cultural superiority: a clean water supply, more schools reaching more children, better nutrition, more health care, etc.

Ironically perhaps, convinced of Western, that is, American, superiority in these cultural institutions, American missionaries during the waning years of the nineteenth and first years of the twentieth centuries sanctioned greater cultural imperialism than they had before or have since. Military assistance by American armed forces to protect and foster American missionary 'good will' was even encouraged in such places as Turkey (1894–5) and China (1900–01). Likewise, the expansion of American 'interests' in Cuba, Puerto

[8] Schlesinger Jr., A., 'The missionary enterprise and theories of imperialism', in J. K. Fairbank (ed.), *The Missionary Enterprise in China and America* (Cambridge, MA: Harvard University Press, 1974), 350–1.

Rico, and the Philippines after the Spanish-American War (1898) allowed United States Protestants to engage in missionary work in the newly acquired territories under a denominational comity arrangement, surely in the belief that advanced American ways were superior to the natives' ways.

By the 1920s, however, the established American Protestant missionary thrust peaked in the deployment of personnel. Mission theorists, having seriously questioned the nineteenth-century notion of theological superiority, now questioned the subsequent assumption of cultural superiority. Daniel J. Fleming, a professor at Union Seminary in New York and a former missionary to India, articulated the new theory. America, like all societies, was 'less-than-Christian', and hence, 'the whole world is the mission field'. Also, Fleming redefined the objectives of missionary activity—away from conquest of land masses—to defeating 'nationalism, materialism, racial injustice, ignorance, war, and poverty', wherever they are to be found.[9]

Whether theological or cultural in form, imperialism was being attacked, most notably from within the American foreign missionary establishment itself. As Schlesinger describes pre-World War II Protestant missiology:

Missionaries now retreated from the view that faith could be served by force or that missions shared a common cause with national states. Confronted by anti-Christian riots in Nanking in the 1920s, missionaries opposed American military intervention and, by calling for a revision of the unequal treaties, signified a readiness to renounce specific diplomatic protection. By the 1930s the Hocking Commission said it was 'clearly not the duty of the Christian missionary to attack the non-Christian systems . . .'. In 1935 a professor at the University of Chicago Divinity School could even write a piece for *The Christian Century* stirringly entitled, 'I Don't Want to Christianize the World'.   (Schlesinger Jr., A., 'The missionary enterprise', 359.)

It is difficult to overestimate how great an ideological shift this was. Not too many years before, just prior to World War I, a British mission pamphlet was published with a vivid color illustration showing the Cross, British flag, and United States flag side by side.[10] No longer would that be possible for American or British establishment religion. If, in the enthusiasm of the earliest twentieth century, the ecumenically minded American Protestants could have the goal of 'evangelizing the world in this generation',[11] by the 1920s, revisionist thinking was articulating a new agenda for world missions.

The watershed for revisionist mission theory was the report, funded by J. D. Rockefeller, Jr., entitled *Re-Thinking Missions: A Laymen's Inquiry After One Hundred Years* and written under the leadership of a Harvard

---

[9] Hutchison, W. R., *Errand to the World* (Chicago, IL: University of Chicago Press, 1987), 152.

[10] Hutchison, W. R., *Errand to the World*, 138.

[11] Handy, R., *A Christian America*, 2nd edn. (New York, NY: Oxford University Press, 1984), 113.

philosopher, William Ernest Hocking. Presented in 1932, the message, while meeting mixed reactions among American Protestants, none the less said what knowledgeable missiologists already knew: Christianity, though encouraged to continue evangelizing anywhere it might choose, should no longer claim religious or cultural superiority:

For a part of the life of any living religion is its groping for a better grasp of truth. . . . We desire the triumph of that final truth: we need not prescribe the route. It appears probable that the advance toward that goal may be of the immediate strengthening of several of the present religions of Asia, Christian and non-Christian together . . . He [the Christian] will look forward, not to the destruction of these religions, but to their continued co-existence with Christianity, each stimulating the other in growth toward the ultimate goal, unity in the completest religious truth. (Hocking, W. E., *Re-thinking Missions: A Layman's Inquiry After 100 Years*, 44.)

The *Laymen's Inquiry* consisted of seven volumes, but the one-volume summary favored Hocking's personal agenda for the collaboration of world religions. His underlying concern was to find a 'world faith' to counter the growing secularization of the times. Critics chastised the report for this perspective, claiming that it would undermine the uniqueness of the Christian faith. Nevertheless, changes internationally and domestically had altered the parameters of, and motivations for, missionary work, and Hocking merely offered a rationale.

From the peak year of 1925, when the establishment denominations holding membership in the Federal, now National, Council of Churches maintained 6,794 foreign missionaries, the number has dropped, until by 1985 only 2,467 remained. Differences of opinion are held regarding why this decline occurred,[12] but irrespective of which opinion is correct, none conforms to a world system perspective or the implied Peter Smith thesis. Great Britain may have been the last empire that could missionize in accordance with its world political-economic position, but, whether or not the United States could, it is certainly a major player in the game that *failed* to do so. The simplest explanation would seem to be—to cite Schlesinger again—'the autonomy of the missionary impulse';[13] American mainline churches changed international strategies long before America's political and economic elites changed theirs.

Schlesinger cites two kinds of evidence that show how the American, Protestant, establishment missionary movement did not coincide with America's world system position. First, he shows that the deployment of foreign mission personnel held no correlation with patterns of United States

---

[12] See M. Burdick, 'Overseas mission: Failure of nerve or change in strategy?' In R. Michaelsen and W. C. Roof (eds.), *Liberal Protestantism* (New York: Pilgrim Press, 1986), 102–14.

[13] Schlesinger Jr., A., 'The missionary enterprise', 350.

imports and exports.[14] He does this for 1840, 1880, and 1900; we have checked more recent years and found the same lack of relationship. The second kind of evidence is really Perry Miller's, whom Schlesinger quotes: 'the peculiarity, more striking in America than anywhere else in Christendom, of a continuous admonition to the merchant classes, who contributed the finances for missionary endeavors, that they were at heart the secret foes of the sacred enterprise.' In short, Schlesinger goes on, at least in particular times and places, missionary zeal was strongly at war with the secular interests in acquisition and exploitation.[15]

Even more than in the British case, therefore, the rise and fall of American establishment religion's foreign missions operation simply do not accord with the world order model. One might note a possible exception: the correlation following World War II between the United States government's rising position in the world's political economy and its growing involvement in a church activity analogous to foreign missions. The United States, partly through the United Nations, was increasingly extending relief to refugees and famine-stricken populations. To a significant degree, such aid was given through already existing agencies of mainline Protestant, Catholic, and Jewish organizations. Cold War objectives were perceived to be taking precedence over humanitarianism, however, which led to a cutting back by many of these mainline groups in their co-operation with the government. By the late 1960s, 'The work of Christian and Jewish agencies overlapped with less frequency; differing views over the proper disposition of the Palestinian refugees created underlying tensions. Mainline Protestant and Catholic efforts were styled differently from the often brash efforts of evangelical Protestants. And the expanding work of secular agencies such as Save the Children, the International Rescue Committee, Oxfam, and others diminished the pride of place religious agencies had long held in the field'.[16] Therefore, establishment church co-operation with the United States government in these efforts peaked just as Peace Corps volunteers peaked in 1966–67, probably for the same reasons. The United States, it could be argued, had lost its hegemonic position, but, just as clearly, other forces were at work, too. As has been shown, the rise and fall of mainline Protestant missionary activity occurs well before the ascendance and then challenge to America's hegemonic position in the world's economy. Hutchison, noting that the real changeover occurred in the 1920s and reverberated for a few more decades, points to: theological innovation, organizational restructuring, the emergence of a world culture, and the rise of nationalism in the

---

[14] Schlesinger Jr., A., 'The missionary enterprise', 421.   [15] Ibid., 344.
[16] Nichols, J. B., *The Uneasy Alliance* (New York, NY: Oxford University Press, 1988), 116.

Third World as accounting for this change.[17] As Wuthnow has pointed out,[18] the world itself increasingly set the agenda for North American churches, which in some sense undercut the liberal religious rationale for evangelizing that world.[19]

In addition to such ideological challenges to American mission theory, one can note the creation of the World Council of Churches in 1947, and later its Commission on World Mission and Evangelism. Not only was a worldwide, ecumenical structure thereupon available as a conduit for denominational participation, but—more importantly perhaps—Third World nations, especially their Christian leaders, had an organized opponent to combat. By the 1970s, therefore, infused both with rising nationalism and theologies of liberation, these leaders called for a 'mission moratorium'. Missionary colonialism had long since lost its usefulness, they claimed. As one Indian church leader declared, 'The mission of the church is the greatest enemy of the gospel'.[20] Though never really implemented, this moratorium symbolized the completion of a transition by American mainline Protestant churches. Begun in the nineteenth century with the goal of *conversion,* their mission strategy had become, by the 1920s, one of *compassion*. By 1970, these churches, if they were to remain in the mission field at all, had to become *companions* to those to whom they would minister.[21]

REGARDING AMERICAN FOREIGN MISSION (NON-ESTABLISHMENT)

If establishment Protestantism's systematic dismantling of its foreign missions, beginning in the 1920s, calls into question the world system perspective, the missionary thrust by non-establishment Protestants offers an astonishing contrast. If modernity dominated the ecumenical, mainline mission theorists, evangelicals adamantly adhered to older theological priorities: the primacy of the supernatural, a definitive social orientation, an open hostility to modernity, and thus a continued conviction that conversion of

[17] Hutchison, W. R., *Errand to the World*, 161.

[18] Wuthnow, R., 'Religious movements and the transition in world order', 77.

[19] Without doubt, the most telling example was the grant of $85,000 by the World Council of Churches' Committee to Combat Racism to the Rhodesian Marxist rebels. Whatever else it meant, it certainly meant revisionist thinking in any mission theory dating from early in the century.

[20] Verghese, P., 'A sacramental humanism', *Christian Century*, 87 (September 1970), 1118.

[21] Hartley, L. H., 'Popular mission philosophies and denominational mission policy', in C. Jacquet (ed.), *Yearbook of American and Canadian Churches, 1988* (Nashville, TN: Abingdon Press, 1987), 273–85.

others to Christianity was their chief objective. Schlesinger's notion of 'the autonomy of the missionary impulse' is amply, if ironically, illustrated by the evangelicals' dominance of foreign missions since World War II.

About 1925 when the so-called mainline American denominations were at maximum personnel strength, other American Protestant bodies had reached parity and then continued a remarkable growth that has yet to stop. Put another way, in 1890 the denominations that were to become members of the National Council of Churches outnumbered their competitors by a 7:1 ratio. In 1985, the competitors enjoyed a 14:1 lead (see Table 8.3). Just as non-establishment, sectarian, evangelical religion has continued its penetration of the domestic religious market, so has its share of the foreign religious market shown few signs of slowing down. While this growth was most pronounced between World War II and 1968—a trend commensurate with the world order model—the growth continues, a fact that does not accord with that model.

Argentina represents a special case. During World War II, heightened anti-Americanism included a virulent hostility towards Protestantism. The government's neutrality was a ruse to conceal their pro-Axis sympathies. By March 1945, fearing post-war isolation, Argentina's military government declared war against Germany and signed the Act of Chapultepec, the Pan-American agreement. Prominent right-wing Catholic nationalists—feeling betrayed by the military for their capitulation to the 'colossus of the north'—wrote that Pan-Americanism was based on 'the messianic Protestantism of the Pilgrim Fathers and the Masonic enlightenment of the XVIII Century'.[22]

Protestants, liberals, Masons, and Jews were repeatedly blamed for the ills that had befallen the country. As late as 1959, a pastoral letter issued by a leading bishop stated: 'To be Argentine is to be Catholic; to deny Catholicism is to deny the Fatherland'. The Second Vatican Council, however, ushered in a new era of ecumenical relations. The traditional Protestants of the country were welcomed, perhaps begrudgingly, because a new 'enemy'—after Marxism that is!—threatened the fatherland: the '*sectas*'.

The sects that have 'invaded' Argentina range from the Moonies to the Mormons, from the electronic church to Latin America's own Tradition, Family and Property, an ultraconservative Catholic group founded in Brazil. Over 1,900 non-Catholic religious bodies are registered in the country. The prominent North American groups are perceived—even by moderate reli-

---

[22] Protestantism has a long history in Argentina. As British investments aided the development of the country, Anglican and other Protestant missionaries ministered to the expatriate community and missionized the Indians of Tierra del Fuego. Also, Welsh settlers had inhabited the Chubut valley of central Argentina, bringing with them their Protestant religion. In 1986 the Argentine Methodist church celebrated its 150th anniversary in the country. See M. Navarro Gerassi, 'Argentine nationalism of the right', *Studies in Comparative International Development*, 1 (1966), 191.

Table 8.3. American foreign missionary personnel deployed by establishment and non-establishment Protestant agencies for selected years (N)

Agency	1854	1890	1900	1905	1920	1925	1938	1952	1960	1968	1980	1985
Establishment denominations	756	2,331	3,001	3,411	4,945	6,764	5,852	5,541	5,249	5,454	2,511	2,467
Non-establishment denominations	5	357	497	1,216	3,877	6,843	4,699	7,896	11,968	23,533	32,078	35,079

Sources: ATS, *Ecumenical Missionary Conference*; Beach, H. P., and Fahs, C. H. (eds.), *World Missionary Atlas* (New York, NY: Institute of Social and Religious Research, 1925); Beach, R., *Foreign Missions Yearbook*; Bliss, E. M., *Encyclopedia of Missions*; Coote, R. T., 'The uneven growth of conservative evangelical missions', *International Bulletin of Missionary Research*, 6 (July 1982); Dayton, E. R. (ed.), *Mission Handbook: North American Protestant Ministries Overseas*, 13th edition (Monrovia, CA: MARC, 1986); Newcomb, H., *Cyclopedia of Missions*; Parker, J. I., *Interpretive Statistical Survey*; Wright, H. O., *Blue Book of Missions*.

gious observers—as a cultural extension of the domination of peripheral countries by the United States. An editor of a progressive Latin American Catholic journal stated: 'We share . . . in the challenges that confront us; from the international usury of the external debt to the invasion of the sects, both are the destruction of our ethos'.[23] Latin American Catholics fear the loss of their religio-cultural heritage. Most Argentines, moreover, are acutely sensitive to their country's position in the world political economy.

Another journalist offers a more strident analysis for Latin America's predicament. After the 1960s' upsurge of left-wing nationalist movements, the 'oligarchy'—acting in consort with United States imperialist policies—implemented widespread repression. In addition to state-sponsored terror under the aegis of the National Security Doctrine, 'hundreds of sects and individualistic and apocalyptic credos [belief systems] were implanted. The memory is the strength of the people and what better than religion to erase that conscience'.[24] The sects—like the International Monetary Fund—symbolize the continued erosion of their nation's political sovereignty, economic independence, and cultural heritage.

A POSSIBLE RESOLUTION

No reasonable alternative theory comes to mind that retains the world order perspective as outlined here and also explains: American establishment Protestant missionary decline before the 1960s, and American non-establishment missionary growth since the 1960s. One obvious adjustment is to change the world system theory regarding religious institutions, but if that would bring order out of disorder in these materials, we, at least, do not see the way to accomplish it.

Another kind of adjustment is possible, however, and that is to revise our notions of what is establishment religion. Perhaps one of the lessons to be learned from Table 8.1—which shows that so-called mainline churches have been losing proportionately to sectarian competitors throughout the twentieth century—is that mainline churches are no longer so mainline, and so-called sectarian churches are assuming increasingly representative status. While such an adjustment does not solve all the discord we have encountered here, it none the less alerts us to what may be a significant change in the religio-political nexus in today's America.

[23] Methol Ferre, A., 'Editorial', *Nexo* (September 1987), 3.
[24] Silletta, A., *Las Sectas Invaden la Argentina* (Buenos Aires: Editorial Contrapunto, 1987), 145.

Actually, our point is more easily made if we start from another perspective—that of 'civil religion'. Peter Smith himself noted that by establishment religion he meant something approximating the concept of civil religion: '[It] may also be thought of as the religious element in . . . the "dominant ideology," that is, the ideological framework by which the coherence of a dominant or ascendant social class is maintained'.[25] Perhaps the label *legitimating myth* is the clearest rendering we can offer of this concept.

Certainly America has had a legitimating myth, and certainly America's churches have participated in that myth's creation, content, promulgation, and modification.[26] Without doubt, moreover, the enthusiastic missionary thrust by the mainline churches in the nineteenth and early twentieth centuries, and the continued domestic growth of *all* churches in America until the mid-1960s, reflected the vitality of that myth. As Robert Wuthnow has written, the core of the myth, 'the millennial future of America', and its role as beacon and harbinger, came under increasing challenge until, by the 1960s, its unifying power was gone. In its place: 'Religious conservatives and liberals offer competing versions of American civil religion that seem to have very little of substance in common'.[27]

Another way to describe this process is to say that, until the 1960s, presidents, other leaders, and perhaps even people in general, were able to blend together, or at least hold in tension, the disparate elements of a single legitimating myth. After the Vietnam protests, the collapse of the civil rights movement, and the rise of the counter-culture as examples on the domestic front; and after our defeat in Vietnam, the turnabout in the export-import ratio, and the spread of nuclear weaponry as examples on the international front, such containment in a single myth was no longer possible. Instead, *two* renditions of the legitimating myth have emerged. While the links of each rendition to class, partisan politics, and general policy dimensions are not all that clear yet, the links to Protestantism are rather obvious: there is a conservative Christian right and a liberal, erstwhile mainline Protestant left. The latter suffers from a failure of nerve, while the former is chiefly concerned domestically about returning the US to an earlier, 'better' time. Internationally it has few qualms about holding out the US as still the world's leader.[28]

[25] Smith, P., 'Anglo-American religion and hegemonic change', 91.

[26] See Albanese, C., *Sons of the Fathers* (Philadelphia, PA: Temple University Press, 1976); Bellah, R., 'Civil religion in America', *Daedalus*, 96 (1967), 1–21; Hammond, P., 'The sociology of American civil religion', *Sociological Analysis*, 37/2 (1976), 169–82.

[27] Wuthnow, R., *The Restructuring of American Religion* (Princeton, NJ: Princeton University Press, 1988), 244.

[28] Wuthnow (ibid., 247) quotes from Jerry Falwell: 'We have the people and the resources to evangelize the world in our generation', thus echoing the sentiments of his liberal counterparts of three-quarters of century earlier.

The implication is clear, even if it cannot be adequately documented here: Evangelical Protestantism in its several forms is replacing liberal Protestantism as the establishment religion of America. Only in the South did liberal denominations gain members during the decade of the 1970s, no doubt in part because of the in-migration of non-southerners. Everywhere else those denominations declined significantly, while evangelical denominations, especially those with roots in southern culture, rose spectacularly. Evangelical religion has dominated the South for a long time, of course, but who would have thought it had more than a quarter the strength of liberalism in the North-east, nearly half the strength in the North-central region, and approaching double the strength in the West?[29]

To the degree such evangelicalism is becoming established, therefore, something of the world order perspective on religious institutions with which we began this discussion would seem at least partly to fit the evidence. As the United States gained its leadership position in the world economy, so was there an increase in the number of missionaries going out from the United States. These missionaries were going out under the sponsorship not of the old establishment religion but of the new. Similarly, throughout this period of ascendancy and hegemony, this new establishment religion gained disproportionately on the domestic front as well. World order theory is lingering in these materials somewhere, but just where and how are not yet as clear as they should be.

[29] See Egerton, J., *The Americanization of Dixie* (New York, NY: Harper's Magazine Press, 1974); Streicher, L. D., and Strober, G. S., *Religion and the New Majority* (New York, NY: Association Press, 1972); Shibley, M., *Resurgent Evangelicalism in the United States: Mapping Cultural Change since 1970* (Columbia, SC: University of South Carolina Press, 1996).

NINE

The Cultural Consequences of Cults

In 1983, David Bromley and I co-hosted a conference devoted to speculation about the future of new religious movements. The proceedings were published in a volume by that title.[1] This essay is one of my contributions to that volume.

The prospectus sent to participants in the conference on the future of new religious movements included the statement that we were 'to anticipate what the future holds for these groups and, by extension, *for American society as a whole*'. Those highlighted words are the subject of this essay, the only essay in the originally published volume that blithely ignores the new religious movements (NRMs) themselves, so to speak, and instead speculates generally about the US in the twenty-first century in light of the fact that NRMs came on the scene during the final third of the twentieth. How might the culture and institutions of this country not just the US, but, by extrapolation, any country that has experienced the influx of NRMs during the 1960s and 1970s, be influenced? One consequence, of course, has been much discussed: the emergence of an anti-cult movement, which has left residues of its own.[2] What might be other consequences?

My concern here will be focused on socio-cultural reverberations somewhat removed from the NRMs themselves. Because of the distance between cause and effects, therefore, the links may be less observable—requiring an analysis such as this even to make visible their potential—but, at the same time, those links may be decidedly more vulnerable to manifold other influences. None the less, if for no other reason than the 'spirit of the game' invites it, some speculation into the direct influences of NRMs on the broader society seems appropriate.

It should be clear that I am estimating neither what the future holds for today's NRMs nor the likelihood of the NRM's own goal achievement, a somewhat different issue. Rather, I am trying to assess what, if any, unintended cultural consequences follow from the fact that during the 1960s, 1970s, and into the 1980s, the industrial nations of the world experienced a

---

[1] Bromley, D., and Hammond, P. (eds.), *The Future of New Religious Movements* (Macon, GA: Mercer University Press, 1987).

[2] For example, see Beckford, J., *Cult Controversies* (London: Tavistock, 1985); also Shupe, Jr., A., and Bromley, D., *The New Vigilantes* (Beverly Hills, CA: Sage Publications, 1980).

range of new religious movements in their midst. As J. Milton Yinger tells us regarding 'deviant religious groups' generally, their importance rests 'on the nature of their cultural challenges, not their memberships'.[3] We might expect, therefore, that it is precisely in the arena of unintended outcomes where their impact will, in the long run, be more lastingly felt. Such, in any event, is what this essay is about.

THE AMERICAN PAST AND ITS TRAJECTORY

Benton Johnson, writing in 1981 about NRMs, notes that, generally speaking, they have no 'adequate theory of society', and thus—even though they may have revised some people's religious consciousness—they are unlikely to produce the social changes they themselves seek.[4] As he recognized, however, to assert that NRMs will fall short of *their* societal aims is not at all to say that they will have no societal *impact*. Assessment of impact is, to be sure, the privilege of the historian looking backward. But, if American history is any guide, one can venture some guesses, informed by the unintended consequences of prior periods when new religious impulses were felt and expressed.

Thus, during the First Great Awakening (*c.* 1730–1760), the ostensible theological thrust was evangelical, but the unintended consequence was the further and irrevocable disestablishment of Puritan Protestantism. During the Second Great Awakening (*c.* 1800–1830), the theological impulse was again evangelical, but the broader outcome was a pattern of religious voluntarism that has persisted to this day. Similarly, in the decades following the Civil War, the theology took a radical turn in the direction of liberalism, but the more lasting impact could be said to be the institutionalization of religious pluralism. If one were to summarize two centuries of religious change, then, one might say that whatever were persons' theological intentions, the periods of religious ferment led to ever greater levels of individual choice.

And what of the late twentieth century? Accepting McLoughlin's analysis that it is, indeed, a period of religious ferment[5]—a period in which the ostensible thrust is toward 'eastern', 'mystical', or at least unconventional theologies—we might note that the long-range consequences of this thrust may

---

[3] Yinger, J. M., *Countercultures: The Promise and Peril of a World Turned Upside Down* (New York, NY: Free Press, 1982), 233.

[4] Johnson, B., 'A sociological perspective on the new religions', In T. Robbins and D. Anthony (eds.), *In Gods We Trust* (New Brunswick, NJ: Transaction Books, 1981), 62.

[5] McLoughlin, W. G., *Revivals, Awakenings, and Reform* (Chicago, IL: University of Chicago Press, 1978).

well be quite otherwise. Just as the previous awakenings have capitalized on an ever-increasing individualism—whatever their doctrinal definition of the situation—so, too, do the NRMs of the current day not only flow from this individualism but also help institutionalize it yet another notch higher. Their impact on the culture at large, then, may lie not so much with the substance of their novel theologies as with the increased demands they make on the ethic of individualism.

A GENERAL CULTURAL OUTCOME

A first observation to be made, therefore, stems from Rodney Stark's point regarding the regulation of the 'religious economy': just as NRMs have a greater chance of emerging and thriving in a relatively unregulated religious economy, so does the appearance of NRMs serve to further deregulate that economy. At the individual level, this increase in individual religious freedom means simply that ever greater choice—in whether and how to be religious—is likely to ensue. At the cultural level, however, it may mean more. It may, by offering novel religious choices, be offering broader value choices as well. Thus Glock and Wuthnow, after comparing the 'conventionally' religious and the 'nonreligious' with the 'alternatively' religious in their Bay Area survey, note:

By and large, to be alternatively religious represents a sharper and more pervasive break with the conventional than does being nonreligious. The differences between the conventionally and alternatively religious on canons of personal morality are in every instance greater than between the conventionally religious and the nonreligious. The same applies to political outlook and political attitudes . . . . Unlike the nonreligious, the alternatively religious break with the conventionally religious in other realms of life. Thus, the alternatively religious in all comparisons are the least likely of the three orientations to attach great importance to the 'creature comfort' items. . . . Openness to alternative life-styles is also more characteristic. . . . These results . . . are not an artifact of group age. . . . Among both youths and matures, the alternatively religious are more sharply and pervasively in conflict with the conventionally religious on all of the issues examined.   (Glock, C. Y., and Wuthnow, R., 'Departures from conventional religion', 62–3.)

One might say, using the parlance coming out of the 1960s, that NRMs have provided an avenue for a counterculture to take root and be expressed. The consequence in the next century will be a yet more variegated culture.

More precision than this is desirable, however, because, over and beyond the sheer addition of religious options, there might be a multiplier effect with reverberations felt elsewhere in society as well. I think at least two such reverberations can be identified and predicted with fair accuracy. They are: the further weakening of the link between religion and family, and the further erosion of 'established' religion. In neither instance can it be said that these outcomes are intended by any NRM, yet both will be more characteristic of our society in the next century, in part because of the NRMs in this one. No doubt there will be many other cultural consequences as well, but these two seem almost certain.

THE LINK BETWEEN RELIGION AND THE FAMILY

In one of the most seminal essays in all of sociology of religion, Talcott Parsons wrote:

. . . it is to be taken for granted that the overwhelming majority will accept the religious affiliations of their parents—of course with varying degrees of commitment. Unless the whole society is drastically disorganized there will not be notable instability in its religious organization. But there will be an important element of flexibility and opportunity for new adjustments within an orderly system which the older church organizations . . . did not allow for.   (Parsons, T., 'Christianity and modern industrial society', 65.)

The 'element of flexibility' Parsons had in mind is the ease with which persons can switch denominations without charges of family heresy. For the Lutheran-raised son or daughter, a change to the Methodists is not a rejection of parental religion, for example, but merely a culturally circumscribed choice. Similarly, Catholics raised in an ethnic parish can remain Catholic even while leaving their ethnic parochial background, and Jews have at least Orthodox, Conservative, and Reform options without dropping out of their familial faith. However wrenching individual cases may be, the religious culture of America, Parsons asserted, made room for adjustments in the religion-family link; one did not have to reject family in order to make a change in religion. All of this flexibility rested on a fairly low rate of defection from all religion, however. That is to say, the assumption that one denomination is about the equivalent of any other presumes that only a few in each generation will exercise the option of rejecting religion altogether. Otherwise, an important cultural feature of Americans—visible at least since Tocqueville's visit in 1831—would be seriously challenged. 'Each sect worships God in its own fashion', Tocqueville observed, 'but all preach the same morality.'[6] President Eisenhower was merely echoing the same sentiment in 1952 when

---

[6] Tocqueville, A. de, *Democracy in America*, G. Lawrence (ed.) (Garden City, NY: Doubleday Anchor, 1969), 290.

he declared our government to be 'founded in a deeply felt religious faith—and I don't care what it is'.[7]

New religious movements in the sixties, seventies, and eighties *have* challenged this cultural assumption, however. Surely it is no coincidence that the strongest expressions of anti-cult feeling come not from mainstream churches but from families who, in seeing their children join a religious group far outside of the mainstream, regard those children as somehow 'lost'. Cults, in other words, call into question the link between religion and family.

And well they might. While the number of cult members is still so small as not to show up in samples of the national population, we have already seen in Essay One in this volume (Tables 1.1 and 1.2), that the cultural assumption of only negligible defection from all religion is seriously in doubt. That evidence makes clear that defection among Catholics and Jews has risen from the generations born before 1931 to the generations born since. Approximately 10 per cent in the older group departed their religious legacy, whereas nearly 20 per cent, and then 25 per cent in subsequent groups have done so. Protestants, however, show no such trend. Is this because they are religiously more loyal? Probably not, inasmuch as their 'defection' rate, while not increasing through time as do those of Catholics and Jews, is consistently much higher. The explanation would seem to be in the far greater options available to Protestants to change from parental denomination while still remaining Protestant. If, therefore, we look not at all kinds of defection from parental religion but just at the proportion of such defections that constitute departure from all religions, we find that Protestants are not that different from Catholics and Jews.

Catholics and Jews lead the way, of course, their choices being restricted once departure from parental religion occurs. None the less, the figures of Table 1.2 in Essay One are remarkable across the board because *in every denomination defection into no religion is on the increase among those departing from parental religion*. Moreover, these defections double and then triple across the three age cohorts. The strong, if flexible, link Parsons could assume in 1963 is now obviously greatly weakened.

Where do new religious movements (NRMs) fit in? They would appear to be both product and producer of this weakened link. First of all, only with the link weakened were NRMs able to recruit members and become a visible force. Research showed that many who were recruited were already estranged from their families, for example, even more estranged from their parents' religion.

---

[7] Quoted in Herberg, W., *Protestant, Catholic, Jew* (Garden City, NY: Doubleday Anchor, 1960), 84.

Second, the cults' very success no doubt contributes to the further weakening of the family-religion link. It is important to recognize that this last assertion is cultural, not individual, however. No doubt the enthusiastic early generations of NRM members have taken great care to raise *their* children in the parental religion. The proximate consequence for members of NRMs may therefore be fewer defections from parental religion. But the wider consequence—of demonstrating that, indeed, children can depart markedly from parents' affiliations—is surely to weaken even further the tie between family and religion.

One might raise the question, therefore, following Parsons's trenchant analysis early in the 1960s, whether or not we have experienced a 'notable instability in . . . religious organization'. In other words, have new religious movements contributed to the disruption of a long-standing cultural pattern in the United States linking the family with religion? Robbins and Anthony, who have followed closely this particular aspect of NRMs, would suggest that the answer is yes:

Cults operate as surrogate extended families and, moreover, provide novel therapeutic and spiritual mystiques which confer meaning on social processes . . . no longer . . . easily legitimated by . . . traditional ideologies. In so doing, however, they exploit the weaknesses of existing institutions (churches, nuclear families, psychiatry) and perhaps pose a threat to these institutions.   (Robbins, T., and Anthony, D., 'Cults, brainwashing, and counter-subversion', 88–9.)

One cultural consequence of the emergence of new religious movements since the 1960s, therefore, will probably be a dramatic further loosening of the link between religion and family.

EROSION OF ESTABLISHED RELIGION

A second cultural consequence of current NRMs will likely be the erosion, through legal decision-making, of the power of those religions with long-standing roots in the American culture—the so-called mainline denominations, including Catholicism and Judaism. More accurately, perhaps, what will happen is *the further erosion* of such religion, because what is occurring is, in reality, but another step in the same direction well-established religions have already been forced to go on previous occasions. Thus, in a quite literal sense, when the framers and ratifiers agreed on the Establishment Clause of the First Amendment, they assured a decline in the power and prestige of whichever denomination *would* have been chosen had an established church been allowed. Similarly, the passing of all vestiges of state establishment—

completed finally in Massachusetts in 1833—left all denominations on a voluntary footing, a decline in power if not in prestige.

The kind of legal erosion being brought on by contemporary NRMs is more subtle than in these earlier instances, however. A closer parallel with the present is the case of Mormon polygamy, wherein the court, confronted by the unprecedented claim to plural marriage,[8] responded not only by declaring the practice unconstitutional but also by making explicit the fact that governments, not churches, determine which behaviors are acceptable. Churches retained their power to *preach* doctrines of choice, but it was now clear they had lost the power necessarily to act on them. In a similar fashion, I would argue, the great number of legal challenges brought by NRMs in our own day—even though, by and large, the courts have upheld the right of NRMs to be different—will have the consequence of further eroding religious power.

The context for this argument is the well-known tension between the Free Exercise Clause and the Establishment Clause of the First Amendment. Put baldly, the argument is that every extension of what is permitted as free exercise of religion by *individuals* leads to a diminution in the rights of religious collectivities because it calls into question their prior privileged position. The more widespread a benefit becomes, in other words, the relatively less value that benefit will have to those who were earlier its sole beneficiaries. This argument is complicated, however, and no doubt controversial as well, so we must proceed slowly.

The idea is hardly new, that legal decisions may lead unintentionally to consequences quite at odds with those decisions' stated purposes. Thus, for example, court cases enabling Native Americans to extend their tribal sovereignty give rise to that sovereignty's possible arbitrary use, which gives rise to the need to protect individual rights, which then undermines tribal sovereignty.[9] The decision is made that children attending schools in poor districts are entitled to the same enriched education received by students in wealthy districts, but local communities therefore no longer control admissions, curriculums, or standards of excellence. This notion—that individual rights are won at the expense of those collectivities intermediary between persons and central governments—is well known.

In the church–state scene, however, there is an additional element inasmuch as the individuals whose rights get recognized in ground-breaking cases are oftentimes representatives of the religious collectivities whose power *as collectivities* is being compromised. As James A. Beckford says, 'Religious groups . . . voluntarily take their testimony into courtrooms and

[8] *Reynolds v. United States*, 98 US 145 [1879].
[9] Medcalf, L., *Law and Identity: Lawyers, Native Americans, and Legal Practice* (Beverly Hills, CA: Sage Publications, 1978).

are thereby seduced into rationalizing their deepest convictions in return for legal credibility'.[10]

This phenomenon is easier to see *ex postfacto,* of course. Thus, in upholding the right to proselytize in hostile neighborhoods, the court made explicit the right of government to control proselytizing.[11] Or in granting conscientious objector status to persons not 'religiously' motivated, the court took on the *de facto* task of defining religion,[12] a task it had hitherto assiduously claimed to avoid.[13] Viewing with alarm these threats to 'established' religious communities that often result unintentionally from the further broadening of individual rights, some 'conservationists' have called for a purposive strengthening through legal recognition of so-called 'mediating structures'. Inevitably, however, such an argument runs into the following problem.

In general, we are more relaxed about 'no establishment' than is the present approach of the courts, and more adamant about 'free exercise'. We would wish the courts to take more seriously the institutional integrity of religion, rather than its current tendency of privatizing religion by focusing on individual beliefs and motivations.   (Kerrine, T., and Neuhaus, R. J., 'Mediating structures: A paradigm for democratic pluralism', 14.)

Kerrine and Neuhaus express this wish, but it is not at all clear how one can be 'more adamant' about individual free exercise and at the same time insist on continued or renewed recognition of religion's 'institutional integrity'—not, at least, if religion retains a single meaning. If the courts will grant the right of conscientious objection to someone who does not believe in God, what special right can be claimed by someone who does believe in God? Or by one belonging to a group based on such a belief? The current Rehnquist Supreme Court of the US is striving to move in what is called the 'nonpreferentialist' direction—that is, neutrally preferring religion over irreligion—but I think such movement runs counter to the history of American church–state jurisprudence.

New Religious Movements, I am asserting, have intensified this historic process by requesting—and, for the most part, being granted—recognition of their religious rights. Thus, on issues not only of evangelizing but also of soliciting funds, tax exemption, and political involvement by religious groups, NRMs have stretched existing boundaries, with the consequence that government feels the need, or is asked, to intervene in matters that once were entirely internal to churches.[14] Ironically, it is an Establishment case

---

[10] Beckford, J. A., 'The state and control of new religious movements', *Acts of the 17th Congress* (Paris: International Conference for the Sociology of Religion, 1983), 10.

[11] *Cantwell v. Connecticut,* 310 US 296 [1940].

[12] *United States v. Seeger,* 380 US 163 [1965]; *Welsh v. United States,* 398 US 333 [1970].

[13] *United States v. Ballard,* 322 US 78 [1944].

[14] See Kelley, D. M. (ed.), *Government Intervention in Religious Affairs* (New York, NY: The Pilgrim Press, 1982) for discussions of these matters.

involving Transcendental Meditation that allows us to see how this erosion process works.

The circumstances of this case were peculiar, to say the least. Followers of Maharishi Mahesh Yogi were teaching meditation techniques in five public schools in New Jersey. Upon examination by the Federal courts, this practice was declared 'religious' and thus in violation of the Establishment Clause. All three judges agreed that Transcendental Meditation (TM) is religious because its 'substantive characteristics' resemble those of other systems found to constitute religion in prior cases. For one of these concurring judges, however, this 'look-alike' test was not enough.

I am convinced that this appeal presents a novel and important question that may not be disposed of simply on the basis of past precedent. Rather . . . the result reached today is largely based upon a newer, more expansive reading of 'religion' that has been developed in the last two decades in the context of free exercise . . . cases but not, until today, applied by an appellate court to invalidate a government program under the establishment clause. *Malnak v. Yogi*, 592 F. 2d 197 [1979].)

Judge Adams then proceeded to write a fairly lengthy opinion that, at the end, offers a legal definition of religion: precisely an outcome established religious traditions would avoid, and will no doubt resist. Along the way, however, the judge considers the 'mediating structures' position of two understandings of religion—a 'broad' one with respect to Free Exercise issues so that individual conscience is given greatest rein, and a 'narrow' one with respect to Establishment issues, thus protecting the favored status of religious collectivities clearly recognized as such. The result, he says, would be a 'three-tiered system of ideas': those that are unquestionably religious and thus free from government interference but also barred from government support; those that are unquestionably nonreligious and thus subject to government regulation and eligible for support; and those that are religious only under the dual definition, thus free from government regulation but eligible for government support. The hypothetical outcome is that the third category would get favorable treatment, which leads to clearly unconstitutional preferences.

The point is, something like this situation already occurs, leading the government to outlaw more and more of what is religious on Establishment grounds *because* it has been recognized as religious on Free Exercise grounds. Thus, says Beckford, many governments used to

. . . justify a variety of arrangements for giving *bonafide* (i.e., generally recognized) religious groups a number of official privileges. Indeed, the privileges used to make very good sense from the States' point of view at a time when religious groups served as the foremost defenders of general culture and as agents of socialization. (Beckford, J. A., 'The state and control of new religious movements', 7.)

Insofar as the substance of 'general culture' is *challenged*, however, then the 'official privileges' are also challenged.

In the realm of education alone, first publicly funded but church-operated schools, then clerical teachers, then a religious curriculum, then sponsored devotionals, have been outlawed from public schools because the *de facto* Protestant nature of such things was challenged by Catholics, Jews, and non-believers whose Free Exercise rights became increasingly clear.

After the fact, the process is not mysterious; the particularism assumed to be universal is shown to be a particularism by the act of recognizing yet other particularisms. NRMs since the 1960s, I am suggesting, are hastening this process by revealing in yet new ways how 'Judeo-Christian' has been our conception of religion. As non-Judeo-Christian variations gain legal status, therefore, the effect will be further erosion of heretofore-established religion.

There is an even larger irony on this point, exposed by those fundament-alists who would reimpose school prayer, declare the US to be 'Christian', or otherwise restore religious particularism—of just what stripe they, of course, dare not say. The irony comes from the failure of these people to recognize their lineage in the left-wing, egalitarian, nonconforming, and sectarian branch of Protestantism that was at least half of the impulse for the First Amendment in the first place. What Robert Bellah calls 'romantic cultural particularism'[15] joined forces with secular individualism two centuries ago to create the church-and-state situation we have today. Considering the path of development since 1789, NRMs are hardly unusual, then, but instead rep-resent simply further occasions by which established religion is eroded.

CONCLUSION

On the basis of the above two predictions, one might generalize further. New religious movements in the last third of the twentieth century have led to yet another increase in institutionalized individualism, just as previous episodes of religious ferment did. And if this is so, are we not led to conclude even more generally that, just as NRMs could take root and grow only in an already secularized soil, so does the success of those NRMs—however lim-ited—indicate even further secularization? After all, we have just argued that individuals will experience even greater freedom from family obligations, and churches will experience even greater loss of influence. Is it not reason-able to conclude, therefore, that religion will decline yet another step?

---

[15] Bellah, R.,'Cultural pluralism and religious particularism', in H. Clark (ed.), *Freedom of Religion in America* (Los Angeles, CA: Center for the Study of the American Experience, University of Southern California, 1982).

Bryan Wilson has been the most eloquent spokesman for this point of view,[16] and probably the majority of sociologists of religion agree. Yet the appearance of NRMs on the contemporary scene has led some observers to the opposite conclusion—that the 'sacred' may be 'returning'.[17] Surely both sides cannot be correct.

Or can they? Perhaps the arguments advanced in the foregoing pages suggest a resolution of this apparent contradiction. Imagine that the 'sacred' is always and everywhere being encountered. That is to say, with Durkheim, social life lived entirely on the profane level is impossible, which means that the 'unquestioned', that is, the sacred, is forever intruding in human affairs.[18] But whether this unquestioned sacred realm is regarded as 'religion' depends upon the accretion of a number of other characteristics, foremost among them being the degree to which the sacred impinges upon lives, and the degree to which it is expressed in supernatural terms.

Looking backward, moreover, we can see yet other accretions: the supernatural expression of the sacred has often been elaborated into systematic theology, which, in the West, has been largely Christian, embodied primarily in the church, the 'purest American' branch of which is Protestant evangelicalism. As long as religion, with these accretions, remained highly institutionalized—as long as Protestant evangelicalism retained a near-monopoly, to use Rodney Stark's formulation—then as new encounters with the sacred occurred, they were likely to be perceived in the culturally prescribed manner, and one person's God resembled the next person's God, one church acted much as all other churches, and so forth.

Given this view, secularization might thus be conceived as the systematic dismantling—or 'unpeeling'—of these accretions. Thus in the US, Protestant evangelicalism lost hegemony; the church had to compete with other Christian bodies; Christianity became but one religion in the marketplace; and informal expressions of the sacred came to exist alongside systematic theology, much of which could in fact be rendered in 'natural' terms, which finally may have lost all relevance in some people's lives. This development did not mean the disappearance of the sacred but rather the loss of its accretions and thus its recognizability as religion.

In the resulting 'secular' setting, new encounters with the sacred may take place, but, insofar as they draw upon cultural traditions some distance from Western Christian traditions, they appear to some as not religious at all and

---

[16] B. Wilson, 'The secularization debate', *Encounter*, 45 (1975), 77–83; *Contemporary Transformations of Religion* (Oxford: Oxford University Press, 1976); 'The return of the sacred', *Journal for the Scientific Study of Religion*, 18 (1979), 268–80.

[17] For example, D. Bell, D., 'The return of the sacred?' *British Journal of Sociology*, 28 (1977), 419–49.

[18] Durkheim, E., *The Elementary Forms of Religious Life*, trans. K. E. Fields (New York, NY: The Free Press, 1995) (originally published in Paris in 1912).

to others as a 'return' of the sacred. The new religious movements in the last third of the twentieth century seem to have met with such mixed reactions, as indeed they would if they are simultaneously two things: both authentic efforts to express the sacred, and believable *because* of the dismantling of previous accretions of the sacred.

The NRMs can never duplicate the course taken by, say, Christian sects in the US, therefore. Even more doubtful is their likelihood of achieving cultural hegemony. But these new religious movements must be seen as intrusions of the sacred into cultural life, even if they are, at the same time, both products of the secularization preceding their appearance and facilitators of yet more to come. Even if the NRMs manage to hang on as religious alternatives, in other words, they carry the cultural implication, not that sacralization is taking place, but quite the opposite.

TEN

Religion and Ethnicity in
Late Twentieth Century America*

After four decades of heightened ethnic consciousness by African Americans, Mexican Americans, Asian Americans, and Native Americans, asserting that assimilation in America remains the greater trend in ethnic relations may seem absurd. Indeed, controversies over 'multiculturalism' in the college curriculum, the 'rise' of 'unmeltable' white ethnics, and the persistence of vibrant ethnic organizations, ethnic newspapers, and ethnic fund appeals would suggest that ethnicity remains a powerful force in American society. And so it does.

None the less, such persistence defies the larger and more prevalent trend toward assimilation. Unlike the long-standing situation in Belgium or Northern Ireland, for example—or the situation more recently exposed in certain African nations or in the former Yugoslavia—US society was not formed by territorially combining already existing ethnic populations. Rather, the vast majority of American citizens are immigrants, or the children of immigrants, who, upon arriving on this continent, found an ongoing culture to which some kind of accommodation was, and is, required. As Stephen Steinberg puts it, such transplanted minorities, 'ripped from their cultural moorings and lacking a territorial base', could hardly survive here with their culture intact. 'American society provided only a weak structural basis for ethnic preservation. The very circumstances under which ethnic groups entered American society virtually predestined them to a gradual but inexorable decline.'[1]

Inexorable decline need not be uniform, however. Common sense alone would suggest that various groups differentially diminish their differences with the host culture, by accommodating to it and/or having it accommodate in return. Moreover, events can occur that in some sense reverse the assimilation process. Seen vividly in the case of Jews during and since the Holocaust, such episodes of ethnic renewal may be long- or short-term, widespread or narrowly experienced, but they may also temporarily halt or

---

* Kee Warner collaborated on this essay.

[1] Steinberg, S., *The Ethnic Myth* (Boston, MA: Beacon Press, 1981), 43.

redirect the inexorable decline. Thus, for example, the percentage of American Jews marrying non-Jews went down from 7 per cent in 1941–50 to 6 per cent in 1956–60, but it then returned to an escalating rate: 17 per cent in 1961–65, 32 per cent in 1966–71, and is even higher now.[2]

ASSIMILATION AND SECULARIZATION

A parallel exists between ethnic assimilation and religious secularization. While there are many meanings of secularization, we mean by the term simply the decline of religion's social significance. Thus both ethnicity and religion, we are saying, are vulnerable to forces that diminish their *social* importance. Individuals may, of course, choose to assign great importance to their ethnicity and/or their religion, but the processes of assimilation and secularization minimize the likelihood that such personal importance translates into generalized social significance. Indeed, it may be precisely the freedom to choose that renders the choices—whatever they are—less salient in social terms.

This increasing freedom to choose reveals yet another feature common to ethnicity and religion: their declining inheritability. The notion that ethnicity may not be inherited is not as readily apparent as the declining inheritability of religion, which is widely understood and well documented in the United States. In fact, the belief that ethnicity is inherited—passed on through generations—is one of its defining features; the other being the existence of a myth of origin. In the United States, most people claiming an ethnic identity believe that the ethnicity they inherit is traceable to some geographic territory and that their myth of origin is tied to that territory. Such beliefs need not be taken literally, of course, especially in the case of such diaspora peoples as Jews and Armenians, or in the case of a new ethnic group such as Mormons, where territory is real enough in the myth, though disputed as geographical reality. In other words, what matters is the belief, not the actuality.

Thus, while the process of choosing whether to remain loyal to one's parents' religion is fairly obvious, the analogous process in the case of ethnicity, though similar, is not so obvious, probably because of the belief that ethnicity *is* inherited. There are, for example, those cases where the precise nature of the ancestry has simply been forgotten, thus allowing persons to select from a variety of ethnic progenitors or to select no foreign ancestry at all. Not surprisingly, in the United States this last option—of declaring oneself

[2] Mayer, E., *Love and Tradition: Marriage between Jews and Christians* (New York, NY: Plenum Press, 1985), 48.

simply American—is more often found in those border southern, Appalachian, states with sizable Scots-Irish, German, and English immigration in the eighteenth century but relatively little in-migration since. After all, one need back up only four generations to find sixteen different ancestors, and it is a rare American who knows much about even a minority of those sixteen. Genes may be inherited, but the social meaning of those genes will, in some sense, be voluntarily selected in a way that parallels the decision of whether and how to remain loyal to one's inherited religion.

A third feature common to ethnicity and religion is the role played by intermarriage in the processes of assimilation and secularization. Just as marriage across ethnic boundaries need not weaken the ethnic identity of either partner but often does, so may marriage occur across religious lines without weakening religious identity. But religious intermarriage is often discouraged for fear of just such loss because that loss, like lost ethnic identity, frequently occurs.

And how could it be otherwise? One or both partners in an intermarriage are likely to give up a religious connection and a territorial tie. One or both may relinquish a friendship network and possibly a language. Secular ethnic organizations might be abandoned as well, just as might friendships with persons still attached to the inherited ethnicity.

Individual assimilation, like secularization, occurs in a number of interrelated ways: by diminished social interaction, reduced residential propinquity, and declining language use, newspaper reading, organizational memberships, worship, kinship contacts, and so forth. Among empirical investigations, Reitz makes this point very clear in the case of ethnicity in Canada,[3] as do Stark and Glock in the case of religion in the United States.[4] This suggests that, if both ethnic and religious identities weaken, so may the relationship between ethnicity and religion.

ETHNICITY AND RELIGION

Just as some observers deny that secularization occurs in the US, others deny the reality of assimilation. Not surprisingly, therefore, so also have some observers doubted the decline in the relationship between ethnicity and religion. For example, historian J. S. Olson states, 'The relationship between ethnicity and religion in the United States is as powerful today as it has been

[3] Reitz, J. G., *The Survival of Ethnic Groups* (Toronto: McGraw Hill Ryerson, 1980).
[4] Stark, R., and Glock, C. Y., *American Piety* (Berkeley, CA: University of California Press, 1968).

throughout American history'.[5] Of course, as our first paragraph acknowledges, ethnicity does remain a powerful force in the United States. Likewise, who can doubt the continued vitality of religion in this society? But persons who argue for no change—by denying assimilation and secularization—rely too much on mere descriptive statistics, as Olson relies on reports showing that, for example, French, Irish, Italian, and Polish Catholics are significantly different in their practice of Catholicism. Of course! But such reports show only that ethnicity remains influential.

The church or synagogue was not just an insulating device by which assimilation was resisted; in many instances, it was also a vehicle by which assimilation or acculturation could be facilitated, just as for many immigrant Americans, religion has been a major way of expressing one's ethnic identification. The questions addressed here are: is this still the case? And if so, for whom is it stronger, and for whom is it weaker?

PATTERNS OF RELATIONSHIP BETWEEN RELIGION AND ETHNICITY

While it might be assumed that, virtually everywhere, ethnicity and religion are related, it must be acknowledged that this relationship takes several forms, at least in mixed immigrant societies such as the United States. Following Abramson,[6] we can distinguish at least three patterns:

1. Religion is the major foundation of ethnicity; examples include the Amish, Hutterites, Jews, and Mormons. Ethnicity in this pattern, so to speak, equals religion, and if the religious identity is denied, so is the ethnic identity, although there can be exceptions, as the labels, 'jack Mormon', 'banned Amish', or 'cultural Jew', suggest. Let us call this pattern 'ethnic fusion'.

2. Religion may be one of several foundations of ethnicity, the others commonly being language and territorial origin; examples include the Greek or Russian Orthodox, and the Dutch Reformed. Ethnicity in this pattern extends beyond religion in the sense that ethnic identification can be claimed without claiming the religious identification, but the reverse is rare. Let us call this pattern 'ethnic religion'.

3. An ethnic group may be linked to a religious tradition, but other ethnic groups will be linked to it, too. Examples include Irish, Italian, and Polish

---

[5] Olson, J. S., *The Ethnic Dimension in American History* (New York, NY: St. Martin's Press, 1979), 436.

[6] Abramson, H. J., 'Religion', in S. Thernstrom, A. Orlov, and O. Handlin (eds.), *Harvard Encyclopedia of American Ethnic Groups* (Cambridge, MA: Harvard University Press, 1980).

Catholics, or Danish, Norwegian, and Swedish Lutherans. Religion in this pattern extends beyond ethnicity, reversing the previous pattern, and religious identification can be claimed without claiming the ethnic identification. Let us call this pattern 'religious ethnicity'.

As a first generalization, we suggest that the first of these patterns, ethnic fusion, is the most firmly institutionalized—that is, religion and ethnicity remain most strongly related and provide the greatest identity—and the third pattern, religious ethnicity, is least firmly institutionalized. Ethnographic evidence testifies to the strength of religion and ethnicity in the first pattern, but that very strength may keep such groups small and insulated and thus obscured in large-scale quantitative studies—Mormons being an exception. In any event, we examine here only examples of ethnic religion and religious ethnicity, though, as will become apparent, in the United States this still leaves room for considerable variation.

A second generalization can also be suggested: if in the first pattern, religion and ethnicity are more or less fused, in the case of ethnic religion it is more likely that ethnicity helps to uphold religion, while in the case of religious ethnicity it is more likely that religion helps to uphold ethnicity. With ethnic religion, in other words, everyone in a church probably shares an ethnicity as well as a religion, but there are fellow ethnics not found in church; with religious ethnicity, everyone in a church probably shares only a religion, though ethnic parishes were a well-known but now declining phenomenon.

Religion and ethnicity differ culturally in one respect, however, which warrants inquiring into the relative stability versus changeability of the two identities. We have discussed the belief in the inheritability of ethnicity. This belief alone no doubt serves to help maintain ethnicity; at most, one may play down its importance to the point where one even loses track of what was inherited ethnically, but only rarely would a person exchange one ethnicity for another.

For religion, the situation is quite otherwise. National polls report overwhelming agreement with the notion that 'an individual should arrive at his or her own religious beliefs independent of any church or synagogue'. In the survey we introduce shortly, 77 per cent agreed with this statement, a figure that helps to interpret the next finding. When asked, 'Do you see the church as something passed on from generation to generation, or as something that needs to be freely chosen by each person?' two-thirds answered 'freely chosen', and only 23 per cent answered 'passed on from generation to generation'. The Protestant principle of individual religious responsibility permeates American culture, in other words, even for those persons with strong ethnic ties. Consequently, all else being equal, religious loyalty will likely weaken before ethnic loyalty weakens. Thus Greek Orthodox Americans become Roman Catholic, Armenian Americans become Episcopalian,

Japanese Americans become Methodist, or Jewish Americans become secular, often as a result of intermarriage, without necessarily giving up Greek, Armenian, Japanese, or Jewish identity.

Seldom is all else equal, however, so the opposing pattern is also found, especially in America among ethnic Catholics, who of course represent the pattern we called religious ethnicity. Thus, for example, Alba reports that among Italian Americans who are third generation in this country and under 30 years of age, as much as 70 per cent marry non-Italian Americans. Alba further notes that 'intermarrying Italians married freely with other Catholic groups',[7] which is to say that religious loyalty could be said to have been stronger than ethnic loyalty in these instances.

THE STRENGTH OF THE ETHNICITY-RELIGION RELATIONSHIP

If it is a truism that ethnic or religious identity may each range along a weak-to-strong continuum, it is also the case that little is known empirically about the relationship of the two identities. Of course, as with many major challenges in the social sciences, this one would be best addressed with time-series data, especially across two or more generations. Ideally, researchers would have measures of the strength of both ethnic and religious identities at several chronological points in order to observe which changed first, why, and with what effect. But studies of this sort are rare in the annals of social research, and surrogate studies must often take their place.

AN EMPIRICAL INQUIRY

Although the data about to be reported were collected in 1988 and 1989 for another purpose,[8] they permit at least a provisional investigation of the issues raised earlier in this essay. The sample comes from four states—California, Massachusetts, North Carolina, and Ohio—via randomly dialed telephone interviews with about 650 adults between the ages of 25 and 63 in each state. From the resulting 2,600 interviews, 1,691 cases can be classified on measures of ethnic identity and religious identity.

---

[7] Alba, R. D., *Italian Americans* (Englewood Cliffs, NJ: Prentice-Hall, 1985), 89.
[8] Hammond, P. E., *Religion and Personal Autonomy* (Columbia, SC: University of South Carolina Press, 1992).

Ethnic Identity Measure

Three pieces of information were used to classify people on an index of ethnic identification. One question asked, 'From what country or part of the world did your ancestors come?' We noted whether persons claimed single or multiple foreign ancestry. A second question asked about spouse's ethnic ancestry. We noted whether respondents married within their ethnic group. The third question asked, 'Would you say, in general, that you feel pretty close to other people from the same national background, or that you don't feel much closer to them than to other people?' We noted whether respondents reported feeling closer or not.

Persons judged to be high in ethnic identification included those who reported feeling closer to fellow ethnics and those who claimed a single foreign ancestry and/or had in-married. This way, unmarried persons could be classified as high in ethnic identity provided they regarded themselves as having a single ethnic ancestry and felt closer to fellow ethnics. Similarly, persons could also score as high despite mixed ethnic ancestry provided they were married to someone sharing one of those ethnic heritages and felt closer to people of that heritage.

By this rather stringent measure, only 16 per cent of our 1,691 cases score as high, though this percentage ranges from 36 per cent, in the case of Mexican Americans, to 3 per cent, in the case of Swedish Americans. This is a much lower rate of strong ethnic identity than common sense would suggest. For example, the rate for blacks, 35 per cent, seems unexpectedly low. The explanation—for blacks, anyway—probably does not lie in low levels of in-marriage or not feeling closer to fellow ethnics but lies instead in the question about foreign origin. For persons whose ancestors emigrated from Sweden, Japan or Italy, little ambiguity exists. But for blacks in America, the situation can be quite unclear. African Americans, of course, came from somewhere other than these shores, but Africa is not a 'country', nor were the 'parts of the world' from which they came identifiable as nation-states at the time. Add the history of slavery, forced marriage, separation, transience, and inadequate record keeping, and it is understandable that many blacks in America do not readily name Africa as the source of their ethnic identity. Only if they did name Africa in this survey as their country of origin, however, could they then affirm the same identity for their spouses, report feeling closer to persons like themselves in this respect, and thus score high on our measure. Even though this measure is thus too blunt to detect nuanced ethnic sentiments, it nevertheless is relatively accurate; persons scoring high are, in fact, likely to be higher in ethnic identity than others.[9]

---

[9] A similar complication forced us to exclude Jews from this analysis. Jews answered the question of national origin with 'Germany', 'Russia', and so on, requiring us to use religious

Religious Identity Measure

Our measure of religious identity is not as indirect as the ethnic identity measure. As with the ethnic measure, however, the upshot is a conservative device that, to the degree that it works, doubtlessly underestimates the phenomenon it purports to measure. Conceptually, at least, it is straightforward.

Many countries from which Americans emigrated had, and may still have, established churches. Other countries were fundamentally homogeneous in religion even if they gave no formal recognition to a single religion. To varying degrees, therefore, immigrants to the United States often had a religion by which and through which they could carry on old-country culture. The current linkage between religion and ethnicity in America is, of course, the topic of this article, but the historical fact of such linkages provides us with our measure. We consider simply whether people remain attached to the religious tradition historically associated with the countries of their ancestral origins.

This operation was simplified by our decision to use, from our sample, only those ethnic groups with twenty-five or more respondents. After Jews were excluded, for the reason given in note 9, only twelve groups qualified, which could be religiously characterized as follows: Lutheran, from Norway, Sweden, or part of Germany; Roman Catholic, from France, Ireland, Italy, Mexico, Poland, or part of Germany; Anglican or Episcopalian, from England; Presbyterian, from Scotland; and black Protestant, from Africa.

Of course, not everyone with roots in a given country is part of that country's religion—for example, this is true of Irish American Protestants—but if persons seek to express their ethnicity religiously, these twelve groups have fairly clear-cut guidelines. Germany, with historically strong Lutheran and Catholic churches, may appear an exception, but by first asking German Americans in our sample if they were raised Lutheran or Catholic, we can classify them as still loyal to their religious tradition or religiously something else. In the case of persons with African roots, we follow the considerable literature testifying to the central role played by black Protestant churches in the history and lives of black Americans. Our assumption, in other words, is not that all African Americans are affiliated with a black Protestant denomination—nor are all Norwegian Americans Lutheran. Rather, we are assuming that remaining with or returning to the religion culturally and historically associated with one's ethnic origins, rather than departing to another religion or to no religion at all, may to some degree express one's ethnicity.

To the extent that these two indices fall short of measuring exactly what

identification to determine their ethnicity. That, in turn, meant we could not investigate their ethnicity and religion separately.

we seek—the strength with which people identify themselves with an ethnic group on the one hand, and with the religion historically linked to that ethnic group on the other hand—we underestimate the true strength of both types of identity as well as the true strength of the relationship between the two types. Our goal *per se* is not to estimate these things with exactness, however, but to discover for various ethnic groups their relative strengths and the reasons for differences in these strengths. Better measures might do this job more effectively, but it is doubtful that they would discover a different ordering of well-documented differences.

Table 10.1. *Strength of identity and religious affiliation, and their relationship in twelve ethnic groups*

Ethnic origin	% high in ethnic identity	% affiliated with historical religion	Correlation	N
Mexico	36	67	0.33	42
Africa	35	68	0.18	77
Italy	23	61	0.10	115
Poland	19	56	0.18	63
Ireland	15	54	0.13	309
Norway	14	31	0.39	29
England	11	0	0.04	373
Scotland	10	15	0.14	125
Germany (Lutheran)	10	12	−0.01	332
Germany (Catholic)	8	87	0.08	110
France	8	30	0.18	83
Sweden	3	18	0.21	33
Total	16	33	0.15	1691

WHAT THE DATA SHOW

Table 10.1 supplies the data necessary for the ensuing analysis. For each of twelve ethnic groups, it provides the number of respondents in the group, the percentage who score high in ethnic identity, the percentage who are affiliated with the historical religion of that ethnic group, and the correlation between ethnic identity and religious affiliation.

Visual inspection of Table 10.1 suggests that religious identity tends to be strongly related to ethnic identity at the group level (Pearson's r = 0.70). In other words, groups with high rates of ethnic identity tend also to have high rates of religious identity. At the individual level, by contrast, the average for the total sample at the bottom row of Table 10.1, is a much lower 0.15, ranging from 0.39 for Norway, to effectively zero, for German Lutherans. Since, however, some groups are fairly small, making their scores unreliable when treated alone, we aggregated groups by category for more reliable analysis.

The first category includes the first two populations listed in Table 10.1, persons tracing their ancestry to Mexico or to Africa. They exhibit not only the highest rates of ethnic identity but also the highest rates of historical religious affiliation. It can also be noted that, of the twelve ethnic groups listed in Table 10.1, these two are most likely to be regarded, by themselves and by others, as racial groups and most subject to political, economic, and social discrimination in American society at large. They are thus more likely than other groups listed to live in ethnic neighborhoods, have friends who are fellow ethnics, and so on. Combined, the two groups' correlation score between ethnic and religious identity is a significant 0.23; that is, persons in these groups who are most strongly identified ethnically are also more likely to be affiliated with their ethnic group's religion.

The characteristics of this first category suggest an antithetical second grouping made up of those ethnic groups that, unlike the first category, have low rates of both ethnic and religious identity. England, Scotland, German Lutherans, and Sweden all seem to fit here without squeezing. Norway, too, qualifies except for a moderately high rate, 31 per cent, of religious attachment to Lutheranism, though with only 29 respondents, this percentage is unreliable. These five groups also share, of course, a history of early entry into the United States, white skin, and cultural similarity to the amalgam culture dominant in America. Consequently, these groups show the highest rates of assimilation found among the twelve groups of Table 10.1.

Three of the five remaining groups, Italy, Poland, and Ireland, are in the middle of the table with respect to both ethnic and religious identity. Catholic Germany is anomalous because of its uncharacteristically low ethnic identity rate and high—the highest—religious identity rate. Some of the explanation may lie in the fact that German Catholics in this sample come disproportionately from Ohio, where Cincinnati remains a traditional center of old German American Catholic culture.[10] France is also anomalous, with measures closer to Norway than Italy, Poland, and Ireland, but still higher on religious identity than all others in the second grouping. As rough conjecture, one might say that German Catholics in America are highly assimilated—by intermarriage, for example—but highly distinctive by religious heritage. Correlatively, French Americans are also highly assimilated by intermarriage but relatively low when it comes to identity with their historical religion.

[10] This is not the entire explanation, however, as is seen from a parallel study to be discussed later in this essay. There, with a sample that is national and 50 per cent larger, the same characteristics are found among German American Catholics.

ANALYSIS

What is the historical religion of French Americans? It is, of course, Roman Catholicism—the same as the historical religion of Italian, Polish, and Irish Americans, and those German Americans raised as Catholic. The contrast with the second grouping is all the more striking, therefore, because all five populations in that grouping are Protestant.

Table 10.2. *Strength of identity and religious affiliation, and their relationship in three ethnic groupings*

Category	% high in ethnic identity	% affiliated with historical religion	Correlation	N
Minority (Mexico, Africa)	35	67	0.23	119
Catholic (Italy, Poland, Ireland, Catholic Germany, France)	15	57	0.13	680
Protestant (Norway, England, Scotland, Lutheran Germany, Sweden)	10	8	0.05	892

If we thus combine all five Catholic ethnic groups, not including Mexican Americans, and all five Protestant ethnic groups, not including African Americans, we can observe that, while the ethnic identity rate of the Catholics is only modestly higher than that of the Protestants—15 per cent versus 10 per cent—the religious identity rate is significantly higher: 57 per cent versus 8 per cent.[11] The inference is strong, therefore, that—to use the terminology of earlier pages—Catholic Americans have assimilated at nearly the rate of Protestant Americans, but they have secularized at a lesser rate. Religious identity, if this inference is correct, thus helps to maintain ethnic identity more than non-religious ethnic identity helps to maintain religious identity, at least in the case of Catholic Americans. For them, the religious identity lingers longer than the non-religious ethnic identity. We are perhaps historically too late to observe this pattern among the greatly assimilated and greatly secularized Protestants. Correlatively, the very low rates of assimilation and secularization of Mexican and African Americans mean that it is too soon to tell, should that point come, whether ethnic or religious identity will erode first.

[11] The procedure of combining ethnic groups this way gives greater weight to groups having more members. If, instead, the individual group scores are first averaged, then added together, and averaged for the category, the results are nearly identical.

A REPLICATION

The analysis just presented was replicated using data from the General Social Surveys, 1983–90, of the National Opinion Research Center at the University of Chicago. Not only was this sample three times the size of the four-state sample—5,235 compared to 1,691—but it also allowed the inclusion of Puerto Ricans in the minority category, the inclusion of Spain and French Canada in the Catholic category, and the inclusion of Denmark in the Protestant category. Measures of ethnic identity and affiliation with historical religion were nearly identical in the two analyses. Remarkably similar percentages and correlations appeared, especially in the comparison with the findings in Table 10.2.

On the basis of these two studies, therefore, it would seem plausible to argue that religion and ethnicity maintain a significant relationship in late-twentieth-century America, but it is just as plausible to note that this relationship systematically varies from one kind of ethnic group to another. Three generalizations seem warranted. First, ethnic identification and loyalty to the religion of one's ethnic group have tended to diminish together in the American context—that is, assimilation and secularization are correlated. Second, the processes of assimilation and secularization occur at a slower pace in ethnic groups regarded as minorities and thus discriminated against. Finally, decline of ethnic identity appears to precede decline of ethnic religious loyalty, though—given the nature of the two samples of data used here—we cannot establish whether this sequence is true only of Catholics in America or is a general process already undergone by Protestant ethnics. This is just one more thing we have yet to learn about the complex relationship of religion and ethnicity in America. Historical data might provide an answer.

THE FUTURE

Neither religion nor ethnicity will disappear in the near future, of course, but the linkage between the two is almost certain to decline. That is to say, as religion becomes more and more a matter of individual choice, and persons become increasingly selective in making that choice, ethnicity, along with other background characteristics, will have a declining effect in determining religious identity. This process will be most obvious in suburban, non-denominational churches and in amorphous spiritual groups, but the inroads made by Pentecostal Protestantism into Hispanic Catholicism, and by Black Muslims into African American Protestantism also signal further weakening of the link between religion and ethnicity.

As mention of Black Muslims reminds us, however, such a weakening linkage does not mean that religion necessarily fades in importance as a vehicle for expressing ethnic concerns. Indeed, just as black Americans have long used their Protestant churches as organizing devices on a range of issues, so may we expect the growing populations of Arabs and Asians in America to use their religions for such purposes. Moreover, it does not necessarily follow that, just because religion is a matter of choice, its importance declines; it may actually take on greater psychological significance even as its social and ethnic importance diminishes.

The overall trend is predictable, however. The decreasing importance of ascribed characteristics, and the correlative increase in individuals' autonomy, diminishes the inheritability of both religion and ethnicity, and that means the decline in their relationship.

ELEVEN

Religion and Family Values
in Presidential Voting*

The term New Christian Right (NCR), since it came into widespread use
during the 1980s and 1990s, has generally been understood to encompass far
more than a renewal of the fundamentalist–modernist split early in this century. The Bible can still evoke bitter controversy, to be sure, but the so-called
'Christian' perspective on communism, education, welfare, race relations,
the criminal justice system, and—above all, perhaps—the spheres of sex and
the family, have in recent years been blended into the theological divide. In
this essay, we assess both this blend and the amount of *separate* impact in
presidential voting the various components of the NCR ideology have had in
the last five elections. We investigate specifically the separate effect of the theological aspect of the NCR (called here the Christian Right component) and
the family-sexual moral aspect of the NCR (called here the Family Values
component).

THE ISSUE IS JOINED

Post-election analyses aim to dissect and explain who voted for whom and
for what reasons. Merely showing that persons holding attitude X voted
disproportionately for candidate Y is never adequate to establish that their
voting was motivated by X, however. It is usually the case that attitude X is
embedded in a bundle of circumstances that would have led to a vote for Y
anyway, with or without attitude X. The following opinion column comment, written by me and Mark Shibley and published on 27 September
1992 by the Santa Barbara *News Press,* describes how complicated it can be
to make sense of voting patterns. Even there, the analysis is handicapped by
the absence of party identification. However, on the pages that follow this
opinion column piece we try to look specifically at the role played in recent
presidential elections by two different, though related, attitudes: a

* Mark Shibley and Peter M. Solow collaborated on this essay.

Christian Right theological perspective and a conservative Family Values perspective.

Vice Presidential candidate Al Gore's speech on 13 September 1992, at the University of Missouri was remarkably reflective of the 'family values' issue.

For his largely youthful, educated audience, Gore noted that American culture is undergoing a significant revolution, and their generation is ahead of earlier generations in both recognizing the inadequacy of the old and accommodating the new. What Gore might also have said is that before the new cultural perspective gains widespread acceptance, a countering effort—often called a revitalization movement—emerges in an effort to reassert the old cultural values even as they are being replaced. This cultural tug-of-war dates back to the 1960s, of course. It picked up heat during the Reagan years, but it has emerged full-blown in this 1992 campaign. Significantly, Clinton and Gore are young enough to have grown up in the '60s and reached maturity after the Vietnam War ended. It was perhaps inevitable that this campaign thus would include sharper disagreement over moral values than we have observed in the past. Put another way, we might have expected the Republican platform to be 'captured' by radical traditionalists, wanting to 'revitalize' an earlier moral code, and we should not be surprised to hear Al Gore assert that today's youth are the lead generation in accepting the emerging moral code.

What may be less obvious is that 'family values' is largely a repackaging of the issue that gave rise to much-noted Reagan Democrats in 1980 and '84 and thus stands to be a big factor in this election. The fact is that so-called pocketbook issues are fairly straightforward, and voters can estimate whether, in paying taxes for example, they gain or lose more than they pay. With some exceptions (for example, the Pentagon) the Republican Party since the 1930s has been the low-tax, low-spend party, and the Democrats have taxed and spent. However, there being more Americans who benefit from government expenditures than who lose, Democrats on this issue alone have an edge, especially if we note that the low-income ranks are joined by some high-income persons who agree with Justice Oliver Wendell Holmes' statement that taxes buy civilization.

Because of this Democratic advantage, therefore, Republicans must find one or more 'wedge' issues to pry away sufficient numbers of otherwise Democrat-inclined voters. Nixon used anti-communism to a 'silent majority', a strategy that Reagan adopted and added to by courting the religious right. In 1988, Bush inherited many of these Reagan Democrats, but developed the 'morality' theme less than he did law-and-order and the containment-of-enemies-abroad. Now in 1992, the wedge issue—in part chosen by Bush and in part thrust upon him in a Party Platform dictated by convention delegates with a traditional view of morality—has sharpened greatly. It is the combined issues of abortion, homosexuality, sex outside of marriage, and gender equality, and it is known as 'family values'. Will it work in this election?

As it happens, a 1988 survey of 2,600 adults drawn randomly from the populations of Massachusetts, North Carolina, Ohio, and California asked about exactly these four issues, allowing a 'family values index' to be constructed, ranking people from strongly supportive of the traditional morality in these four areas of behavior to strongly supportive of new morality. Males and females do not differ on this index, but age is modestly related, and in the direction Al Gore suggests; respondents his age and younger are half again as likely to support the new morality as respondents aged 60 and older. Persons in the middle age group are in between. Gore was especially correct in seeing education as facilitating rejection of the old and adoption of the new; people with college degrees are more than three times as likely to support the new morality as people who never finished high school. Theological position is also involved. People who believe that the Bible is to be taken literally (this, of course, being negatively correlated with education) are only one-fourth as likely to support the new morality as people dissenting from the inerrancy position.

But so what? Will people who might otherwise be inclined to vote Democratic instead vote Republican if they hold to the traditional morality? That, needless to say, is what George Bush is counting on by seeming to embrace a moral position he is known earlier to have rejected and that his wife rejects now.

The question is, will it work in this campaign? A reasonable estimate might be made from the same survey. While respondents were not asked their party identification, they were asked to identify themselves politically as liberal, moderate, or conservative. We also know whether, as of October 1988, they intended to vote for Dukakis or Bush. Let's see what influence their moral views had on their vote intention.

In 1988, among persons who regarded themselves as politically liberal, twice as many moral traditionalists (as measured by the family values index) declared an intention to vote for Bush as did liberals holding the newer morality. This is not a trivial number since more than a third of these self-assigned liberals were moral traditionalists, perhaps persons who, though liberal on economic matters, foreign affairs, the environment, etc., had not yet found a way to accommodate the sexual revolution of the 1960s. Just as significant, Bush lost no support from self assigned conservatives on the moral issue; though overwhelmingly in his camp, whatever their sexual moral views, those who expressed the new morality were, if anything, even stronger in their support for Bush.

But there lies the rub. In 1988 the sexual morality theme was not so starkly an issue, embedded as it was in other 'social' issues such as gun control, prison leaves, and welfare payments. Today, however, the Republicans have taken the 'nativist' or 'revitalization' position. They claim to want to stem a cultural change that, in some fashion, is inexorable. Though involving choices, this cultural change also reflects the fact that the world has changed. The automobile and motel, for example, have made sexual encounter easier, but so too have earlier sexual maturity (by as much as three years in this century) by both males and females. This, coupled with delayed age at marriage, has greatly expanded the period of time adolescents are exposed to serious sexual conduct with serious potential consequences. The increased availability of divorce through no-fault laws is a socially engineered analog. The near disappearance of the chaperone is another.

All of this, moreover, is accompanied by an awakened sense of individual freedom—to engage sexually without regard to traditional expectations, to look upon marriage and parenthood as negotiable sources of pleasure, and—most dramatically—to regard abortion and same-sex relationships as governed by much the same individual ethic. This is a severe challenge to the sexual ethic that prevailed since at least the emergence of the middle-class in the 19th Century. Bush sees, however opaquely, that such a morality still appeals, and he has chosen it as a wedge issue in 1992. In Richard Nixon's campaign recommendation to Bush that he dump the 'religious fanatics', however, is the warning that 1992 may not simply repeat 1988; erstwhile conservatives comfortable with the new morality may be more inclined to vote Democratic this time around, and erstwhile liberals may now recognize that their 'liberalism' has been co-opted in the name of some very intolerant ideas. Bush's 'family values' tactic, in other words, is a distinct gamble.

Toward the end of this essay we will took specifically at the role played by religion and family values in the 1992 election, then the 1996 election. First, however, we take a closer took at the three preceding presidential campaigns.

IDEOLOGY AND THE POLITICAL PROCESS

American culture places great emphasis on making up one's own mind, on being independent in thought and deed. Thus, a person who has purchased five Buicks in succession will nonetheless insist that each 'decision' was independently arrived at. Likewise, many life-long Democratic or Republican voters will claim to debate in their own minds at each election which candidate to favor yet consistently pull the lever of their 'own' party.

Does this mean that only party identification and not ideological positions determine presidential vote? Of course not. What it does mean, however, is that ideological positions, along with such other factors as family and community allegiances, 'steer' persons toward one or another party, and unless there are significant ideological shifts in the voters and/or the parties, voters' loyalties remain reasonably fixed.

Shifting of party loyalties does occur, of course, but contrary to popular perception, such shifts are unlikely to take place over a 'single' issue. John F. Kennedy's Catholicism may have been an exception to this generalization, but certainly most Catholic Republicans who voted for JFK in 1960, and Protestant Democrats who voted against him, returned to their respective parties in later elections. Those that did not return contributed to a potential party realignment, but that is a phenomenon occurring on a massive scale only rarely in American political history. It is not clear whether such a realignment is occurring in the late twentieth century, but claims are frequently heard that a party realignment may be taking place over the issues of religion or family values, or both.

In any discussion of the role of religion and family values in recent presidential voting, however, it is not enough to determine whether right-wing Christians or anti-abortionists voted Republican more than Democrat. It is entirely possible that such persons 'always' voted Republican and would have done so again and again even if Reagan or Bush had not endorsed evangelical Protestantism and not opposed abortions. As we said above, 'single' issues seldom lead to a change of vote, and rarer yet do they lead to a change in party identification.

This perspective is nicely illustrated by the research of Benton Johnson and Mark A. Shibley on the role of 'Christian Right' ideology in the presidential elections of 1972, 1976, and 1980.[1] They show that persons holding Christian Right views are far more likely to hold conservative political views as well. When party affiliation is then examined, however, they find that, while the general conservative political viewpoint powerfully influences Republican Party identification, the Christian Right viewpoint has no *independent additional* effect. Similarly, party identification itself 'explains' the bulk of the presidential vote, leaving little additional impact for conservative political viewpoint to play. In their research, just as party identification 'mediated' most of the effect of political ideology, so did political ideology 'mediate' all of the effect of Christian Right views.

A further complexity arises, however, a point that experienced survey researchers recognize but others may not. It is bound up in what Paul F. Lazarsfeld called 'the doctrine of the interchangeability of indices'.[2] The basic notion is that all measures of so-called dispositional concepts—for example, 'intelligence' as distinct from 'age', 'group cohesion' as distinct from 'membership size'—are impure. Multiple probes, with answers combined, are preferable to a single probe, therefore, but multiple probes create their own ambiguities. Take, in this instance, the notion of 'conservatism'. If a single question is asked in a survey, for example, 'On a scale of 1 to 10, how conservative would you say you are?', objection can be raised that conservatism has many meanings and therefore respondents probably had different meanings in mind in answering that question. If multiple probes are used, on the other hand, it becomes apparent that, since answers are not perfectly correlated, maybe 'conservatism' is not a unitary thing at all. Just as in the Graduate Record Exam, where we distinguish 'verbal' from 'quantitative' from 'analytic' skill, so may we want to distinguish economic conservatism from religious conservatism or anti-communist conservatism.

But here lies the complexity. Though verbal, quantitative, and analytic scores are not perfectly correlated, they are positively related, so questions designed to measure verbal skill will tap quantitative and analytic skill as

---

[1] Johnson, B., and Shibley, M. A., 'How new is the new Christian right?' in J. K. Hadden and A. Shupe (eds.), *Secularization and Fundamentalism Reconsidered* (New York, NY: Paragon Press, 1989), 178–98.

[2] Lazarsfeld, P. F., 'Problems in methodology', in R. K. Merton (ed.), *Sociology Today* (New York, NY: Basic Books, 1958), 60–7.

well. Similarly, in measuring economic conservatism we are also tapping into religious conservatism, anti-communist conservatism, and so forth. Any empirical demonstration of the effect on presidential voting of either religious conservatism or family values conservatism must therefore show the *independent* effect of either or both of these factors—over *and beyond the effect of conservatism generally.* A homely analogy: persons who would attribute their indigestion to the garlic in the sausage must first take into account the effects of other spicy items they ate—for example, the onion in the salad, the paprika in the goulash, or the chili in the salsa. Perhaps any one or any combination of these is capable of producing heartburn. If so, then to diners who eat one or more of these other items, adding garlic sausage may not have any additional effect. Showing that it does, requires first taking into account the effect of spicy food generally, then demonstrating the *additional* effect of garlic.

When asking whether religious conservatism or family values conservatism influenced presidential voting, therefore, we are required to ask:

1. Did conservative ideology contribute to voting decisions over and beyond conservatism's role in steering people into Republican party identification?
2. If conservative ideology did make such an additional contribution, was it 'conservatism' generally, or did religious conservatism or conservative family values play independent roles?

These questions are what we now examine.

CONSERVATIVE IDEOLOGY IN PRESIDENTIAL POLITICS

It must be conceded that no once-and-for-all definition of 'conservatism' is possible. Nevertheless, for specific time periods in specific places, a reasonable grasp can be made of notions of what is conservative and therefore what is liberal. An ideology of either stripe can thus be likened to an umbrella made up of multiple parts. Persons may not feel equally committed to all these component parts and therefore know greater comfort under one part of the umbrella than under others. Moreover, if the particular component that energizes them is singled out, they might readily accept the label 'conservative' or 'liberal', whereas they may balk at accepting such a label if it is attached to some other component—thus the politician who calls himself a 'fiscal conservative' but a 'social liberal', for example.

In the late twentieth century in the United States, a number of components are believed to comprise a conservative ideology—with which the New

Christian Right is often identified—even if different people emphasize different components. One component having a pedigree dating back to World War II might be labeled 'anti-communism'. It seems likely that the conservative 'umbrella' is being reconfigured as a result of the 1989 fall of the Berlin Wall, but China, Cuba, and other entities can still trigger political sentiment. Another component, made popular by Ronald Reagan, might be called 'anti-government', a notion that taxes are too high and government bureaucracy is inefficient. A third component of conservative ideology of recent decades has been termed 'law-and-order', a label that stands for favoring the death penalty, opposing gun control, and generally preferring stiffer sentences and more police presence. There is, fourth, a component that is often called the 'Christian Right', an ideological position that for many decades was quite silent but since the 1970s has been increasingly outspoken. It stands for so-called Biblical values and opposes what it calls 'secular humanism'. Finally, and closely related to a Christian Right outlook, is a 'family values' component. Many persons holding this ideological position find Biblical warrant for their views, but those views are held by many not holding to a literal reading of the Protestant Bible.

More components could be added, drawn from the areas of civil rights, economic justice, immigration policy, education, and so forth. Each additional component provides further refinement of a measure of 'conservatism', to be sure, but it does so at a diminishing return rate when it comes to social research analysis. Moreover, in secondary analysis we are limited to the use of items contained in existing survey questionnaires, so some compromises have to be expected. Items measuring the five components discussed above happen to be available, while potentially worthy items measuring other components of conservatism simply are not. We work with what we have.

Even what we have is far from what would be desirable in an ideal research project. But surveys asking about: presidential vote, political party affiliation, and a number of attitudes bearing on political conservatism, including religion and family values—that also extend over a range of years and thus several presidential elections—are hard to come by. Indeed, only the General Social Survey, by the University of Chicago's National Opinion Research Center fills the bill. From them, for the presidential elections analyzed here, we have used the following questions to measure:

Presidential Vote

Did you vote for Carter, Reagan, or Anderson (Mondale or Reagan; Dukakis or Bush; Clinton, Bush, or Perot; Clinton or Dole)?

Party Identification

Generally speaking, do you usually think of yourself as a Republican, Democrat, independent, or what?

Anti-communist Component

Thinking about the different kinds of governments in the world today, which of these statements comes closest to how you feel about communism as a form of government? Choosing 'It's the worst kind of all' = Anti-communism.

Do you think our government should continue to belong to the United Nations, or should we pull out of it now? Choosing 'Pull out now' = Anti-communism.

Antigovernment Component

We are faced with many problems in this country, none of which can be solved easily or inexpensively. I'm going to name some of these problems, and for each I'd like you to tell me whether you think we're spending too much money on it, too little, or about the right amount. [How about] on welfare? Choosing 'too much' = Anti-government. Half the sample was asked not about welfare spending but spending on 'poor people', which elicited greater generosity.

Same as above but asked about 'Improving conditions of Blacks'. Choosing 'too much' = Anti-government.

Law-and-Order Component

Would you favor or oppose a law which would require a person to obtain a police permit before he or she could buy a gun? Choosing 'oppose' = Law-and-Order.

Do you favor or oppose the death penalty for persons convicted of murder? Choosing 'Favor' = Law-and-Order.

In general do you think courts in this area deal too harshly or not harshly enough with criminals? Choosing 'Not harshly enough' = Law-and-Order.

Christian Right Component

The US Supreme Court has ruled that no state or local government may require the reading of the Lord's Prayer or Bible verses in public schools. What are your views on this—do you approve or disapprove of the court ruling? Choosing 'Disapprove' = Christian Right.

There are always some people whose ideas are considered bad or danger-
ous by other people. For instance, somebody who is against all churches and
religion. If such a person wanted to make a speech in your community
against churches and religion, should he be allowed to speak or not?
Choosing 'Not allowed' = Christian Right.

Family Values Component

Please tell me whether or not you think it should be possible for a pregnant
woman to obtain a legal abortion if she is married and does not way any
more children. Choosing 'No' = Family Values.

There's been a lot of discussion about the way morals and attitudes about
sex are changing in this country. If a man and a woman have sex relations
before marriage, do you think it is always wrong, almost always wrong,
wrong only sometimes, or not at all? Choosing 'Always' or 'Almost always
wrong' = Family Values.

What about sexual relations between two adults of the same sex—do you
think it is always wrong, almost always wrong, wrong only sometimes, or
not wrong at all? Choosing 'Always' or 'Almost always wrong' = Family
Values.

Do you agree or disagree with this statement? Women should take care of
running their homes and leave running the country up to men. Choosing
'Agree' = Family Values.

Of course objections can be leveled against these particular indicators as
being too few in number, too contaminated or too restrictive, and so on. But
they are the best available, and we must use them or give up our search.

A first observation to be made is that, while the five components are
clearly reflective of a conservative ideology, they are distinct from one
another yet related. Table 11.1 shows how each component is correlated with
the other four components. For this part of our analysis, we have combined
the three surveys covering the elections of 1980, 1984, and 1988.

The Anti-communist component is the only one of the five components
that has statistically significant (beyond 0.01) relationships with all four others. There is a surprising, though small, *negative* correlation between the

Table 11.1. *Correlation matrix for components of conservative ideology*

	Anti-communist	Anti-government	Law-and-Order	Christian Right
Family Values	0.24	insig.	0.09	0.47
Anti-communist		0.11	0.15	0.24
Anti-government			0.24	−0.07
Law-and-Order				insig.

Christian Right component and the Anti-government component. And there are two correlations, between Family Values and Anti-government, and between Law-and-Order and Christian Right, too small to reach statistical significance. What stands out, however, is the huge, by survey research standards, relationship between Family Values and Christian Right. Those two components, especially if joined by the Anti-communist component, probably 'absorb' much of the conservative ideological spectrum; certainly persons scoring high on all three of these components can logically be called conservative and probably regard themselves as such.

In an important way, the above correlations make the point we made earlier: neither the NCR nor 'conservatism' is a unitary thing, an ideological entity that can be measured by a single dimension. But neither are its multiple dimensions independent of one another, which means that in classifying respondents in a survey on one dimension, a researcher is automatically classifying them to some degree on the other dimensions. The question thus becomes again whether any one dimension of conservatism has some independent effect on the presidential vote after the combined other dimensions of conservatism are already taken into account. This question is exactly parallel to the question that logically precedes it: since conservatives are more likely to be Republicans and thus vote for the Republican candidate, does conservative ideology have any independent effect on voting after party identification is already taken into account? We are now in a position to address those two questions for the elections of 1980, 1984, and 1988.

Using all of the information about voters that we discussed above—their vote, their party identification, and their scores on conservative ideology measured five different ways—we can 'explain' an average of about 46 per cent of the direction of vote in the three elections. The overwhelming proportion of this 'explanation' is found in party identification alone; that is, to know a person's political affiliation goes most of the way in providing whatever accuracy an observer might have in predicting their vote. But while the overwhelming proportion is provided by party identification, there is a significant contribution made by the five combined measures of conservatism over and beyond party identification. Though differing slightly from one election to the next, the strength of this independent ideological impact averages about 13 per cent of the strength of party identification. Put another way, party identification has about 3.5 times the strength of 'leftover' conservative ideology, as measured here, in the presidential voting in 1980, 1984, and 1988. While relatively small, therefore, conservative attitudes were significant beyond any doubt, which indicates that ideological posturing and positions on issues did play a role that went beyond the attitudinal and value forces that steered people into one or another party and kept them loyal to it.

But we have yet another question to ask: did the kinds of conservatism described above as the Christian Right component and/or the Family Values component have any *independent* impact on presidential vote over and beyond the role played by a generalized conservative ideology? To answer that question we reanalyze the data from the three election years pretty much as before, except this time separately by election. After assessing the impact of party identification, we look at the combination of all the components of conservative ideology *minus* the Christian Right component, so we can examine its *separate* effect. Then we put the Christian Right component back into the combination of components, and remove the Family Values component in order to see if it has separate impact. A glance at Figure 11.1 will help convey this process. It is as if we look at the whole 'pie' with, first, the Religion (Christian Right) slice taken out and looked at separately, then we put back in the Religion slice and repeat the process but assessing this time the separate impact of Family Values. What did we find?

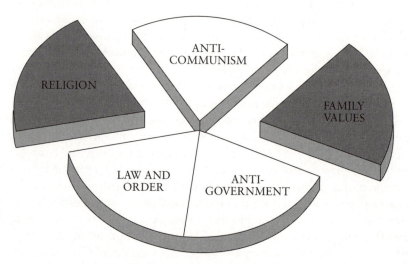

Fig. 11.1 Components of conservative ideology.

In none of the three elections did the Christian Right component have any statistically significant *additional* impact on presidential vote once party identification and an ideological measure consisting of the other components are taken into account. The Family Values component fared similarly; though it showed a statistically significant impact in the 1984 election, the impact was less than half that of the combined other four components and only one tenth the impact of party identification in that year's election.

Nor is this unexpected in light of what was earlier called the 'interchangeability of indices'. Following the procedure just outlined, we looked at the independent impact of each of the other three components in each election. With few exceptions, that impact was statistically insignificant, and in only one instance did a single component outweigh the combined impact of the other four, that being the role played by Anti-government sentiment, which overwhelmed all other ideological factors in the election of Ronald Reagan in 1980.

Once again, this analysis does not reveal the impotence of ideological factors in elections. It merely shows that after such factors help establish a party identification, there is little additional force left to expend. Similarly, once research gets a broad-gauged measure of a conservative ideology, and then assesses its impact, there is even less role to play by any particular component of that ideology. The question now is whether, as was widely reported in the press and elsewhere, Christian Right or Family Values conservatism had any impact in the 1992 presidential election.

THE 1992 PRESIDENTIAL VOTE

Analysis of the 1992 election data leads to nearly identical results. The total amount of voting pattern that can be 'explained' is slightly less than in the combined 1980–1984–1988 analysis: 40 per cent compared with 46 per cent. In like fashion, the interrelationships among the five ideological components shifted hardly at all from the pattern observed in Table 11.1. The effect of party identification on the vote remains huge, relative to the impact of all ideological components combined, although the independent effect of ideology in 1992 nearly doubled from 13 per cent of party identification's impact in the earlier elections to 22 per cent in 1992. It is in the analysis of the independent effects of the *separate* ideological components, however, that significant change is to be seen.

We noted that the Christian Right component had no additional effect in any of the three previous elections and that the Family Values component was similar; though statistically significant in 1984, its impact was still less than half that of the other four components combined. Indeed, of the fifteen separate analyses possible (5 components x 3 elections), only the Anti-government component in 1980 exceeded in impact the combined effect of the other four components. What do we find in 1992?

In the case of the Anti-communism, Law-and-Order, and Anti-government components—looked at separately—there is no statistically significant effect over and beyond the effect of the combined other components.

In the case of the Christian Right and Family Values components, the situation is the reverse: each not only proved to be statistically significant, thus exhibiting an independent effect on voting, but each also exceeded in strength the effect of the combined other components. In other words, in 1992 the religion issue and the morality issue 'stood out' as the dominant components in whatever impact conservative ideology had over and beyond party identification in influencing the presidential vote.

These two issues were not equally dominant however. While the Christian Right component was 33 per cent stronger than the combined other components, the Family Values component was nearly *three times* as potent as *its* combined other components. The suggestion is strong, therefore, that if the New Christian Right is seen as having both theological and moral aspects, it is the latter that has greater political clout. Of course, as we saw throughout all these elections, the components called above Christian Right and Family Values are strongly correlated, so it is no doubt the case that voters who are both theologically and morally conservative were especially committed to Bush in 1992. But it is just as clear that among voters who are, so to speak, conservative in one of these two ways but not both, those who are morally conservative without being on the Christian theological right were obviously more loyal to Bush than those who are on the theological right but not conservative on the moral dimension.

What does this analysis therefore say about the political impact of the New Christian Right? We offer the following generalizations:

1. While in each of the last four presidential elections, a role has been played by conservative ideology over and beyond the effect of party identification, this role has been relatively small. Moreover, apart from specifically anti-government sentiment in 1980 and specifically religious and family value sentiment in 1992, it matters little how this conservative ideology was expressed and measured; *any* reasonable indication of conservatism was adequate to express the *whole* of conservative sentiments.

2. Therefore, the emergence in the 1992 vote of a NCR factor—as indexed here by the Christian Right component but especially the Family Values component—is potentially significant. It is possible that an issue, strongly correlated with evangelical Protestant theology but primarily energized by traditional morality in the family and sexual spheres, is becoming differentiated from a more general or diffuse conservatism.

3. The long-term political impact of such a differentiated factor of conservatism will thus depend upon whether the two major parties continue to adopt opposing positions on the family values issue. Nixon's advice to Bush in 1992 (quoted above) is, of course, a warning to the Republican Party that it stands to lose more than it gains by promulgating the traditional morality that is being challenged on many fronts. Does it?

4. While the analysis supplied thus far shows that the family values issue played an undeniable, and undeniably separate, role in the 1992 vote, it has not indicated whether that role was one that gained Democratic votes for Bush or lost Republican votes for him—or both. On this point, the data are skimpier than we would like, but Table 11.2 suggests that the answer is 'both'. Bush lost some support from Republicans who were liberal on all the ideological dimensions, including the family values issue (read across Line 2), but Republicans who were already conservative on most of the dimensions were not influenced by their views on family values (read across Line 1). By contrast, Bush drew Democrats of both conservative and liberal stripe on the family values issue (read across Lines 3 and 4).

Table 11.2. *The influence of family values on the per cent voting for Bush in 1992*

On the combined other components:	On the family values issue:		
	Conservative	Moderate	Liberal
Republicans			
Conservative	78 (46)	81 (42)	— (0)
Liberal	81 (57)	62 (68)	70 (23)
Democrats			
Conservative	18 (40)	7 (43)	(0) (3)
Liberal	15 (41)	10 (94)	4 (51)

Notes: The number of cases is indicated in parentheses.
Source: General Social Survey, National Opinion Research Center, University of Chicago.

CONCLUSION

Assuming that these four generalizations are correct, we can claim to have identified at least one of the ways by which America's 'culture war' is being fought. James D. Hunter's persuasive argument regarding this culture war anticipated our findings:

The divisions of political consequence today are not theological and ecclesiastical in character but the result of differing world-views. That is to say, they no longer revolve around specific doctrinal issues or styles of religious practice and organization but around our most fundamental and cherished assumptions about how to order our lives.   (Hunter, J. D., *Culture Wars*, 42.)

It would seem that of the various dimensions along which our 'most fundamental and cherished assumptions' might split into liberal and conservative camps the dimension called here Family Values is the likeliest candidate.

The New Christian Right, in other words, is being transformed. It is no longer fundamentalists disagreeing with modernists over biblical inerrancy, but moral traditionalists alarmed over divorce, abortion, school curricula, feminism, sexual liberation, and so on. Culturally the line seems to be clearly drawn; the future political consequences of that line, however, would appear to depend upon how much that line also separates the two major parties.

THE 1996 PRESIDENTIAL VOTE

The 1996 voting pattern was largely a repeat of the 1992 pattern. Once again, about 40 per cent of the direction of vote is 'explained' by party identification plus the combined ideological factor. 90 per cent of this explanation is party identification, however. The *independent* effect of the Christian Right component shrank to insignificance in 1996. The Family Values component was also lower in *independent* effect than it was in 1992, although it still had 20 per cent more impact than the combined other ideological components. As with Bush in 1992, it is clear that Bob Dole lost support among Republicans liberal on the family values issue, but there is no evidence that Dole picked up Democratic votes because of the issue.

The second generalization above—regarding the emergence of the Family Values component in partisan politics—appears still to be valid, though the strength of its independent impact may be on the wane, as the backpedaling of some Republican politicians would suggest.

TWELVE

Church, State, and the Dilemma of Conscience*

In 1960, the Maryland Court of Appeals, the highest court in that state, upheld the denial of a notary public commission for Roy R. Torcaso because of his failure to declare his belief in God as required by state law for positions of 'profit or trust'. Among other justifications, the court noted:

To the members of the [Maryland Constitutional] Convention, as to the voters who adopted our [State] Constitution, belief in God was equated with a belief in moral accountability and the sanctity of an oath. We may assume that there may be permissible differences in the individual's conception of God. But it seems clear that under our [State] Constitution disbelief in a Supreme Being, and the denial of any moral accountability for conduct, not only renders a person incompetent to hold public office, but to give testimony, or serve as a juror. The historical record makes it clear that religious toleration, in which the State has taken pride, was never thought to encompass the ungodly. (*Torcaso v. Watkins*, 223 MD 49 [1960].)

This decision, hardly out of step with the legal reasoning of the century preceding it, was overturned by the US Supreme Court the following year in *Torcaso v. Watkins*.[1] In effect, the Court reaffirmed its 1947 position in *Everson v. Board of Education* that 'neither a State nor the Federal Government can constitutionally force a person to profess a belief or disbelief in any religion'.[2] While the state of Maryland could not countenance disbelief in God, the Supreme Court recognized that the umbrella of First Amendment protection covered various levels of belief, extending even to disbelief. Torcaso could therefore rely on the religion clauses to protect his sincerely held conviction of disbelief. Religion, it would seem, need not necessarily bear the form traditionally held, and might be found in a variety of expressions throughout society. The static, institutional, generally Protestant definition of religion in large part disappeared with the *Torcaso* ruling. It seemed that traditional notions of church–state separation required rethinking.

In this essay we first take issue with those who, because of their reluctance to engage in such rethinking, regard decisions such as *Torcaso* as indicative

---

* Eric M. Mazur collaborated on this essay.

[1] *Torcaso v. Watkins*, 367 US 488 [1961].

[2] *Everson v. Board of Education*, 330 US 1 [1947].

of a willful diminution of religion in public affairs. Second, we suggest that
if 'religion' has diminished in public affairs, 'conscience' has been recognized
as its functional equivalent, and we discuss the process by which these
changes occurred and the reasoning behind them. Finally, we introduce what
we call the 'middle level of potential resolution' in order to address the issue
of how claims of conscience might be adjudicated without violating either of
the two religion clauses.

IS RELIGION DISAPPEARING FROM PUBLIC AFFAIRS?

Much of the discussion in recent years of the proper relationship of church
and state has taken place between so-called 'separationists' and 'accommodationists'. Separationists are often portrayed as those who want religion
removed from the public sphere and are pleased that American society grows
ever more 'secular', while accommodationists, regretting the diminished role
religion plays in public affairs, would restore religion's presence in some
measure.

With notable exceptions, much of this debate is carried on as if people
need to be convinced to adopt one or the other of the two positions—that
citizens should see the merits of a society in which religion is increasingly privatized and removed from public affairs or, by contrast, should see the merits of a society 'informed', perhaps even indirectly governed, by the religious
sentiments of its citizens. Insofar as some persons, out of social sensitivity
perhaps, refrain from injecting their religious feelings into conversations or
otherwise refrain from displaying their religion, there may be room to argue
that such restraint is or is not desirable. But surely the restraint felt by many,
and the restraint imposed by law, that reduces religion's presence in public
affairs is less a matter of choice than of necessity. Not only do people sense
the need to 'privatize' religion if religious freedom is to prevail, but also leg-
islatures and courts are compelled in the interests of religious liberty to con-
strain religion. Thus, a 'secular' society results from a robust freedom of
religion. Paradoxical it may seem, but by whatever label, it is inescapable in
contemporary American society.

Failure to understand this inescapable paradox is found in the work of
accommodationists such as Richard John Neuhaus's *The Naked Public
Square* and Stephen Carter's *The Culture of Disbelief*.[3] These works fail to
appreciate the social structure of religious pluralism, a social structure that

---

[3] Neuhaus, R. J., *The Naked Public Square* (Grand Rapids, MI: Wm. B. Eerdmans, 1984);
Carter, S., *The Culture of Disbelief* (New York. NY: Basic Books, 1993).

can best, though not exclusively, be observed in the US in Supreme Court decisions specifically, and judicial actions more generally. Put another way, these works fail to appreciate the sociology of religious pluralism, as distinct from what might otherwise be called the *demography* of religious plural-ism—that is, how religiously heterogeneous are the American people?—or the *psychology* of religious pluralism—that is, how do Americans feel about religious pluralism?. This failure allows the misperception that if persons only willed its involvement in public affairs, religion would not be 'left out', 'excluded', or 'privatized' but would instead play a vibrant and beneficial role in societal decision-making.

It might be argued otherwise. It is suggested here that religion is very much present—but in a form that requires a new lens to be observed. The 'absence' of religion from the US public square, or the religious disbelief 'apparent' in US culture, stems not from feeble religion but from religion that, in a pluralistic setting, is often transmuted into something else. The *perception* of secularity in public affairs is thus really a failure of focus, which, with proper adjustment, reveals instead a great deal of religion in US life. In other words, religious *motivation* remains free to enter the public arena precisely because religious *language* adds nothing of intrinsic value in any pluralistic debate and therefore is curtailed. Thus, analysts like Neuhaus overlook the restraints imposed on religion-in-society by the very lack of restraints on religion-in-individuals. The premise of Neuhaus's book—that 'The naked public square is the result of political doctrine and practice that would exclude religion . . . from the conduct of public business'[4]—is there-fore questionable. Similar in its misunderstanding is Carter's claim:

One good way to end a conversation . . . is to tell a group of well-educated profes-sionals that you hold a political position . . . because it is required by your under-standing of God's will. In the unlikely event that anyone hangs around to talk to you about it, the chances are that you will be challenged on the ground that you are intent on imposing your religious beliefs on other people. (Carter, S., *The Culture of Disbelief*, 23.)

It seems more likely to imagine that those well-educated professionals would hang around expecting to hear just what it is that links 'God's will' to one's 'political position'. Or, as Neuhaus himself says, seemingly unaware that he is demolishing his own thesis, 'Those who want to bring religiously based values to bear in public discourse have an obligation to "translate" those values into terms that are as accessible as possible to those who do not share the same religious grounding'.[5] But fulfilling that obligation, of course, mutes the religious language and renders the 'accessible terms' more impor-tant *in that setting* than the 'religiously based values'.

---

[4] Neuhaus, R. J., *Naked Public Square*, vii.   [5] Neuhaus, *Naked Public Square*, 125.

Kent Greenawalt aptly makes this very point:

Why should political decisions in liberal democracies be based on shared premises and accessible reasons? The claim is that this is an aspect of a common, equal citizenship. If there is reliance on other reasons—religious reasons or reasons derived from other controversial comprehensive views of life—then those who do not recognize the reasons are being treated unfairly. They are being imposed upon on the basis of reasons they cannot be expected to share.   (Greenawalt, K., 'The Role of Religion in a Liberal Democracy', 517.)

Once again, however, it must be stated that the situation Greenawalt describes is not a matter of individual choice once a society commits itself to the legitimacy of plural 'religious reasons' or plural 'comprehensive views of life'. All societies, including those that grant religious liberty, require premises that are shared and reasons that are accessible if the public's business is to get conducted. In religiously plural societies, however, those premises cannot be religious in the ordinary sense.

This paradox, it might further be said, is hardly new. Garry Wills makes this point clear in his discussion of Roger Williams and the Rhode Island colony:

There is something inadvertent about much of Williams' achievement. He cared most about leading a reformed church, and could never form such a thing. He cared comparatively little about a secular power, yet that is what he set up. . . . The process by which those zealous for religion separated it from government presented in microcosm the process that would be worked out in America over the next centuries. The secular state came from the zeal of religion itself . . . it was the most religious community that produced the most religiously neutral state, just as—a century later—it would be a very religious nation that produced the first secular state. (Wills, G., *Under God. Religion and American Politics*, 352.)

A similar analysis is given by political scientist Ralph Lerner reflecting on the First Amendment and Article VI of the US Constitution prohibiting religious tests for officeholders:

. . . at least as far as federal constitutional law was concerned, the focus of attention was to be shifted from groups to individuals, from sects to consciences. The new enlightened regime . . . made a new world safe, not for church or chapel or synagogue, but for each and every believer, indeed for each and every person's private conscience. . . . American society under the Constitution was open to all kinds of voluntary associations, and . . . religionists who meant to enjoy the benefits of that regime had to quietly accept their place as one kind of association among many. Those unable to bear this muting of their clarion call would soon discover that society was equally uncomfortable with them. . . . Eschewing any pretensions to holiness or divine direction, this system of secular, enlightened indifference is large enough and generous enough to shield almost any kind of holiness so long as it minds its civil manners.   (Lerner, R., 'Believers and the Founders' Constitution, 88–9.)

It is in 'minding its civil manners', so to speak, that religion seems to fade from view in the public square.

Conscience is Recognized

Angela C. Carmela has recently articulated the dilemma that inheres in the US church–state situation:

> The jurisprudential inconsistencies occur not simply because of changes in court composition or ideological shifts, but because the Court is attempting to balance two larger political principles: deference and limitation. 'Deference' says the state should defer on matters of religion to individual conscience and churches. . . . The other political principle—'limitation'—says the state has the authority to limit the definition of religious conduct, and to decide what are secular activities and therefore within its competence to regulate, to monitor, or to prohibit.   (Carmela, A. C., 'The Religion Clauses and Acculturated Religious Conduct', 23.)

Carmela goes on to say that 'The balance of deference and limitation is hardest with respect to acculturated conduct',[6] by which she means religiously motivated activity that resembles activity carried on also by persons or organizations not religiously motivated. Thus, is a nursery school run by a church free of regulations with which a secular school must comply? Will a person whose conscientious objection to war is religiously-based be exempt while a person who conscientiously objects to war on other grounds will not?

Actually, the Supreme Court's response to the second of these questions—in the *Seeger* and *Welsh* cases—brought into high relief the dilemma American society faces in this area of church and state.[7]

In the first of these two conscientious objector cases, the Court accepted Seeger's contention that, while he did not believe in a Supreme Being, he did have a 'faith in a purely ethical creed'. This, the justices agreed, was equivalent to a religion, which they characterized in the oft-quoted phrase: a 'sincere and meaningful belief which occupies in the life of its possessor a place parallel to that filled by the God of those admittedly qualifying for the exemption'.[8] Five years later, Welsh specifically claimed that his beliefs were not religious but based on his reading of history and sociology, and the Court responded much as it had in *Seeger*, though not without three dissenting votes. The upshot was that, as one legal scholar has put it, the Court left

---

[6] Carmela, A. C., 'The Religion Clauses and Acculturated Religious Conduct', in J. E. Wood, Jr. and D. Davis (eds.), *The Role of Government in Monitoring and Regulating Religion in Public Life* (Waco, TX: J. M. Dawson Institute of Church–State Studies, Baylor University, 1993), 33.

[7] *United States v. Seeger*, 380 US 163 [1965]; *Welsh v. United States*, 398 US 333 [1970].

[8] *Seeger* at 166.

'no room for any residual doubt'. It 'viewed deeply and sincerely held moral or ethical beliefs as the functional, and thus the legal, equivalent of religious beliefs. The justices had obfuscated any distinction between religion and all other belief systems'.[9]

In deciding as it did, the Court was only advancing an already pressing trend that was becoming more and more apparent. For example, in 1944 the Court determined that the credibility of religious beliefs was less important than the sincerity with which they were held, thus expanding the scope of what might qualify as religion.[10] A year earlier, in a Federal District Court, an atheist was granted conscientious objector status on the grounds of 'a conscience which categorically requires the believer to disregard elementary self-interest and to accept martyrdom in preference to transgressing its tenets. . . . [This] may justly be regarded as a response of the individual to an inward mentor, call it conscience or God, that is for many persons at the present time the equivalent of what has always been thought a religious impulse'.[11] We have already seen that in 1961 the Supreme Court ruled unconstitutional Maryland's law requiring a belief in God in order to qualify as a notary public. Four years earlier a lower court had extended tax exemption to humanistic, that is, non-theistic, 'religious' organizations. Not to do so, the court reasoned, would be to favor theism over non-theism, something now understood as clearly prohibited by the Establishment Clause because it required a judgment about the *content of* belief. Instead, said the Court, the judgment should be based on the belief's function— 'whether or not the belief occupies the same place in the lives of its holders that . . . orthodox beliefs occupy in the lives of believing majorities'.[12] This wording—and reasoning—it might be surmised, was known to the justices who decided *Seeger* eight years later. As noted above, the law responds to the pressures applied to it, and in the area of church and state these pressures encouraged the expansion of religious liberty. Paradoxically one effect of this expansion was seemingly to mute religion's public role.

As legal scholar Marc Galanter perceived soon after the *Seeger* decision, the shift from a substantive to a functional definition of religion is really a 'dual movement'. Not only has the Court gone from 'a narrower to a more permissive definition of religion',[13] which some might see as a discretionary change on the Court's part, but, in fact, it was *obliged* to do so once it abandoned the so-called 'belief-action' distinction that had prevailed in American

---

[9] Ingber, S., 'Religion or Ideology: A Needed Clarification of the Religion Clauses', *Stanford Law Review*, 41 (1989), 260.

[10] *United States v. Ballard*, 322 US 78 [1944].

[11] *United States v. Kauten*, 133 F. 2d. 703 [1943] at 708.

[12] *Fellowship of Humanity v. County of Alanteda*, 153 Cal. App. 2d 673 [1957] at 692.

[13] Galanter, M., 'Religious Freedoms in the United States: A Turning Point?' *Wisconsin Law Review*, 1966: 2 (1966), 270.

legal thought since colonial times, and in Supreme Court doctrine since the 1878 Mormon polygamy case. There, the Court had declared that while laws 'cannot interfere with mere religious belief and opinions, they may with practices', and this distinction was maintained, says Galanter, until 1940.[14] In that year, in *Cantwell v. Connecticut*,[15] the Court reversed the conviction of a Jehovah's Witness who was clearly violating a breach-of-the-peace ord-inance by playing in public a religious message on a portable phonograph. Before 1940, courts would have rendered a guilty verdict, merely noting the violation of a secular regulation applicable to all, but in *Cantwell* the Supreme Court reversed the verdict, acknowledging that *religiously* motiv-ated behavior might be constitutionally protected even as the same behavior, otherwise motivated, is not. Thereby, 'having given up the belief-action dis-tinction and with it the secular regulation rule, and forswearing an absolute immunity, the Court had to find some way to weigh or balance the interests involved'.[16] Thus began a series of cases in which religious motivation was found to allow certain persons to be exempt from what the law says others must do—for example, salute the flag—and allow certain persons to do what others may not do—for example, use peyote. Not only did these cases lead to the doctrine of 'compelling interest' wherein the government must identify a significant reason for restricting religious action, but—far more complicated—they also required some way for courts to identify which actions are *religious*. This second requirement had never arisen as long as 'belief' and 'action' were sharply differentiated, but now the free exercise of religion was understood to include a freedom to act on one's religion, so 'religion' itself became problematic. Thus, the expanding jurisprudential definition of religion has been, as Galanter perceived, embedded in a correl-ative shift that found constitutional privilege for at least some religious actions that earlier would have been disallowed.

These shifts resulted not from mere changes of court personnel nor from mere volition; they instead resulted from pressures built into American his-tory and social structure, at least two of which are notable: vastly increased religious pluralism in the US, and the vast increase of governmental regula-tion and thus government intrusion into citizens' lives, including their reli-gious lives. Before, religion had merely to be protected—everyone 'knew' what religion was. Now religion must be accommodated, and the line between religion and non-religion is not at all clear. Before, 'free exercise' meant absolute freedom to believe as one wanted, but religious behavior could be regulated as long as the 'establishment' clause was not violated by differential treatment of religions. Now, by privileging religious behavior, the

---

14 *Reynolds v. United States*, 98 US 145 [1878].
15 *Cantwell v. Connecticut*, 310 US 296 [1940].
16 Galanter, M., 'Religious Freedoms', 237.

question inevitably arises as to whether such privilege 'establishes' some religions over others, or if—to avoid that situation—the law denies the privilege to everyone, is it thereby denying the right to 'free exercise'? What we now face is the dilemma that arises when government would give special treatment to profoundly held convictions that may or may not be seen as religious, even by their possessors.

In the previous decision of *US v. Kauten* (1943), it was noted that a conscientious objector status was granted to an atheist—anticipating the more famous *Seeger* and *Welsh* cases a quarter-century later—which held that whatever 'categorically requires the believer to disregard elementary self-interest and to accept martyrdom in preference to transgressing its tenets' is equivalent to religion. Such an 'inward mentor', the decision went on to say, might even be called 'conscience or God'. Might it be said that the District Court in *Kauten*—like the Supreme Court in *Seeger* and *Welsh*—was recognizing 'conscience' as more or less a synonym for 'religion'? Might it also be surmised that in its 1961 *Torcaso* decision, the Court was suggesting that a notary public can be 'morally accountable' that is, with conscience, without believing in God? Such a jurisprudential development should not really be surprising.

A plausible argument might be made that the Founding Fathers regarded conscience and religion as synonyms. James Madison, the chief architect of both Virginia's 1776 Declaration of Rights and the 1785 Memorial and Remonstrance—opposing Virginia's proposed General Assessment Bill—referred to the 'free exercise of religion' according to the dictates of 'conscience'. Not surprisingly, Madison retained the word 'conscience' in reworking the various wordings that eventuated in the First Amendment. It is true that by the eighth version of that Amendment, the word 'conscience' was dropped and did not reappear in the tenth and final version,[17] but it is doubtful that, as Ingber contends, the dropping of the word shows that the framers meant something distinctively different by 'conscience' and 'religion'.[18] Indeed, of the thirteen states that had constitutions in place before the adoption of the Bill of Rights in 1789, nine used the word 'conscience' in their sections dealing with religion, typically in phrasing to the effect that religion was free to be practiced 'according to the dictates of conscience'. Of the thirty-five states that joined the Union between 1789 and 1912, when New Mexico and Arizona were added, only seven, or 20 per cent, failed to use the word conscience in the religion sections of their constitutions.[19] Not

---

[17] Malbin, M. J., *Religion and Politics: The Intentions of the Authors of the First Amendment* (Washington DC: American Enterprise Institute, 1978), 22–6.

[18] Ingber, S., *Religion or Ideology*, 252.

[19] Moehlman, C. H., *The American Constitutions and Religion* (Beme, IN: privately printed, 1938).

until Alaska and Hawaii became states in 1959 was the wording of the federal constitution essentially duplicated in state constitutions. 'Conscience', therefore, might even be said to have been the preferred label for whatever American citizens wanted to protect in the sacred sphere.

Of course the meaning of conscience in the eighteenth and nineteenth centuries was not the meaning of that word in the late twentieth century. Probably most Americans at the time of the nation's founding would have imagined most 'consciences' to be 'Christian', and saw as most important protecting the right of people to express their Christianity in whatever manner their consciences dictated. Nevertheless, more than Christian conscience was of concern; indeed, more than theism. As Derek Davis says, 'Some of the founders clearly sought religious freedom for non-theists' and quotes Jefferson about the necessity of protecting 'the Jew and Gentile, the Christian and Mahometan, the Hindoo, and infidel of every denomination'.[20] It is a fair inference that Americans wanted and expected special treatment for that core element in persons that animates and compels them.

Having made this argument, however, we must acknowledge that until *Kauten*, *Seeger*, and *Welsh*, 'conscience' was no doubt assumed to be expressed religiously. Put another way, animating and compelling motives expressed in non-religious terms were not thought to deserve constitutional protection. As discussed above, only recently have consciences expressed in terms other than ordinary religion been accorded the same rights as consciences expressed in ordinary religious terms. Understandably this development has led to a vigorous debate; the issue is whether every profound moral conviction qualifies as 'religion', or the equivalent of religion, and thus commands constitutional protection.

We are not here entering that debate except to note that the legal cloudiness is not lifted by changing the needed distinction from 'religion vs. non-religion' to 'conscience vs. non-conscience'. That is, just as in an earlier time it was necessary to determine when a conviction was *religiously* held and when it was not, under the new formulation it is necessary to determine when a conviction is *conscientiously* held and when it is not. Now, people can claim the right to exercise conscientiously compelled activity, and the government may not 'establish' one kind of conscientiously compelled activity over other kinds. In 1985, Justice John Paul Stevens put the matter succinctly in *Wallace v. Jaffree*, in which several Alabama school statutes authorizing periods of silence, meditation, or leading 'willing students' in prayer were declared unconstitutional:

---

[20] Davis, D., 'The Courts and the Constitutional meaning of "religion"', in J. E. Wood, Jr. and D. Davis (eds.), *The Role of Government in Monitoring and Regulating Religion in Public Life* (Waco, TX: J. M. Dawson Institute of Church–State Studies, Baylor University, 1993), 92.

At one time it was thought that this right [to choose one's 'own creed' or 'to refrain from accepting the creed established by the majority'] merely proscribed the preference of one Christian sect over another. . . . But when the underlying principle has been examined in the crucible of litigation, the Court has unambiguously concluded that the individual freedom of conscience protected by the First Amendment embraces the right to select any religious faith or none at all.   (Wallace v. Jaffree, 472 US 38 [1985].)

Upsetting as this interpretation is to many, this broader understanding of what is constitutionally protected by the religion clauses would seem to be essential in modern, pluralistic US. Conceiving of religion as 'conscience', or conscience as 'religion', is necessary, as Derek Davis says, 'to provide constitutional protection to the endless variety of religions, both old and new, foreseen and unforeseen, that carry transcendent meaning for people'.[21]

While the state must therefore be as neutral toward 'conscience' as it must be toward 'religion', this does not mean that every profound conviction a person may hold is deserving of protection. It is tempting to make this point by simply saying that only 'religious ' consciences are so protected, but this formulation, of course, is no help at all, since it is those consciences that are not ordinarily seen as religious that the judicial system has reached out to embrace *as if they were religious*. The issue is how to distinguish conscientious claims that deserve such protection from those that do not.

In principle at least, the distinction is not difficult to make. When in 1943 the atheist Kauten was granted conscientious objector status on First Amendment grounds, Judge Augustus Hand wrote then of a conscience that 'categorically requires the believer to disregard self-interest and to accept martyrdom in preference to transgressing its tenets'.[22] Thus a protected conscience, far from being manipulated self-interest, is precisely an obligation to sacrifice the self rather than violate a profoundly held rule. That rule stems not from idiosyncratic whimsy, but indeed will be regarded as binding on others as well as the self. If challenged, moreover, the rule will be justified in terms of a larger moral scheme, believed to emanate from a realm beyond the self and worthy of promulgation. Such a view of conscience coincides with Madison's assertion in his 1785 *Memorial and Remonstrance* that 'It is the duty of every man to render to the Creator such homage and such only as he believes to be acceptable to him. This duty is precedent, both in order of time and in degree of obligation, to the claims of Civil Society'.[23] What coincides in Madison's and Judge Hand's formulations is not their choice of words but the notion that persons can and do believe in a realm of obligation

---

[21] Davis, D., 'The Courts', 115.   [22] Quoted in Davis, D., 'The Courts', 96.
[23] Madison is quoted in Flowers, R., *That Godless Court?* (Louisville, KY: Westminster John Knox Press, 1994), 147–52.

that transcends both self and society. It is those consciences informed by such a realm that warrant constitutional protection as if they were religion.

Why would objections be raised against an expansion of what is covered by the religion clauses of the First Amendment? In all likelihood, given their nature and source, the objections have less to do with recognizing as religion what once was not so recognized, but they have more to do with the consequent decline in the relatively privileged position held by traditional religion. Schoolhouse religious practices such as teacher-led prayer or Bible-reading are perhaps the clearest examples. Apparently it is difficult for some, especially those on the Christian Right, to conceive of fellow citizens who are conscientiously opposed to those practices, citizens who desire not that religion be driven out of public life but merely that it not enjoy tax-funded sponsorship. The consequence, however, is seen as systematic diminution of religion in public life. Richard John Neuhaus states the case very well:

As time went on . . . the court's references to religion had less and less to do with what is usually meant by religion. That is, religion no longer referred to those communal traditions of ultimate beliefs and practices ordinarily called religion. Religion, in the court's meaning, became radically individualized and privatized. Religion became a synonym for conscience. . . . Thus religion is no longer a matter of content but of sincerity. It is no longer a matter of communal values but of individual conviction. In short, it is no longer a public reality and therefore cannot interfere with public business. (Neuhaus, R. J., *The Naked Public Square*, 80.)

Except for the disapproving tone of Neuhaus's statement, in content its message differs little from the foregoing pages of this essay. When he goes on to say, 'Such a religious evacuation of the public square cannot be sustained',[24] however, not only is his disapproval obvious, but he invites the rhetorical response: 'So, what would you change without violating the religion clauses of the First Amendment?' It is true that when unemployment benefits are awarded to a person who refuses to work on Sunday because he is a Christian though not a member of any church, the clout once enjoyed by churches of which other Christians are members is diminished, at least relatively.[25] So is the clout of so-called peace churches when members of other churches are also granted conscientious objector status, or of all churches, when agnostics and atheists have the privilege extended to them. To the degree that people have freedom to be religious in their own way, including the freedom not to be religious at all in the ordinary sense, the *public* importance of 'ordinary' religion will decline. That is the consequence of America's

---

[24] Neuhaus, R. J., *Naked Public Square*, 80.
[25] *Frazee v. Illinois Department of Employment Security*, 489 US 829 [1989].

church–state policy as it has unfolded over two centuries. In Neuhaus's words, the more 'individual conviction' is recognized, the less 'communal values' will be given special treatment in the legal sphere. To do otherwise is to prefer one kind of religion over another.

THIRTEEN

Conscience and the Establishment Clause

By now it seems reasonably clear that what the Free Exercise Clause protects is increasingly understood to refer not just to religion but to conscience; and that this enlarged understanding of free exercise was compelled once the Courts rejected the belief-action distinction, thus requiring the law to differentiate between actions that are secularly motivated from actions reflecting true conviction, whether articulated in religious language or not. Once it is recognized, however, that it is 'conscience' that is protected—and not just 'religion' as traditionally understood—a rather startling implication becomes apparent: if conscience is what can be freely exercised, is it therefore also conscience that Congress must not establish? If so, just what does that mean? Those questions are what I explore here. In doing so, I shall be showing how, with the subtle decline of religious institutions as presumptive definers of the sacred, an even more subtle process is occurring—the increased role of legal institutions in defining the sacred. While no one would confuse a court with a church, none the less the court's 'religious' functioning is unmistakable.

Here is an opportunity, therefore, to examine closely one aspect of some 'received wisdom' in the sociology of religion—that secularization means stripping away from religious institutions many erstwhile functions such as education, physical and mental therapies, demographic record keeping, etc., finding them instead carried out by other institutions.[1] In this transition, however, seldom has it been doubted that religious institutions at least retain a monopoly on defining, protecting, and celebrating the sacred realm. I want here to challenge that assumption. I shall argue that defining the sacred realm is now shared by legal institutions in the United States, especially by the Supreme Court.

---

[1] For just three examples, see Parsons, T., 'Christianity and modern industrial society', in E. A. Tiryakian (ed.), *Sociological Theory, Values and Sociocultural Change* (Glencoe, IL: Free Press, 1963); Wilson, B., *Religion in Sociological Perspective* (Oxford: Oxford University Press, 1982); and Stark, R., and Bainbridge, W. S., *The Future of Religion: Secularization, Revival and Cult Formation* (Berkeley, CA: University of California Press, 1985).

NONPREFERENTIALISM EXPOSED

The greatest support for the free exercise of religion could be expected to come from persons who assign greatest importance to religion. In one sense that is true, as exemplified in the very broad range of religious leaders included in the support given to the Rev. Sun Myung Moon in his tax evasion case:

A stranger group of bedfellows would be hard to imagine: the Reverend Jerry Falwell, former Senator Eugene McCarthy, the late Clare Booth Luce, Harvard law professor Laurence Tribe, and Senator Orrin Hatch. . . . [A] single thread also ties together the liberal American Civil Liberties Union and the Southern Christian Leadership Conference with the conservative Freemen Institute. The same thread connects Baptists and Presbyterians, the Roman Catholic Church and the National Council of Churches, not to mention the avowedly Marxist Spartacist League as well as the states of Hawaii, Oregon, and Rhode Island. Between 1982 and 1984 all of the above and more than thirty other individuals and organizations entered amicus curiae . . . briefs [on Moon's behalf]. (Sherwood, C., *Inquisition*, 377–8.)

Moon lost his case despite this outpouring of support, but the reason for the support is simple to understand. All the sponsors of those briefs could see that if the Internal Revenue Service could punish the founder and leader of the Unification Church on the grounds charged, then it could similarly punish them; in the case of religious leaders, it was their own free exercise of religion that was in jeopardy. In any avowedly pluralistic society, then, each religion is likely to recognize that its welfare depends upon upholding the free exercise of all religions. All consciences deserve governmental respect.

At least some people of religious conviction, however, decry the circumstances whereby 'conscience' becomes entitled to the legal protection heretofore extended only to 'religion'. For Richard John Neuhaus, this means that courts look not at the content of belief but at the sincerity with which belief is held. 'Individual conviction', he says, has replaced 'communal values'.[2]

When individual conviction or conscience is regarded as religion's legal equivalent, religion as a 'communal value' does not disappear, as Neuhaus seems to suggest. Rather, upon close inspection it turns out that communal religion—that is, the 'church', or organized religious activity—merely has to give up the governmental privilege it once enjoyed: a recognition now seen to be unconstitutional. The more sensitive the state becomes in protecting conscience, in other words, the more likely it is to uncover heretofore unacknowledged 'established' religion, which is then found to be in violation of

[2] Neuhaus, R. J., *The Naked Public Square* (Grand Rapids, MI: William B. Eerdmans, 1984), 80.

the Establishment Clause. People who regret this jurisprudential development are often called 'nonpreferentialists' because, while they agree that
government cannot prefer one religion over another, they do believe government can and should prefer religion over non-religion. They do believe that
religious, not legal, institutions alone determine the sacred. Thus, following
his lament that, when conscience became a synonym for religion, 'communal
values' were replaced by 'individual conviction', Neuhaus goes on to say that
religion 'is no longer a public reality and therefore cannot interfere with
public business'.[3] This fact Neuhaus laments, but he is mistaken; it is not
that religion is no longer a public reality but rather the courts now have a
broader conception of religion in that reality.

It is not surprising that when free exercise doctrine extends far enough to
recognize consciences not articulated in traditional religious language, some
people are vexed—not so much because conscientious persons receive benefits, but because traditional forms of religion seem to lose benefits. This, of
course, is not the wording used by those who are troubled. They would say,
rather, that government is no longer accommodating traditional forms of
religion. It is renewed accommodation of *their* religion that they desire, not
the newly discovered accommodation of heretofore unprotected consciences. Marvin Frankel makes this point with bombast. Labeling as
'access-seekers' persons who want the wall of separation lowered to a previous height, Frankel claims that 'the concrete goals of the access-seekers
reflect mainly crabbed demands for status, authority, and petty but maddening superordination'.[4]

Frankel's criticism may be harsh, but it does point up the inherent tension
between the Free Exercise Clause and its Establishment counterpart, or—as
some have put it—between the accommodation of religion that the Free
Exercise Clause *requires*, and the accommodation of religion that the
Establishment Clause *permits*. It seems that persons who support an interpretation of Free Exercise broad enough to extend to 'conscience' are likely
to support an interpretation of Establishment that finds unconstitutional
many religious actions that have previously been accommodated. When the
rights of free exercise are extended to conscience or conviction, whether
articulated religiously or not, then heretofore religious actions that have
been shown preference because they are *religious* are vulnerable to the charge
that they represent an unconstitutional establishment of religion. The conscientious objection cases illustrate this point exactly;[5] if conviction alone,
and not identification with a *particular* kind of religious belief, is sufficient
to claim conscientious objector status, it means that persons holding those

---

[3] Ibid.
[4] Frankel, M. E., *Faith and Freedom* (New York, NY: Hill and Wang, 1992), 639.
[5] *United States v. Seeger*, 380 US 163 [1965]; *Welsh v. United States*, 398 US 3331 [1970].

particular beliefs were earlier enjoying an unconstitutional special privilege that was being denied others who did not hold those beliefs.

FREE EXERCISE VS. NO ESTABLISHMENT

This inherent tension between the two clauses is illustrated in an unusually vivid way in a 1989 Supreme Court case, *County of Allegheny, et al., v. American Civil Liberties Union, et al.*[6] At issue was the constitutionality of a nativity scene installed in the lobby of Pittsburgh's City-County Building, and a Chanukah menorah placed just outside that building, next to a Christmas tree and a sign saluting liberty. The Court, with four dissenting votes, ruled to outlaw the nativity scene as clearly sending a message of governmental 'endorsement' of an obviously Christian symbol, but it ruled in favor of the menorah on the grounds that the menorah, like the Christmas tree, has secular as well as religious connotations and thus could be interpreted as merely a symbol of the winter holiday season.

Because the Justices arrive at their opinions after circulating drafts of each other's tentative views of a case, it is not uncommon in cases having dissenting minorities for the final majority and minority opinions to include counter-arguments as well as arguments. The Allegheny nativity case provides us with an especially vigorous, not to say vituperative, illustration of the point I am making. Let us take a close look.

After Justice Blackmun introduces the facts of the nativity and menorah case, he begins to develop the line of reasoning he and other members of the majority have employed in arriving at their opinion. He begins:

This Nation is heir to a history and tradition of religious diversity that dates from the settlement of the North American continent. Sectarian differences among various Christian denominations were central to the origins of our Republic. Since then, adherents of religions too numerous to name have made the United States their home, as have those whose beliefs expressly exclude religion. Precisely because of the religious diversity ... the Founders added ... a Bill of Rights, the very first words of which declare: 'Congress shall make no law respecting an establishment of religion, or prohibiting the free exercise thereof ...' Perhaps in the early days of the Republic these words were understood to protect only the diversity within Christianity, but today they are recognized as guaranteeing religious liberty and equality to the infidel, the atheist, or the adherent of a non-Christian faith such as Islam or Judaism. ... It is settled law that no government official in this Nation may violate these fundamental constitutional rights regarding matters of conscience. (*County of Allegheny, et al. v. American Civil Liberties Union, et al.* 492 US 573 [1989] 589–90.)

[6] *County of Allegheny et al. v. American Civil Liberties Union, et al.*, 492 US 573 [1989].

Blackmun thus sets the stage by giving great weight to religious pluralism and the need to safeguard everyone's religious free exercise. Not so obvious is the implicit loss of privilege once enjoyed by Christianity.

Blackmun then goes on to a lengthy discussion of how the nativity scene violates the Establishment Clause because it so obviously suggests governmental endorsement of Christianity. But it is just as clear that he regards such an endorsement as also violating the Free Exercise Clause because it communicates to non-Christians that their religions are *not* endorsed. The sacred sphere of non-Christians must be accorded equal treatment by the government; else limitations are placed on true religious liberty.

Justice Kennedy, joined by Chief Justice Rehnquist and Justices White and Scalia, offers several counter-arguments, but the one of interest here is Kennedy's claim that, in failing to accommodate the nativity scene in a government building, the majority opinion misinterprets the Establishment Clause:

Rather than requiring government to avoid any action that acknowledges or aids religion, the Establishment Clause permits government some latitude in recognizing and accommodating the central role religion plays in our society. . . . Any approach less sensitive to our heritage would border on latent hostility toward religion, as it would require government in all its multifaceted roles to acknowledge only the secular, to the exclusion and so to the detriment of the religious. . . . [The consequence is] Those religions enjoying the largest following must be consigned to the status of least-favored faiths so as to avoid any possible risk of offending members of minority religions.   (*County of Allegheny, et al. v. American Civil Liberties Union, et al.* 492 US 573 [1989] 657.)

Blackmun rises to this bait and in so doing reveals how deeply embedded in the sacred sphere is this church–state case:

Although Justice Kennedy repeatedly accuses the Court of harboring a 'latent hostility' . . . toward religion. . . . nothing could be further from the truth, and the accusations could be said to be as offensive as they are absurd. Justice Kennedy apparently has misperceived a respect for religious pluralism, a respect commanded by the Constitution, as hostility or indifference to religion. No misperception could be more antithetical to the values embodied in the Establishment Clause. . . . In his attempt to legitimize the display of the crèche . . . Justice Kennedy repeatedly characterizes it as 'accommodation' of religion. But accommodation of religion, in order to be permitted under the Establishment Clause, must lift an identifiable burden *on the exercise of religion*. . . . One may agree with Justice Kennedy that the scope of accommodations permissible under the Establishment Clause is larger than the scope of accommodations mandated by the Free Exercise Clause. . . . But a category of permissible accommodations of religion not required by the Free Exercise Clause aids the crèche . . . not at all. Prohibiting the display of a crèche at this location . . . does not impose a burden on the practice of Christianity (except to the extent some Christian sect seeks to be an officially approved religion), and therefore permitting the display is not an 'accommodation' of religion in the conventional sense. (*County of Allegheny, et al. v. American Civil Liberties Union, et al.* 492 US 573 [1989] 610.)

Justice Blackmun is accusing Justice Kennedy of defending nonpreferentialism, or what Marvin Frankel, as we saw a few pages back, called 'crabbed demands for status, authority, and petty but maddening superordination'.

In 1992, three years after the *Allegheny* nativity decision, a similar issue came before the Supreme Court, and once again nonpreferentialism was debated. What was being challenged in *Lee v. Weisman*[7] was the practice in a Providence junior high school of the principal's inviting local clergy to offer prayer at graduation ceremonies.

Splitting pretty much as they had in *Allegheny,* the Justices declared 5-4 that such prayers are unconstitutional. This time the dissent was written by Justice Scalia, who reiterated the nonpreferentialist credo that 'government policies of accommodation, acknowledgment, and support for religion are an accepted part of our political and cultural heritage'. Scalia's dissent has been nominated as the 'high-water mark' for its 'impatient distaste for deviant sensibilities getting in the way of majority preferences',[8] and it is exactly that impatient distaste that raised the ire of Justice Souter to the point of writing a rebuttal as a majority concurring opinion in *Lee v. Weisman*. Souter's claim:

Since *Everson,* we have consistently held the [Establishment] Clause applicable no less to governmental acts favoring religion generally than to acts favoring one religion over others. Thus in *Engel v. Vitale* . . .(1962), we held that the public schools may not subject their students to readings of any prayer however 'denominationally neutral'. . . . More recently, in *Wallace v. Jaffee* . . . (1985), we held that an Alabama moment-of-silence statute passed for the sole purpose of 'returning voluntary prayer to public schools' . . . violated the Establishment Clause even though it did not encourage students to pray to any particular deity. We said that, 'when the underlying principle has been examined in the crucible of litigation, the Court has unambiguously concluded that the individual freedom of conscience protected by the First Amendment embraces the right to select any religious faith or none at all'. (*Lee v. Weisman,* 505 US 577 [1992] 610.)

It seems that what strict separationists see clearly, the nonpreferentialists do not see—that once conscience is accorded the same protection that religion receives, then Establishment Clause cases necessarily broaden the conception of the sacred. David A. J. Richards claims that this broader notion of the sacred was known, at least to some, from the very beginning of the republic. Thomas Jefferson, Richards says

---

[7] *Lee v. Weisman,* 505 US 577 [1992].   [8] Frankel, M. E., *Faith and Freedom,* 12.

elaborates the underlying moral ideal of respect for conscience to indulge not only free exercise, but any form of religious qualification for civil rights or any compulsion of tax money for support of religious beliefs, even one's own. Since Jefferson believes that the rights of conscience are inalienable rights . . . he regards any state financial or other support for the propagation of religious belief as tyranny. (Richards, D. A. J., *Conscience and the Constitution*, 12.)

According to James Washington, most of Jefferson's colleagues would have agreed that the 'rights of conscience' are natural and inalienable. 'But this did not forestall nearly 150 years of theological and philosophical debates about the meaning of this phrase'.[9] While the debates go on, therefore, and the role of conscience is by no means yet fixed in law, this new understanding of the sacred does seem to be emerging, as the Free Exercise implications found in Establishment cases are recognized. Granted, it has taken a long time to understand that when, say, a nativity scene is supported by public tax money, it is not just non-Christian believers whose truly free exercise of religion is being limited; also limited is the truly free exercise of Christian believers who can observe their government dictating—however gently—how their Christianity is to be conceived and practiced. And that, as Jefferson would say, is 'tyranny'.

FREEDOM OF CONSCIENCE AND THE ESTABLISHMENT CLAUSE

To this point, we have been looking at cases in which unconstitutional state endorsement has been bestowed on practices that are obviously religious—a nativity scene in a county building, prayer at a public school commencement, etc.—and I have argued that just as these are clearly Establishment cases, so are they clearly Free Exercise cases also, inasmuch as they represent government-mandated practices that deny conscientious discretion to persons entitled to such. This is the line of reasoning by which the Supreme Court declared unconstitutional the 1928 Arkansas law prohibiting the teaching of evolution in any public school in the state.[10] Justice Fortas, who wrote the unanimous opinion, perceived the law's purpose as preventing teachers from discussing evolution 'because it is contrary to the belief of some that the Book of Genesis must be the exclusive source of doctrine as to the origin of man'. But such a law, he said, conflicts with the Free Exercise Clause and not just the Establishment Clause. Indeed, in an analysis of Fortas's opinion,

---

[9] Washington, J., 'The crisis in the sanctity of conscience in American jurisprudence', *DePaul Law Review*, 42 (1992), 21–2.

[10] *Epperson v. Arkansas*, 393 US 97 [1967].

Kyron Huigens, in a law review article significantly entitled 'Science, Freedom of Conscience and the Establishment Clause', says that Fortas was suggesting 'that orthodoxy, indoctrination, and conformity – *in themselves, and not merely as features of an established church* – are effects of government actions which it is the function of the establishment clause to prevent'.[11]

This principle—that violations of the Establishment Clause may violate the Free Exercise Clause by infringing on conscience—can also be seen in the 1984 *Grand Rapids School District v. Ball*,[12] where publicly paid teachers were disallowed from teaching secular subjects in parochial schools. In the majority opinion Justice Brennan noted that if any religious indoctrination were to occur, it 'would have devastating effects on the right of each individual voluntarily to determine what to believe (and what not to believe) free of any coercive pressure from the state'.

Thus, Free Exercise implications that arise in Establishment cases are relatively easy to discern once conscience is seen as the legal equivalent of religion. Such implications are less obvious in other kinds of cases, however, especially cases that technically lie outside the realm of church and state. I turn next, therefore, to a discussion of three examples. Constitutionally, these cases were decided not on First Amendment grounds but on the Due Process Clause of the Fourteenth Amendment. Ostensibly, then, they deal with 'liberty', not 'religion', but it will be seen that conscience or the sacred, plays a constant role in these cases. Significantly, it can be noted that all three examples are found on the battleground of what James D. Hunter calls America's 'culture wars'.[13] That is to say, they are among the issues that currently exercise American citizens greatly, suggesting that though they may not generally be perceived as church–state issues, they none the less are debates about the 'soul' of Americans and of America; they are deeply embedded in the sacred sphere. I am referring to abortion, euthanasia, and homosexuality.

Abortion

In 1979, the US Supreme court, by a vote of 5-4, upheld the constitutionality of the Congressional legislation known as the 'Hyde Amendment', which prohibits federal funding for Medicaid abortions.[14] Cora McRae, a pregnant indigent woman eligible for Medicaid, desired an abortion for therapeutic

[11] Huigens, K., 'Science, Freedom of Conscience and the Establishment Clause', *University of Puget Sound Law Review*, 13 (1989): 89. Emphasis added.
[12] *Grand Rapids School District v. Ball*, 473 US 373 [1984].
[13] Hunter, J. D., *Culture Wars* (New York, NY: Basic Books, 1991).
[14] *Harris v. McRae*, 448 US 297 [1979].

reasons but was turned down. She brought suit on several grounds: that she was denied due process, and that both the Establishment Clause and the Free Exercise Clause were violated in her case. The majority rejected all three of these claims. They said McRae's due process was not violated because she was not denied an abortion, only the federal funds to pay for it. The claim based on the Establishment Clause was rejected because, while some religions do regard abortion as sinful, that fact does not prevent government from passing laws outlawing abortion. Finally, McRae's Free Exercise argument was rejected because she did not allege, let alone prove, that she sought an abortion 'under compulsion of religious belief'. As will now be shown, the four dissenters in this case have a markedly different picture of this case.

It is, I submit, not far-fetched to suggest that, contrary to the majority view, McRae's free exercise of religion *was* violated, if 'conscience' is what it is that can be freely exercised. A hint of this perspective is found in the dissents of Justices Stevens and Brennan. Both accept the view that McRae was being treated unfairly because she was poor, and, as Stevens writes,

the government must use neutral criteria in distributing benefits. . . . [I]t may not create exceptions for the sole purpose of furthering a governmental interest that is constitutionally subordinate to the individual interest that the entire program was designed to protect.   (*Harris v. McRae*, 448 US 297 [1979] 356.)

And what is the individual interest in this case? It is the provision of health care to indigent citizens. Once such a provision is in place, the dissenters agree, the state may not use its financial power to influence a woman's freedom to choose whether to have an abortion. That freedom, needless to say, is constitutionally guaranteed by *Roe v. Wade*.[15] Justice Brennan goes further in his dissent, however:

My focus . . . is upon the coercive impact of the congressional decision to fund one outcome of pregnancy—childbirth—while not funding the other—abortion. . . . [T]he Hyde Amendment is a transparent attempt by the Legislative Branch to impose the political majority's judgment of the morally acceptable and socially desirable preference on a sensitive and intimate decision that the Constitution entrusts to the individual.   (*Harris v. McRae*, 448 US 297 [1979] 330.)

Might Brennan have been comfortable tacking on the word 'conscience' or 'sacred' to that last sentence? This is not a legal analysis in the usual sense but rather an effort to extract a cultural interpretation using legal cases. Obviously, I do not know how Justice Brennan would have responded to my hypothetical question, but the hint to which I referred a few paragraphs back is found further on in Brennan's dissent when he draws a parallel between McRae and a Seventh-day Adventist, Sherbert, who was found eligible for

---

[15] *Roe v. Wade*, 410 US 113 [1973].

unemployment compensation when she resigned her job rather than work on Saturdays. Brennan quotes from the majority opinion that he himself wrote in that case:

The ruling [denying her benefits] forces her to choose between following the precepts of her religion and forfeiting benefits, on the one hand, and abandoning one of the precepts of her religion in order to accept work, on the other hand. Governmental imposition of such a choice puts the same kind of burden upon the free exercise of religion, as would a fine imposed against the appellant for her Saturday worship.   (*Harris v. McRae*, 448 US 297 [1979] 335.)

I am *not* suggesting that McRae's free exercise of her religion, in the narrow sense, was assaulted by the Hyde Amendment; I *am* suggesting that the Hyde Amendment represents an unconstitutional establishment of one conscientious position over alternative conscientious positions—which violates McRae's freedom of conscience, and thus the Free Exercise Clause as interpreted here.

This interpretation is more clearly illustrated in another abortion case nine years later.[16] The same four justices dissented in that case, but it is Justice Stevens's dissent we attend to here. *Webster* resulted from a Missouri legislative bill, the preamble of which declared that the life of 'each human being begins at conception'. Three other provisions stipulated certain regulations to be followed in abortion cases: that no public funds be used to encourage abortion, that no public employees or facilities be used in performing abortions, and that a viability test be performed on the fetus of any woman seeking abortion if reason exists to believe she is twenty or more weeks' pregnant.

Justice Stevens is bothered chiefly by the preamble. He writes

I am persuaded that the absence of any secular purpose for the legislative declarations that life begins at conception and that conception occurs at fertilization makes the relevant portion of the preamble invalid under the Establishment Clause. . . . This conclusion does not, and could not, rest on the fact that the statement happens to coincide with the tenets of certain religions . . . or on the fact that the legislators who voted to enact it may have been motivated by religious considerations. . . . Rather, it rests on the fact that the preamble, an unequivocal endorsement of a religious tenet of some but by no means all Christian faiths, serves no identifiable secular purpose. That fact alone compels a conclusion that the statute violates the Establishment Clause.   (*Webster v. Reproductive Health Services*, 492 US 490 [1989] 566.)

It is important to note that Justice Stevens is not choosing secularism over religion. He is not stating that life does *not* begin at conception. Rather, he is saying that whether or not life begins at conception is necessarily a con-

---

[16] *Webster v. Reproductive Health Services*, 492 US 490 [1989].

science issue, not because religions have views on this issue but because no secular purpose has been identified. The implication is that even if the 'pro-choice' supporters in this case did not regard their position as 'religious', it was conscientiously held and therefore, in Justice Stevens's view, entitled to the same First Amendment protection enjoyed by their opponents—the right to 'select any religious faith or none at all'. Justice Stevens recognized that the question of when life begins involves at least two conflicting positions, each entitled to be freely exercised, and neither entitled to be 'established' in law. Clearly, Justice Stevens is redefining the sacred.

As I said above, I am using examples—that of abortion thus far—to illustrate a more general perspective on conscience and thus the sacred. It is time now to address this general perspective.

The General Perspective

Is it possible, we can ask, to believe profoundly that abortion is evil and still leave the decision to abort to the pregnant woman whose life and conscience are most directly connected to the choice? That pair of views, writes Ronald Dworkin, 'is not only consistent but is in keeping with a great tradition of freedom of conscience in modern pluralistic democracies'.[17] What is really at issue in abortion cases, Dworkin insists, is

> whether state legislatures have the constitutional power to decide which intrinsic values all citizens must respect, and how, and whether legislatures may prohibit abortion on that ground. . . . *[F]reedom of choice about abortion is a necessary implication of the religious freedom guaranteed by the First Amendment.* [Emphasis added] (Dworkin, R., *Life's Dominion*, 25–6.)

Peter Wenz makes the same argument in his book, *Abortion Rights As Religious Freedom*.[18]

David A. J. Richards makes the case more generally. The moral basis of the Free Exercise Clause, he writes, is 'immunizing from state coercion the exercise of conceptions of life well and ethically lived and expressive of a mature person's rational and reasonable powers'.[19] Likewise, the Establishment Clause prohibits the state from interfering with the 'forming and changing of those conceptions'.[20]

I have illustrated this perspective thus far with the abortion issue. I turn next to a similar issue: euthanasia.

---

[17] Dworkin, R., *Life's Dominion* (New York, NY: Alfred A. Knopf, 1993), 15.
[18] Wenz, P., *Abortion Rights as Religious Freedom* (Philadelphia, PA: Temple University Press, 1992).
[19] Richards, D. A. J., *Conscience and the Constitution*, 140.   [20] Ibid.

Euthanasia

Less space is needed for the euthanasia illustration because, as has often been noted, the legal and moral issues are much the same as those in the case of abortion. Both involve competing interests that must be weighed and a balance found. Moreover, in both instances these interests change through time, which alters the balance and thus also alters the state's interest in intervening. As a Ninth Circuit Federal Court decision regarding assisted suicide recently stated: 'both types of case raise issues of life and death, and both arouse similar religious and moral concerns. Both also present basic questions about an individual's right of choice'.[21]

As in the case of abortion, the significant issue in euthanasia is this: on what basis may the state restrict an individual's right of choice? The first case we examine involved a Missouri law that required 'clear and convincing evidence' of an unconscious, terminally ill person's wish to have life-sustaining treatment withdrawn before any such withdrawal can be approved.[22] Nancy Cruzan was a victim of an auto accident that had left her for six years in a 'permanent vegetative state'. The testimony of her parents and her one-time housemate, that Nancy often expressed her desire to avoid being kept alive by such means, was found insufficient by a lower court, and a five-person majority of the Supreme Court could find no Constitutional basis for finding otherwise. As in other cases we are examining here, however, the cultural meaning I am identifying is found not in the majority opinion but in the dissent. It is, of course, no coincidence that the dissenters in this case are the same four whose views we have already encountered—Brennan, Blackmun, Marshall, and Stevens. In *Cruzan*, it is Stevens's dissent that best illustrates my argument here. He writes:

Missouri's regulation is an unreasonable intrusion upon traditionally private matters encompassed within the liberty protected by the Due Process Clause. . . . [N]ot much may be said with confidence about death unless it is said from faith, and that alone is reason enough to protect the freedom to conform choices about death to individual conscience. . . . Missouri asserts that its policy is related to a state interest in the protection of life. In my view, however, it is an effort to define life, rather than to protect it, that is the heart of Missouri's policy. Missouri insists, without regard to Nancy Cruzan's own interests, upon equaling her life with the biological persistence of her bodily functions . . . [T]here is a serious question as to whether the mere persistence of their bodies is 'life' as that word is commonly understood, or as it is used in both the Constitution and the Declaration of Independence. It is not within the province of secular government to circumscribe the liberties of the people by regulations designed wholly for the purpose of *establishing a sectarian definition*

---

[21] *Compassion in Dying v. State of Washington*, 96 Journal DAR 2639 [1996].
[22] *Cruzan v. Director, Missouri Department of Health*, 497 US 261 [1990].

of life. [Emphasis added].   (*Cruzan v. Director, Missouri Department of Health,*
497 US 261 [1996] at 338; 343; 344–5; 350.)

It is hardly surprising that in this dissent Justice Stevens footnotes his dissent in the *Webster* abortion case already discussed. In both cases, he sees legislation that arbitrarily defines life—when it begins in *Webster,* when it ends in *Cruzan*—with the effect being the unnecessary and unconstitutional establishment of an ultimate perspective not shared by all. If not an establishment of a religion in the narrow sense, it *is* an establishment of one conscientious position, disregarding—even outlawing—alternative conscientious positions. That is what Justice Stevens objects to: governmental encroachment on an expanded understanding of what is sacred.

In 1996 the Ninth Circuit Court of Appeals declared unconstitutional the Washington State law making a felony of any physician-assisted suicide.[23] The vote was 8–3, which, along with the fact that this Appellate case challenges the *Cruzan* decision, probably destined it to go to the US Supreme Court. Before turning to that decision—which reversed the Circuit Court's—let us look at the appellate court's reasoning.

The terminally-ill patients who joined their doctors as plaintiffs were in this instance judged competent to make a decision to withhold life-supporting assistance for themselves. They could, for example, have refused medication that extended their lives. What they could not do is expect their doctors to assist them in accomplishing a sure and painless end to life. The majority of the Ninth Circuit judges who heard this case decided that this restriction is unconstitutional.

The Ninth Circuit was mindful of the seriousness of the case before them. After laying out the circumstances of the case, the opinion strikes the seriousness note:

Our decisions involve difficult judgments regarding the conscience, traditions, and fundamental tenets of our nation. We must sometimes apply those basic principles in light of changing values based on shared experience. Other times we must apply them to new problems arising out of the development and use of new technologies. In all cases, our analysis of the applicability of the protections of the Constitution must be made in light of existing circumstances as well as our historic traditions. (*Compassion in Dying v. State of Washington,* 79 F. 3d 790 (9th Cir. 1996) 802–3.)

The Circuit Court then reviewed a great many cases from the past in which 'personal' matters have been adjudicated, deciding that 'Certainly, few decisions are more personal, intimate or important than the decision to end one's life, especially when the reason for doing so is to avoid excessive and protracted pain'. It then quotes from a 1992 Court decision[24] that declared

[23] *Compassion in Dying v. State of Washington,* 96 Journal DAR 2639 [1996].
[24] *Planned Parenthood v. Casey,* 505 US 833 [1992].

the most intimate and personal choices a person may make in a lifetime, choices central to personal dignity and autonomy, are central to the liberty protected by the Fourteenth Amendment. At the heart of liberty is the right to define one's own concept of existence, of meaning, of the universe, and of the mystery of human life. Beliefs about these matters could not define the attributes of personhood were they formed under compulsion of the State.   (*Planned Parenthood v. Casey*, 505 US 833 [1992] 851.)

On this basis, then, the Ninth Circuit Court in this assisted-suicide case wrote the summary statement so widely quoted in news stories about this case:

A competent terminally ill adult, having lived nearly the full measure of his life, has a strong liberty interest in choosing a dignified and humane death rather than being reduced at the end of his existence to a childlike state of helplessness, diapered, sedated, incontinent.   (*Compassion in Dying v. State of Washington*, 79 F. 3d 790 (9th Cir. 1996) 839.)

That such a 'childlike state' should not be imposed by the government because it invades the sacred sphere is evidenced in the decision's concluding paragraph:

There is one final point we must emphasize. Some argue strongly that decisions regarding matters affecting life or death should not be made by the courts. Essentially, we agree with that proposition. In this case, by permitting the individual to exercise the right to choose we are following the constitutional mandate to take such decisions out of the hands of the government, both state and federal, and to put them where they rightly belong, in the hands of the people. We are allowing individuals to make the decisions that so profoundly affect their very existence—and precluding the state from intruding excessively into that critical realm. . . . Those who believe strongly that death must come without physician assistance are free to follow that creed, be they doctors or patients. They are not free, however, to force their views, their religious convictions, or their philosophies on all the other members of a democratic society, and to compel those whose values differ with theirs to die painful, protracted, and agonizing deaths. [Emphasis added]   (Compassion in Dying v. State of Washington, 79 F. 3d 790 (9th Cir. 1996) 840.)

In the minds of the majority of Ninth Circuit judges the sacred issues involved in euthanasia thus transcend the question of life versus death. They include choice, and dignity, and self-direction. They ask of us not whether life is sacred but how the sanctity of life is to be understood.[25]

The Supreme Court saw it differently. In a unanimous 1997 decision, it ruled that the individual states have the authority to make assisted suicide illegal,[26] thus signaling no challenge to Oregon's recent legalization of the

---

[25] Dworkin, *Life's Dominion*, chapter 7; Urofsky, M., *Letting Go: Death, Dying, and the Law* (New York, NY: Charles Scribner's Sons, 1993).

[26] *Compassion In Dying v. State of Washington*, 117 US 2293 [1997].

act. Four of the justices, while agreeing with the majority, nevertheless wrote concurring opinions. As might be expected, Justice Stevens comes closest to the position I have articulated here. He wrote:

A State, like Washington, that has authorized the death penalty and thereby has concluded that the sanctity of human life does not require that it always be preserved, must acknowledge that there are situations in which an interest in hastening death is legitimate. Indeed, not only is that interest sometimes legitimate, I am also convinced that there are times when it is entitled to constitutional protection. (*Washington, et al., v. Glucksberg, et al.*, 521 US 702 [1997] 741–2.)

Several of the Justices noted the increasing attention the euthanasia issue is receiving, brought on both by technological advances in keeping bodies 'alive', and by the greater number persons who are living longer lives and thus experiencing deteriorating, non-curable diseases. The US Supreme Court, as I interpret their words, was not declaring assisted suicide unconstitutional but rather declaring it to be within the jurisdiction of each individual state.

Homosexuality

It has been suggested that the euthanasia issue is now about where the abortion issue was twenty years ago. Dispute continues over abortion, however, even if the principle of a constitutional right to privacy appears to be reasonably secure. That suggests that euthanasia will likewise be debated for years to come. Even newer on the legal front is the issue of homosexuality, an issue having much in common with abortion and euthanasia, at least to those who follow my reasoning here.

One feature the three issues share is a certain divide. In each instance there is one side who finds a certain action objectionable, even evil; and in each instance there is an opposing side who finds the same action desirable, even noble. A major difference between the two sides is that the first side has had its viewpoint not just recognized as the dominant cultural viewpoint but has also been successful getting its viewpoint written into law. This has left members of the second side subject to criminal prosecution as well as social denunciation.

A second feature the three issues share is this: while the first side often articulates its viewpoint in religious language, the second side articulates its viewpoint in the language of conscience that often omits reference to religion. Does this give a constitutional advantage to the first side? I would argue that it has, but it should not. I would argue further that the second side can show its opponents to be enjoying a two-fold unconstitutional privilege: an unconstitutional 'establishment' of the first side's viewpoint and an unconstitutional 'violation' of the second side's right to the free exercise of conscience.

Only recently has homosexuality as an issue joined this company of issues. The Georgia sodomy case[27] was technically not a decision about same-sex activity, since heterosexual sodomy was also outlawed by the Georgia statute, but it none the less stands as a measure of Supreme Court thinking less than two decades ago. The Supreme Court majority voted to uphold the Georgia statute, while four dissenters saw that Georgia was imposing on all a particular viewpoint that by no means was shared by all. The legal standing of homosexuality is obviously 'ripening' as gay and lesbian persons are insisting on their rights as citizens, including the right to marry. As with abortion and euthanasia, these demands touch on the very core of what 'conscience' or the 'sacred' means.

Andrew Sullivan has made the case for this last assertion in his carefully reasoned *Virtually Normal*,[28] an analysis of several stances toward homosexuality to be found in contemporary America. Sullivan says

. . . the vast majority of people engaging in homosexual acts regard those acts as an extension of their deepest emotional and sexual desires, desires which they do not believe they have chosen and which they cannot believe are always and everywhere wrong.

When the subject of homosexuality emerges, it is always subject to emotive passion, and affects matters of religious conscience. . . . The act of openly conceding one's homosexuality is in some ways an act of faith, of faith in the sturdiness of one's own identity and the sincerity of one's own heart. (Sullivan, A., *Virtually Normal*, 30 and 158, 166.)

Near the end of his book, Sullivan admits that homosexuality is not the equivalent of a 'religious calling', but who can doubt that—to him certainly, but obviously to many others as well—it involves the very core of one's being.[29]

CONCLUSION

David A. J. Richards has written: 'The antiestablishment worry is not over regulations of conscience in general, but over sectarian conscience using state power to unfair . . . advantage inconsistent with equal respect for con-

---

[27] *Bowers v. Hardwick*, 478 US 186 [1985].

[28] Sullivan, A., *Virtually Normal* (New York, NY: Alfred A. Knopf, 1995).

[29] Eskridge, Jr., W. N., makes the same in argument in *The Case for Same-Sex Marriage* (New York, NY: Free Press, 1996).

science'.[30] I maintain that when equal respect for conscience is recognized—when, that is, conscience is accorded not just free exercise rights but the full implications of that recognition are perceived—then Establishment Clause jurisprudence is also involved. Moreover, it is involved in a way that leads to a redefinition of the sacred. As a consequence, legal institutions perform a task that traditionally has been a task for religious institutions. There is, as yet, no consensus on whether such an institutional shift of function is good or bad. Indeed, the issues of abortion, euthanasia, and homosexuality are at the very center of a great cultural debate going on among the American people. Two things are clear, however: that debate is undeniably sacred in character, and it is from the domain not of religious institutions but of legal institutions that the resolution—if any—will come.

[30] Richards, D. A. J., *Conscience and the Constitution*, 145.

FOURTEEN

Can Religion Be Religious in Public?

The rhetorical question that is my title must be answered with a qualified 'Yes', but that qualification is a crucial one. It depends upon how one answers this question: is the essence of religion thought to be its *public authority*? Since religion's public authority is precisely what must be relinquished when religion engages in public debate, persons who answer positively this second question will look upon religion in public as tamed to the point of becoming non-religion. Others, however, see the matter in a different way. They can imagine religion having authority over individuals if, in a society such as our own, such individuals voluntarily accept it. What is prohibited is the use of *governmental* authority to enforce *religion's* authority. To do that is to violate the First Amendment's Establishment Clause.

Religion, then, can be religious in public by following the rules implied in the Establishment Clause, which, as we shall see, are by no means obvious. Indeed, they are the subject of much debate and, as Justice Rehnquist's testy dissent in *Wallace v. Jaffee*[1] demonstrates, even incoherent in operation. That situation need not be, however, and I advance here an argument that would bring clarity in the realm of Establishment Clause jurisprudence and, in so doing, show how religion can be religious in public.

Essay Twelve made the case for treating conscience as that which the Free Exercise Clause protects. Essay Thirteen then discussed the implications this proposition has for the Establishment Clause and used abortion, assisted suicide, and same-sex marriage as examples of situations where one conscientious position is written into law at the expense of an opposing conscientious position. These three examples, in my view, illustrate the *improper* role of religion in public.

It is clear from these three examples that 'religion' is involved in the issues in question, not because religious doctrine proclaims when life begins or ends or declares what is a real marriage. Rather 'religion' is involved as conviction, and the state in these examples has lent its authority to prefer one conviction over another. And it has done so without a secular purpose. It has said, in Missouri, that people who are convinced that life does not begin

---

[1] *Wallace v. Jaffee*, 472 US 38 [1985].

until a fetus can be sustained outside the womb cannot act on that conviction. It has said in Washington State that terminally-ill persons must continue to endure their pain or indignity even if they believe that what they regard as 'life' is already over for them. And many states, by passing legislation denying recognition to any same-sex marriage solemnized in another state, are using the government's authority to honor one conviction and deny another.

But surely, some will object, government can override at least *some* convictions and pass legislation declaring *some* actions to be legal and others to be illegal. It may indeed, but—and here is the key point—only when it has a *secular* purpose in doing so. Homicide is thus illegal not because one of the Ten Commandments prohibits killing, but because society reasons that violence is disruptive, and anarchy would prevail if violence is not curtailed. This 'translation step' is the lesson that religion must learn and follow if it wants to be religious in public. It must identify a secular purpose, even if its own reasons are religiously inspired. This is Richard John Neuhaus's meaning when he writes 'Those who want to bring religiously based values to bear in public discourse have an obligation to 'translate' those values into terms that are as accessible as possible to those who do not share the same religious grounding'.[2]

It would appear, then, that for religion to be religious in public it must know how to translate its religious values into secular language. What does that mean? I suggest that it means that claims—whether religiously motivated or not—must, if they are to be made in public and carry authority, have an empirical, logical, or rational basis, including those claims that may also have a religious basis. Claims having an empirical, logical, or rational basis are, in principle, claims that can receive unanimous agreement.

Thus, for example, after the nth week of a pregnancy, a fetus can be shown to have a probability greater than zero of surviving outside the womb. On an *empirical* basis, therefore, a state may declare that life has begun in the nth week and extend legal protection to that life. It may also, on *rational* grounds, decide that even after the nth week, a fetus may be aborted if doing so will save the life of the mother. Having thus rationally judged a life-not-yet-born as less valuable than that of an already living mother-to-be, a state may *logically* extend its reasoning, and also conclude that a fetus known to be so ill-developed as to make life after birth impossible may likewise be aborted after the nth week.

---

[2] Neuhaus, R. J., *The Naked Public Square* (Grand Rapids, MI: Eerdmans, 1984), 125.

TWO EXAMPLES

Perhaps some real-life examples will illustrate the general point. In 1980 the United States Supreme Court struck down Kentucky's law requiring the posting of the Ten Commandments in every public school classroom in that state. Recognizing that such a law could not be justified on the grounds, for example, that the Ten Commandments were handed down by God, the Legislature of Kentucky stipulated that the posters include the following sentence: 'The secular application of the Ten Commandments is clearly seen in its adoption as the fundamental legal code of Western Civilization and the common Law of the United States'.[3] Here, obviously, the Kentucky lawmakers imagined themselves to be 'translating' religious claims into claims having an empirical, logical, or rational basis. And, in the case of the last six commandments, regarding honoring parents, murder, adultery, stealing, lying, and coveting, perhaps the legislators had a point. But the first four commandments—to remember the Sabbath, not to honor other gods, not to make graven images, nor take God's name in vain—because they are incapable of translation into empirical, logical, or rational terms—could be justified only on grounds of conviction.

It is conceivable, in other words, that Kentucky might have prevailed had only the last six commandments been posted. If, in addition, selections from Hammurabi's Code, the Magna Carta, etc. had been included, the display almost certainly would pass constitutional muster. Kentucky, however, was attempting to piggyback four clearly impermissible commandments onto a poster that otherwise might well be said to have a rational purpose: to show the cultural sources of contemporary law.

An Alabama judge recently vowed to keep a display of the Ten Commandments on his courtroom wall despite a circuit court ruling that the display is unconstitutional. The circuit court judge who made the ruling is quoted as saying, 'It is obvious that the sole purpose of the plaques hanging in the courtroom in such a fashion is purely religious'. The circuit court judge even suggested that his opinion might change if the Ten Commandments were displayed differently, 'perhaps with other historic or cultural items'.[4] The Alabama judge, however, had forthrightly declared that his motive was religious, and the basis for the display lies in his conviction that the laws he administers are in turn based on a belief in God.

So, it must be said in this case, the judge's beliefs were the only basis for bringing religion into the public arena. And that is not enough. As Justice

---

[3] *Stone v. Graham*, 449 US 39 [1980] at 41.

[4] Bragg, R., 'Judge Allows God's Law to Mix with Alabama', *New York Times* (13 February 1997), A14.

Harry Blackmun wrote in his dissent in a case upholding a Georgia law prohibiting sodomy, 'The legitimacy of secular legislation depends . . . on whether the State can advance some justification for its law beyond its conformity to religious doctrine'.[5] That is what those who bring religious motives and religious agendas to the public table must recognize. Those motives and agendas are admissible, of course, but there must be 'some justification . . . beyond' their 'conformity to religious doctrine'.

SECULAR VS. RELIGIOUS PURPOSES

David A. J. Richards, in his book, *Toleration and the Constitution*, points to what might be called 'public reason' to get at this issue. Public reasons involve rational principles that give 'necessary and indispensable protection to the interests of adult persons in life, bodily security and integrity, security in institutional relationships and claims arising therefrom, and the like'. Public reasons, in other words, identify what Richards calls 'neutral goods—things all persons could reasonably accept as all-purpose conditions of pursuing their aims, whatever they are'.[6] For Richards, therefore, laws that prohibit the sale or use of contraceptives, that outlaw all abortions or homosexual relations, are unconstitutional not because some religions have moral codes declaring these activities to be sins, but because they reflect no 'neutral goods' that public reason can identify.

Edward B. Foley also utilizes the concept of public reason, which he claims has two components: 'The epistemological component is, essentially, the methods and conclusions of logic and science. The ethical component . . . is the fundamental idea that the interest of all persons count equally for purposes of determining their rights and duties as citizens'.[7] For Foley also, therefore, public reason involves the employment of concepts, principles, and cause-effect relations that all persons can reasonably be expected to accept.

Kyron Huigens advocates another path to much the same end. In a 1989 law review article entitled 'Science, Freedom of Conscience and the Establishment Clause', Huigens borrows the insight of Karl Popper, the philosopher of science who gave us the notion of 'falsifiability'. 'Popper's key insight', Huigens writes, 'was to notice that scientific experiments are

---

[5] *Bowers v. Hardwick*, 478 US 186 [1985] at 211.

[6] Richards, D. A. J., *Toleration and Constitution* (New York, NY: Oxford University Press, 1986), 259, 273.

[7] Foley, E. B., 'Political Liberalism and Establishment Clause Jurisprudence', *Case Western Reserve Law Review*, 43 (1993), 965.

persuasive, not when they verify hypotheses, but when there is a substantial risk that they will have the opposite effect: falsification'. Huigens would apply the falsifiability test to governmental actions and declare invalid under the Establishment Clause any actions having the 'effect of advancing belief not falsifiable in principle'.[8]

Huigens's proposal may seem radical to some, but it conforms nicely to the argument of this essay. The strong separationist position involved in his proposal views the decisions in *Engel v. Vitale* (outlawing school prayer), *Abington Township v. Schempp* (outlawing school devotional Bible-reading), *Epperson v. Arkansas* (permitting the teaching of evolution), *Stone v. Graham* (outlawing the posting of the ten Commandments), and all other cases involving religion in the public schools as fundamentally decisions that involve the *protection of conscience*. All these cases bar government from 'advancing dogmatic belief, not because dogma is the product of an established church or because it might lead to persecution but for reasons having to do with dogma itself'.[9] In other words, dogma, by definition, is not falsifiable and therefore, for establishment reasons, cannot be advanced by the state.

Huigens's proposal goes considerably beyond any accommodationist position. In fact 'accommodation' of religion *as such* would disappear under his scheme, allowing for no governmental benefits to religion except those *required* by the Free Exercise Clause. Thus, under the Huigens doctrine, parochial schools would receive police and fire protection; to deny such protection would burden the free exercise rights of parochial school students and their parents. But tax-supported bus transportation—*Everson v. Board of Education*[10]—would not be allowed, since the state should not assist in the promulgation of sectarian dogma. Similarly, tax-supported military chaplains are constitutional because many military personnel, away from home, are otherwise unable freely to exercise their religious rights. The legislative chaplain in the Nebraska legislature, on the other hand, would be disallowed, contrary to *Marsh v. Chambers*,[11] because it makes the state the sponsor or promulgator of dogma.

Huigens revisits the creation vs. evolution cases[12] to illustrate his falsifiability principle. Any proposal to have public schools teach creationism or 'creation science' is unconstitutional not because a possibility exists that such teaching would become an 'establishment' but simply because—unlike evolutionary theory, which offers falsifiable propositions—creation theory

[8] Huigens, K., 'Science, Freedom of Conscience and the Establishment Clause', *University of Puget sound Law Review*, 13 (1989), 67, 96; cf. Popper, K., *The Logic of Scientific Discovery*, revised edition (London: Hutchinson, 1968).

[9] Huigens, K., 'Science', 90.   [10] *Everson v. Board of Education*, 330 US 1 [1947].

[11] *Marsh v. Chambers*, 463 US 783 [1983].

[12] *Epperson v. Arkansas*, 393 US 97 [1968]; *Edwards v. Aguillard*, 482 US 578 [1987].

offers only immutable-truth dogma. For public schools to teach creationism, then, is to have the state use its power to assault the freedom of conscience. For the state to use its 'power to inculcate, strengthen or perpetuate belief not falsifiable in principle violates deeply held convictions about the state, belief, and the injunction to use others as ends, not means'.[13] Huigens's proposal, read one way, appears hostile to religion, but read another way, gives priority precisely to religious liberty; it requires the state to give a wide berth to the free exercise of conscience.

SACRED PURPOSE AS A RESIDUAL CATEGORY

It is notable that in the several methods just reviewed for determining what is religious or secular for Establishment Clause purposes—and thus what is and is not constitutional—religion is essentially a residual category. That is, the decisive distinction involves finding what is 'secular', with all else being 'religious' in the eyes of the law. This makes for some surprising outcomes, of course, because much that is non-secular is not, in the ordinary sense, religious. We see this vividly in Justice Stevens's dissent in the 1989 Missouri abortion decision. The Preamble portion of the Missouri legislative bill declared that the life of each human being begins at conception. That Preamble, wrote Stevens, happens to coincide with the tenets of one or another religion, but that is not what disqualifies it in his view. Rather, only if the state had a *secular* purpose in adopting the Preamble would that part of the bill be constitutional. Stevens could find no secular purpose and held therefore that the Preamble of the Missouri bill violated the Establishment Clause. Justice Stevens's opinion was the minority view.

It bears repeating, however, that Justice Stevens is not arguing that life does *not* begin at conception, for that statement, like its opposite, also has no secular purpose. And that is exactly the point; since no known reliable and valid way exists to determine just when 'life' begins, people are allowed—up until fetal viability is determined—to answer the question however they wish.

What is the dividing line between the two beliefs—one dealing with fetal viability, which all persons are expected to accept, and the other, dealing with the origin of life—which persons are free to answer as they choose? The best answer to this question is found in Peter S. Wenz's *Abortion Rights as Religious Freedom*.[14] His book's argument—coincident with the argument

[13] Huigens, K., 'Science', 138–9.
[14] Wenz, P. S., *Abortion Rights as Religious Freedom* (Philadelphia, PA: Temple University Press, 1992).

of this essay—is that up until the time of fetal viability—which itself is subject to change, of course, by technological advance—a woman must, based on her free exercise of conscience, have a right to terminate her pregnancy. Wenz thus devotes a great amount of attention to this issue of the dividing line between the two kinds of belief—between secular beliefs and religious beliefs. Like the authors already reviewed on this issue, Wenz defines as religious any beliefs that are not secular. Unlike secular beliefs, Wenz says, religious beliefs

cannot be established solely by appeals to generally accepted methods of coming to know what is true and right. This is the epistemological standard for distinguishing religious from secular belief. Additionally, religious beliefs are those on which agreement is unnecessary for the cooperation required to sustain our society. They are matters on which people sharing our current way of life can agree permanently to disagree. They are not among the threads needed to hold our social fabric together.   (Wenz, P. S., *Abortion Rights as Religious Freedom*, 136.)

Wenz's epistemological standard is the standard Huigens called falsifiability. It is scientific in the sense of employing normal canons of reason and evidence. Secular beliefs, in this light, do not in fact have to obtain 100 per cent agreement, but at least in principle they could.

Beliefs judged to be religious by the fact that differing positions, even contradictory positions, on those beliefs need not be disruptive of social life, represent a quite different category. Included are some obvious instances, such as the capacity of the unitarian, trinitarian, and atheist to live together in harmony if they choose to do so; their dogmatic differences need not interfere in their interactions. The fact that quarrels over religious beliefs do occur does nothing to disqualify that statement.

In sharp contrast are those beliefs about matters for which agreement *is* necessary for a smoothly functioning society. They are therefore secular beliefs. These range from seemingly simple beliefs that nobody claims are religious rather than secular such as which side of the road to drive on, to those beliefs whose origins may be found in religion, such as beliefs about the immorality of murder, robbery, battery, and so on. Many, of course, might still regard these kinds of beliefs to be religious, and in one sense they are for those persons who conceive of their own beliefs about morality as rooted in their religion. From the legal standpoint, however, whether these beliefs are regarded by persons as rooted in their religion is immaterial; society expects people to behave in accordance with these beliefs anyway, as necessary for a stable society.

A SPECIAL CLASS

There is a class of activities involving the state and religious organizations worthy of special note. These are cases where a government agency, in pursuit of its religiously neutral goals, utilizes religious organizations as its agents. Unlike government grants to parochial schools—for example, vouchers, salary assistance, or building maintenance—to aid those schools in achieving *their* goals, government in these cases is not assenting to requests from religious communities but asking those communities to help government achieve *its* goals. In most instances, no doubt, those goals overlap those of the religious communities, but that is for them, not the state, to decide.

Take as a vivid example, the case of refugee relief following the Vietnam War, when thousands upon thousands of Vietnamese, Laotians, and Cambodians sought refuge in the United States and elsewhere. Because some churches already had in place the facilities for 'processing' refugees, the US government found it convenient and cheaper to use those facilities to conduct health examinations, fill out migration forms, and so forth—activities those facilities had been doing earlier, but on a smaller scale and without government financial support.

Before this co-operative endeavor began, the religious organizations could decide whom they would accept and what would be done with those accepted. Now the US government made those decisions, which may have caused some frustration or curtailed some behaviors by religiously motivated personnel. Presumably, in the earlier period, these processing centers were more or less missionary operations by American denominations, and a reasonable assumption was that at least some of those accepted would 'convert'. At least efforts towards that end were not prohibited. Now they were at least limited.

In all probability, what these denominational programs were doing earlier, at their own expense, they regarded as 'religious'. When working in concert with the government, but still engaged in much the same activity, is it still 'religious'? Answers will vary, no doubt, but a reasonable perspective on the matter is this: religious organizations have never been *unlimited* by the state in what they could do, so the question is whether the limitations imposed by the state diminish the religious mission to the point where its religious 'core' is lost. Thus Roman Catholic hospitals receive government subvention, but in exchange they cannot restrict their patients and medical staff to Catholics. Inner-city churches are given tax dollars to help provide food and sleeping quarters to the homeless, but they serve all who qualify by the state's standards. A sectarian college can get financial help to construct buildings, but it must guarantee not to conduct worship in those buildings. In these examples, has the hospital, the church, or the college so compromised its reason-for-being that its core identity is lost?

This question, interestingly, is the mirror image of the question asked in so-called 'establishment' cases. In such cases, the court asks if an activity violates the Establishment Clause of the Constitution's First Amendment and must answer Yes or No. But just because an answer is blunt does not mean the process of arriving at that answer is clear-cut. Of the twenty-five establishment cases heard by the US Supreme Court between 1980 and 1995, only five were decided on 9-0 votes. A full 60 per cent were decided on votes of 5–4 or 6–3, indicating enormous disagreement over what is and what it not a violation of the Establishment Clause.

And so it is with the parallel question of whether a religious organization sacrifices its core identity by accommodating the state's demands of neutrality in order to receive some of the state's largesse. It would seem hopeless to draw a line that will work in all cases. Just as the Court seems to waffle on where to draw the establishment line—for example, the state may lend to parochial schools geography textbooks that contain maps of the United States, but it may not lend maps of the United States for use in geography classes—so do religious organizations seem to waffle on where to draw the compromise line. A hard-line separationist such as the late Leo Pfeffer would outlaw a statue of the Virgin Mary in any Catholic hospital receiving public money, and Bob Jones University lost its tax-exempt status rather than compromise on its policy prohibiting interracial dating by its students.[15]

In asking therefore—concerning this special class of cases in which religious organizations receive government financial help—whether those are instances of religion being religious in public, we must return to the topic of this essay's first paragraph. In accepting public tax money to support its mission, does a religious organization relinquish its authority over the activities for which the money was given? The answer is Yes, meaning—in this very special sense, and only in this sense—religion is being religious in public.

ARGUMENT AND COUNTER-ARGUMENT

Much of the above material was presented orally at the annual joint meeting of the Religious Research Association and the Society for the Scientific Study of Religion in November 1997. Objections were raised along several lines.

[15] Regarding Pfeffer, see Hammond, P. E., *With Liberty for All* (Louisville, KY: Westminster John Knox Press, 1998), 4. Regarding Bob Jones University, see *Bob Jones University v. US*, 461 US 574 [1983].

All, in my view, *sound* valid but upon analysis turn out to be specious. I conclude, therefore with some comments about these objections.

The objection most easily countered is one that asks: 'If all claims of conscience are constitutionally protected, even if not couched in religious language, what is to stop anybody from doing anything in the name of conscience?' The answer is that *not* all claims of conscience are protected; what is protected is the presumption of a conscientious right *unless the state can identify a secular purpose for curtailing that right*. For this reason, judging the legitimacy of a non-religious conscience claim is no harder than judging the legitimacy of a religious claim.

A second objection arises out of a clear misunderstanding of my argument: 'that for religion to be religious in public it must drop its religious language or disguise its underlying religious motives'. This simply isn't so. The public square does not rule out religious words and motives; it simply does not accord them authority until they are translated. In his book *The Dissent of the Governed*, Stephen L. Carter exhibits this misunderstanding. He wonders if the example of the *Reverend* Martin Luther King, Jr., of the Southern *Christian* Leadership Conference (his emphasis) does not show that the United States Constitution allows a religious community to 'use the coercive apparatus of the state to impose its moral understandings on those in the political community who are not co-religionists'.[16] I would respond that it shows religious language and motive *are* admissible in the public square, but that, while King was no doubt granted charismatic authority because of his religious eloquence, his influence came precisely from his translating the Christian gospel message into terms readily understood by non-Christians, even the non-religious. Certainly the coercive apparatus of the state—in enforcing school desegregation, for example—was justified not by King's words but by words interpreting the United States Constitution.

A third objection parallels the misunderstanding of the second: 'that constraining religion in public pushes it further in the direction of privatization'. That the separation of church and state—or the constitutional interpretation of the First Amendment—leads empirically to the privatization of religion is, by now, beyond dispute. Such privatization is not *required,* however, nor is the public square *off limits* to religious persons using religious language. Jose Casanova puts this point nicely: '[W]hichever position . . . it takes, the church will have to justify it through open, public, rational discourse in the public sphere of civil society . . . [Therefore, only] a religion which has incorporated as its own the central aspect of the Enlightenment critique of religion is in a position today to play a positive role in . . . the

---

[16] Carter, S. L., *The Dissent of the Governed* (Cambridge, MA: Harvard University Press, 1998), 29.

revitalization of the modern public square'.[17] Qualification for religious participation, in Casanova's terms, is tantamount to acceptance of the notion that, in the public square, religion must advance its positions on empirical, rational, or logical grounds.

Another objection to my argument says that to insist on placing such a qualification on religion in the public square is to trivialize it and to imply that religion has nothing empirical, rational, or logical to say on public issues. Surely this objection is fallacious. Requiring religion to translate its positions into terms understandable to all implies that its positions may be convincing even to others not sharing the theological suppositions underlying those positions.

Finally, it has been objected that my argument ignores minority faiths and communicates a message of hostility to them. I find this objection surprising because so much of the basis of my argument, as I explained above, comes out of judicial rulings that favored the free exercise of minority, sometimes despised, faiths. Consider the conscientious objection cases: it was the Supreme Court that located the 'faith' element in the consciences of Seeger and Welsh, even when they themselves denied having any orthodox faith. More important, however, the implications of this expanded understanding of the Free Exercise Clause for the Establishment Clause puts the lie to this last objection. Why? Because it turns out that, despite a long history of church–state separation, American society is still riddled with privileges extended to religion over non-religion as well as to some religions over others. Keep in mind that people who articulate their convictions in a language other than religion are *also* required to translate their arguments based on those convictions into empirical, rational, or logical terms. Religions, then, are not being unfairly treated but simply being asked to play by the rules binding on all.

CONCLUSION

This lesson is not easy to grasp. Prejudices so old as to not be recognized as prejudices are difficult to excise. I close with but one example. *Catalyst*, the journal of the Catholic League for Religious and Civil Rights, states in its masthead that 'It defends the right of Catholic—lay and cleric alike—to participate in American life without defamation or discrimination'. Most of the *Catalyst* issue of May 1998, is therefore stories drawn from newspapers,

---

[17] Casanova, J., *Public Religions in the Modern World* (Chicago, IL: University of Chicago Press, 1994), 223, 233.

Hollywood, radio and TV, and other avenues of mass communication where Catholicism is denigrated, or apologies for such denigration are reported. As the League's purpose says, Catholics should be able to participate fully in public life without discrimination. What should be made, therefore, of a contrasting *Catalyst* story, headlined 'No To "Life Partners"', which reads, in part:

The Philadelphia/South Jersey chapter of the Catholic League . . . is supporting the efforts of the Archdiocese of Philadelphia in opposing a life partners' bill. The legislation seeks to put alternative lifestyles on the same legal, social and moral plane as the institution of marriage. The Philadelphia chapter placed an ad in *Catholic Standard* and *Times* urging Catholics to stand behind Cardinal Anthony Bevilacqua. (*Catalyst*, 25/4 (1998), 11.)

The Catholic League, its seems, not only guards against religious discrimination but promotes it as well. Justice Louis Brandeis's admonition still rings true: 'the greatest dangers to liberty lurk in insidious encroachment by men of zeal, well-meaning but without understanding'.[18]

---

[18] *Olmstead v. US*, 277 US 438 [1927] at 479.

Afterword

William Frazee refused a temporary retail position offered him by Kelly Services because the job would have required him to work on Sunday. Frazee told Kelly that, as a Christian, he could not work on 'the Lord's day'. He then applied for unemployment benefits, but his application was denied. This decision was upheld by a review board and two appellant courts on the grounds that 'a refusal of work . . . based on religious convictions . . . must be based upon some tenet or dogma accepted by the individual of some church, sect, or denomination . . .'

The United States Supreme Court reversed. In so doing, it said:

Undoubtedly, membership in an organized religious denomination, especially one with a specific tenet forbidding members to work on Sunday, would simplify the problem of identifying sincerely held religious beliefs, but we reject the notion that to claim the protection of the Free Exercise Clause, one must be responding to the commands of a particular religious organization.   (*Frazee v. Illinois Department of Employment Security*, 489 US 829 [1989], 834.)

BIBLIOGRAPHY

ABRAMSON, HAROLD. *Ethnic Diversity in Catholic America* (New York, NY: John Wiley & Sons, 1973).

——'Religion', in S. Thernstrom, A. Orlov, and O. Handlin (eds.), *Harvard Encyclopedia of American Ethnic Groups* (Cambridge, MA: Harvard University Press, 1980).

AHLSTROM, SYDNEY. *A Religious History of the American People* (New Haven, CT: Yale University Press, 1972).

ALBA, RICHARD D. *Italian Americans* (Englewood Cliffs, NJ: Prentice-Hall, 1985).

ALBANESE, CATHERINE. *Sons of the Fathers* (Philadelphia, PA: Temple University Press, 1976).

AMMERMAN, NANCY. *Baptist Battles: Social Change and Religious Conflict in the Southern Baptist Convention* (New Brunswick, NJ: Rutgers University Press, 1990).

ANTHONY, DICK, and ROBBINS, THOMAS. 'Spiritual innovation and the crisis of American civil religion', in M. Douglas and S. Tipton (eds.) *Religion in America* (Boston, MA: Beacon Press, 1983).

BAINBRIDGE, WILLIAM SIMS. *The Sociology of Religious Movements* (New York, NY: Routledge, 1997).

BARKER, EILEEN (ed.). *New Religious Movements* (Lewiston, NY: Edwin Mellen Press, 1982).

——(ed.). *Of Gods and Men: New Religious Movements in the West* (Macon, GA: Mercer University Press, 1983).

BECKFORD, JAMES A. 'The state and control of new religious movements', *Acts of the 17th Congress* (Paris: International Converence for the Sociology of Religion, 1983).

——*Cult Controversies* (London: Tavistock, 1985).

——and RICHARDSON, JAMES T. 'A bibliography of social scientific studies of new religious movements in the U.S. and Europe', *Social Compass*, 30 (1983).

BELL, DANIEL. 'The Return of the Sacred?' *British Journal of Sociology*, 28 (1977).

BELLAH, ROBERT. 'Civil religion in America', *Daedalus* (Winter, 1967).

——'New religious consciousness and the crisis in modernity', in C. Glock and R. Bellah (eds.), *The New Religious Consciousness* (Berkeley, CA: University of California Press, 1976).

——'Cultural pluralism and religious particularism', in H. Clark (ed.), *Freedom of Religion in America* (Los Angeles, CA: Center for the Study of the American Experience, University of Southern California, 1982).

BELLAH, ROBERT, *et al.* *Habits of the Heart* (Berkeley, CA: University of California Press, 1985).

BENDER, THOMAS. *Community and Social Change in America* (New Brunswick, NJ: Rutger's University Press, 1978).

BERGER, PETER. *A Rumor of Angels: Modern Society and the Rediscovery of the Supernatural* (Garden City, NY: Doubleday, 1969).

——and NEUHAUS, RICHARD JOHN. *To Empower People* (Washington, DC: American Enterprise Institute, 1977).

BIBBY, REGINALD. *Fragmented Gods* (Toronto: Irwin Press, 1987).

BLOOM, HAROLD. *The American Religion* (New York, NY: Simon and Schuster, 1992).

BROMLEY, DAVID G., and HAMMOND, PHILLIP E. (eds.). *The Future of New Religious Movements* (Macon, GA: Mercer University Press, 1987).

BULL, MALCOLM, and LOCKHART, KEITH. *Seeking a Sanctuary: Seventh-day Adventism and the American Dream* (San Francisco, CA: Harper & Row, 1989).

BURDICK, MICHAEL. 'Overseas mission: Failure of nerve or change in strategy?' In R. Michaelsen and W. C. Roof (eds.), *Liberal Protestantism* (New York, NY: Pilgrim Press, 1986).

CAPLOW, THEODORE. 'Contrasting Trends in European and American Religion', *Sociological Analysis*, 46 (1985).

CARMELA, ANGELA C. 'The Religion Clauses and Acculturated Religious Conduct', in J. E. Wood, Jr. and D. Davis (eds.), *The Role of Government in Monitoring and Regulating Religion in Public Life* (Waco, TX: J. M. Dawson Institute of Church–State Studies, Baylor University, 1993).

CARTER, STEPHEN. *The Culture of Disbelief* (New York, NY: Basic Books, 1993).

——*The Dissent of the Governed* (Cambridge, MA: Harvard University Press, 1998).

CASANOVA, JOSE. *Public Religions in the Modern World* (Chicago, IL: University of Chicago Press, 1994).

CHAVES, MARK, and CANN, D. E. 'Regulation, pluralism, and religious market structure', *Rationality and Society*, 4 (1992),

CLARK, ELMER. *The Small Sects in America*, Revised edition (New York, NY: Abingdon-Cokesbury Press, 1949).

DAVIDMAN, LYNN. *Tradition in a Rootless World: Women Turn to Orthodox Judaism* (Berkeley, CA: University of California Press, 1991).

DAVIS, DEREK. 'The Courts and the Constitutional meaning of "religion"', in J. E. Wood, Jr. and D. Davis (eds.), *The Role of Government in Monitoring and Regulating Religion in Public Life* (Waco, TX: J. M. Dawson Institute of Church–State Studies, Baylor University, 1993).

DEMERATH, N. Jay III. 'Religious capital and capital religions', *Daedalus* (Summer 1991).

DURKHEIM, EMILE. *The Elementary Forms of Religious Life*, trans. K. E. Fields (New York, NY: The Free Press, 1995).

DWORKIN, RONALD. *Life's Dominion* (New York, NY: Alfred A. Knopf, 1993).

EGERTON, JOHN. *The Americanization of Dixie* (New York, NY: Harper's Magazine Press, 1974).

ELLWOOD, ROBERT. 'Emergent religion in America: An historical perspective', in J. Needleman and G. Baker (eds.), *Understanding the New Religions* (New York, NY: Seabury, 1978).

EMERSON, RALPH WALDO. *Collected Works*, Vol. 2 (Boston, MA: Houghton Mifflin, 1865).

ESKRIDGE, WILLIAM N., Jr. *The Case for Same-Sex Marriage* (New York, NY: Free Press, 1996).

FERRE, A. METHOL. 'Editorial', *Nexo* (September 1987).

FINKE, ROGER, and IANNACCONE, LAURENCE. 'Supply-side explanations for religious change', *Annals of the American Academy of Political and Social Science (Religion in the Nineties)*, 527 (May 1993).

—— and STARK, RODNEY. 'How the upstart sects won America: 1776–1850', *Journal for the Scientific Study of Religion*, 28/1 (1989).

—— —— *The Churching of America, 1776–1990.* (New Brunswick, NJ: Rutger's University Press, 1992).

FLOWERS, R. *That Godless Court?* (Louisville, KY: Westminster John Knox Press, 1994).

FOLEY, EDWARD B. 'Political Liberalism and Establishment Clause Jurisprudence', *Case Western Reserve Law Review*, 43 (1993).

FRANCIS, JOHN G. 'The evolving regulatory structure of European church–state relations', *Journal of Church and State*, 34 (1992).

FRANKEL, MARVIN E. *Faith and Freedom* (New York, NY: Hill and Wang, 1992).

GALANTER, MARC. 'Religious Freedoms in the United States: A Turning Point?' *Wisconsin Law Review*, 1966: 2 (1966).

GANS, HERBERT. 'American Jewry: Present and future', *Commentary*, 22 (May–June 1956).

GERASSI, M. NAVARRO. 'Argentine nationalism of the right', *Studies in Comparative International Development*, 1 (1966).

GLENDON, MARY ANN. *The New Family and the New Property* (Toronto: Butterworths, 1981).

GLOCK, CHARLES, and WUTHNOW, ROBERT. 'Departures from conventional religion', in R. Wuthnow (ed.), *The Religious Dimension* (New York, NY: Academic Press, 1979).

GORDON, MILTON. *Assimilation in American Life* (New York, NY: Oxford University Press, 1964).

GREELEY, ANDREW. *Why Can't They Be Like Us?* (New York, NY: E. P. Dutton & Co., 1971).

—— *Ethnicity in the United States* (New York, NY: John Wiley & Sons, 1974).

GREENAWALT, KENT. 'The Role of Religion in a Liberal Democracy', *Journal of Church and State* 35 (1993).

HAMMOND, PHILLIP E. *The Campus Clergyman* (New York, NY: Basic Books, 1966).

—— 'The sociology of American civil religion', *Sociological Analysis*, 37/2 (1976).

—— 'The courts and secular humanism: How to misinterpret church/state issues', *Society*, 21/4 (1984).

—— *The Protestant Presence in Twentieth-Century America: Religion and Political Culture* (Albany, NY: State University of New York Press, 1992).

—— *Religion and Personal Autonomy: The Third Disestablishment* (Columbia, SC: University of South Carolina Press, 1992).

HAMMOND, PHILLIP E. 'Of churches, courts, and moral order', in J. R. Stone (ed.), *The Craft of Religious Studies* (New York, NY: St. Martin's Press, 1998).

—— *With Liberty for All* (Louisville, KY: Westminster John Knox Press, 1998).

—— and MACHACEK, DAVID W. *Soka Gakkai in America: Accommodation and Conversion* (Oxford: Oxford University Press, 1999).

HANDY, ROBERT. *A Christian America*, 2nd edition (New York, NY: Oxford University Press, 1984).

HANSEN, M. L. 'The problem of the third generation immigrant', *Commentary*, 14 (1962).

HARTLEY, L. H. 'Popular mission philosophies and denominational mission policy', In C. Jacquet (ed.), *Yearbook of American and Canadian Churches, 1988* (Nashville TN: Abingdon Press, 1987).

HEILMAN, SAMUEL, and COHEN, STEVEN. *Cosmopolitans & Parochials: Modern Orthodox Jews in America* (Chicago, IL: University of Chicago Press, 1989).

HERBERG, WILL. *Protestant, Catholic, Jew* (Garden City, NY: Doubleday Anchor, 1960).

HEXHAM, IRVING, and POEWE, KARLA. *New Religions as Global Cultures* (Denver, CO: Westview, 1997).

HOCKING, WILLIAM ERNEST. *Re-Thinking Missions: A Laymen's Inquiry After One Hundred Years* (New York and London: Harper and Brothers Publisher, 1932).

HUIGENS, KAREN. 'Science, Freedom of Conscience and the Establishment Clause', *University of Puget Sound Law Review*, 13 (1989).

HUTCHISON, WILLIAM R. *Errand to the World* (Chicago, IL: University of Chicago Press, 1987).

HUNTER, JAMES D. *Culture Wars* (New York, NY: Basic Books, 1991).

IANNACCONE, LAURENCE R. 'The Consequences of Religious Market Structure', *Rationality and Society*, 3 (1991).

INGBER, STANLEY. 'Religion or Ideology: A Needed Clarification of the Religion Clauses', *Stanford Law Review*, 41 (1989).

JOHNSON, BENTON. 'A sociological perspective on the new religions', In T. Robbins and D. Anthony (eds.), *In Gods We Trust* (New Brunswick, NJ: Transaction Books, 1981).

—— and SHIBLEY, MARK A. 'How new is the new Christian right?' in J. K. Hadden and A. Shupe (eds.), *Secularization and Fundamentalism Reconsidered* (New York, NY: Paragon Press, 1989).

KELLEY, DEAN. *Why Conservative Churches Are Growing* (New York, NY: Harper & Row, 1972).

—— (ed.). *Government Intervention in Religious Affairs* (New York, NY: The Pilgrim Press, 1982).

KERRINE, T., and NEUHAUS, RICHARD J. 'Mediating structures: A paradigm for democratic pluralism', *The Annals of the American Academy of Political and Social Science*, 446 (1979).

KEYES, CHARLES F. 'The dialectics of ethnic change', In C. F. Keyes (ed.), *Ethnic Change* (Seattle, WA: University of Washington, 1981).

KITANO, H. H., et *al.* 'Asian American interracial marriage', *Journal of Marriage and Family*, 46 (1984).

KOSMIN, BARRY A., and LACHMAN, SEYMOUR P. *One Nation under God : Religion in Contemporary American Society* (New York, NY: Harmony Books, 1993).

LAZARSFELD, PAUL. 'Problems in methodology', in R. K. Merton (ed.), *Sociology Today* (New York, NY: Basic Books, 1958).

——*The Sociology of Empirical Social Research* (Boston, MA: Allyn and Bacon, 1972).

LEONARD, BILL. *God's Last and Only Hope: The Fragmentation of the Southern Baptist Convention* (Grand Rapids, MI: W. B. Eerdmans, 1990).

LERNER, RALPH. 'Believers and the Founders' Constitution', *This World*, 26 (1989).

LIEBERSON, STANLEY. *Language and Ethnic Relations in Canada* (New York, NY: Wiley, 1970).

LUCKMANN, THOMAS. *The Invisible Religion* (New York, NY: Macmillan, 1967).

MALBIN, MICHAEL J. *Religion and Politics: The Intentions of the Authors of the First Amendment* (Washington DC: American Enterprise Institute, 1978).

MARTY, MARTIN. 'Ethnicity: The skeleton of religion in America', *Church History*, 41 (1972).

MAUSS, ARMAND. *The Angel and the Beehive* (Urbana, IL: University of Illinois Press, 1994).

MAYER, EGON. *Love and Tradition: Marriage between Jews and Christians* (New York, NY: Plenum Press, 1985).

McGUIRE, MEREDITH. *Religion: The Social Context* (Belmont, CA: Wadsworth, 1987).

McLOUGHLIN, WILLIAM G. *Revivals, Awakenings, and Reform* (Chicago, IL: University of Chicago Press, 1978).

McNAMARA, PATRICK. *Conscience First, Tradition Second* (Albany, NY: State University of New York Press, 1991).

MEDCALF, LINDA. *Law and Identity: Lawyers, Native Americans, and Legal Practice* (Beverly Hills, CA: Sage Publications, 1978).

MEDHURST, KENNETH, and MOYER, GEORGE. *Church and Politics in a Secular Age* (Oxford: Clarendon Press, 1988).

MELTON, J. GORDON. *The Encyclopedic Handbook of Cults in America* (New York, NY: Garland Publishers, 1986).

——*Encyclopedia of American Religions*, 4th edition (Detroit MI: Gale Research, 1993).

MILLER, RANDALL M., and MARZIK, THOMAS D. (eds.), *Immigrants and Religion in Urban America* (Philadelphia, PA: Temple University Press, 1977).

MOEHLMAN, CONRAD H. *The American Constitutions and Religion* (Beme, IN: privately printed, 1938).

MOL, HANS (ed.). *Identity and Religion* (Beverly Hills, CA: Sage Publications, 1978).

MOSKOS, CHARLES C., Jr. *Greek Americans* (Englewood Cliffs, NJ: Prentice-Hall, 1980).

NEUHAUS, RICHARD JOHN. *The Naked Public Square* (Grand Rapids, MI: William B. Eerdmans, 1984).

NICHOLS, J. BRUCE. *The Uneasy Alliance* (New York, NY: Oxford University Press, 1988).

NIEBUHR, H. RICHARD. *The Social Sources of Denominationalism* (New York, NY: H. Holt and Company, 1929).

NISBET, ROBERT. *The Quest for Community* (New York, NY: Oxford University Press, 1953).

NOVAK, MICHAEL. *The Rise of the Unmeltable Ethnics* (New York, NY: The MacMillan Company, 1971).

OLSON, JAMES S. *The Ethnic Dimension in American History* (New York, NY: St. Martin's Press, 1979).

PADGETT, DEBORAH. 'Symbolic ethnicity and patterns of ethnic identity assertion in American-born Serbs', *Ethnic Groups*, 3 (1980).

PARSONS, TALCOTT. 'Christianity and modern industrial society', in E. A. Tiryakian (ed.), *Sociology Theory, Values, and Sociological Change* (New York, NY: The Free Press, 1963).

PITCHER, ALVIN W. 'The politics of mass society: Significance for the churches', In D. B. Robertson (ed.), *Voluntary Associations* (Richmond: John Knox Press, 1966).

POPPER, KARL. *The Logic of Scientific Discovery*, Revised Edition (London: Hutchinson, 1968).

PRICE, CHARLES A. *Southern Europeans in Australia* (Melbourne: Oxford University Press, 1963).

REITZ, JEFFERY. *The Survival of Ethnic Groups* (Toronto: McGraw-Hill Ryerson, 1980).

RICHARDS, DAVID A. J. *Toleration and the Constitution* (New York, NY: Oxford University Press, 1986).

——*Conscience and the Constitution* (Princeton, NJ: Princeton University Press, 1993).

ROBBINS, THOMAS. *Cults, Converts and Charisma: The Sociology of New Religious Movements* (London: Sage, 1988).

——and ANTHONY, DICK. 'Cults, brainwashing, and counter-subversion', *The Annals of the American Academy of Political and Social Science*, 446 (1979).

————and RICHARDSON, JAMES T. 'Theory and research on today's new religions', *Sociological Analysis*, 39 (1978).

ROBERTS, KEITH. *Religion in Sociological Perspective* (Belmont, CA: Wadsworth, 1990).

ROBERTSON, ROLAND. 'The sacred and the world system', in P. Hammond (ed.), *The Sacred in a Secular Age* (Berkeley, CA: University of California Press, 1985)

——'Church–state relations and the world system', in T. Robbins and R. Robertson (eds.), *Church–State Relations* (New Brunswick, NJ: Transaction, Inc., 1987).

——and CHIRICO, J. 'Humanity, globalization, and worldwide religious resurgence', *Sociological Analysis*, 46/3 (1985).

ROOF, WADE CLARK. *Commitment and Community* (New York, NY: Elsevier, 1978).

——and McKinney, William. *American Mainline Religion: Its Changing Shape and Future* (New Brunswick, NJ: Rutger's, 1987).

——Carroll, Jackson, and Roozen, David (eds.). *The Postwar Generation and Religious Establishments* (Boulder, CO: Westview Press, 1995).

Sandberg, Neil C. *Ethnic Identity and Assimilation: The Polish American Community* (New York, NY: Praeger, 1974).

Schlesinger, Arthur Jr. 'The missionary enterprise and theories of imperialism', in J. K. Fairbank (ed.), *The Missionary Enterprise in China and America* (Cambridge, MA: Harvard University Press, 1974).

Shedd, Clarence P. *The Church Follows its Students* (New Haven, CT: Yale University Press, 1938).

Sherwood, Carlton. *Inquisition* (Washington, DC: Regnerey Gateway, 1991).

Shibley, Mark. *Resurgent Evangelicalism in the United States: Mapping Cultural Change since 1970* (Columbia, SC: University of South Carolina Press, 1996).

Shupe, Jr., A., and Bromley, David, *The New Vigilantes* (Beverly Hills, CA: Sage Publications, 1980).

Silletta, Alfredo. *Las Sectas Invaden la Argentina* (Buenos Aires: Editorial Contrapunto, 1987).

Smith, P. 'Anglo-American religion and hegemonic change in the world system, c. 1870–1980', *British Journal of Sociology*, 37 (1986).

Smith, Timothy. 'Religion and ethnicity in America', *American Historical Review*, 83 (1978).

——'Religion', In S. Thernstrom, *et al.* (eds.), *Harvard Encyclopedia of American Ethnic Groups* (Boston, MA: Belknap Press, 1980).

Stanley, Brian. ' "Commerce and Christianity": Providence theory, the missionary movement, and the imperialism of free trade', *The Historical Journal*, 26 (1983).

Stark, Rodney, and Bainbridge, William Sims. 'Churches, sects, and cults: Preliminary concepts for a theory of religious movements', *Journal for the Scientific Study of Religion*, 18 (1979).

————*The Future of Religion: Secularization, Revival, and Cult Formation* (Berkeley, CA: University of California Press, 1985).

——and Glock, Charles Y. *American Piety* (Berkeley, CA: University of California Press, 1968).

——and Roberts, Lynne. 'The arithmetic of social movements', *Sociological Analysis*, 4 (1982).

Steinberg, Stephen. *The Ethnic Myth* (New York, NY: Atheneum, 1981).

Stout, Harry. 'Ethnicity: The vital center of religion in America', *Ethnicity*, 2 (1975).

Streiker, Lowell D., and Strober, Gerald S. *Religion and the New Majority* (New York, NY: Association Press, 1972).

Sullivan, Andrew. *Virtually Normal* (New York, NY: Alfred A. Knopf, 1995).

Swatos, William. 'Beyond denominationalism', *Journal for the Scientific Study of Religion*, 20 (1981).

——*Into Denominationalism: The Anglican Metamorphosis* (Society for the Scientific Study of Religion Monograph Series, No. 2, 1979).

THOMAS, JOHN L. 'The factor of religion in the selection of marriage mates', *American Sociological Review*, 16 (1951).

TINLIN, PAUL, and BLUMHOFER, EDITH. 'Decade of decline or harvest? Dilemmas of the Assemblies of God', *Christian Century*, 108/21 (1991).

TIPTON, STEVEN. 'The moral logic of alternative religions', in M. Douglas and S. Tipton (eds.), *Religion in America* (Boston, MA: Beacon Press, 1983).

TOCQUEVILLE, ALEXIS DE. *Democracy in America*, G. Lawrence (trans.) (Garden City, NY: Doubleday Anchor, 1969).

UROFSKY, MELVIN. *Letting Go: Death, Dying, and the Law* (New York, NY: Charles Scribner's Sons, 1993).

VERGHESE, FR. P. 'A sacramental humanism', *Christian Century*, 87 (September 1970).

WALLIS, ROY. 'Ideology, authority, and the development of cultic movements', *Social Research*, 41 (1975).

——and BRUCE, STEVEN. 'The Stark–Bainbridge Theory of Religion: A Critical Analysis and Counter Proposals', *Sociological Analysis*, 45 (1984).

WARNER, R. STEPHEN. 'Work in progress toward a new paradigm for the sociological study of religion in the United States', *American Journal of Sociology*, 98/5 (1993).

WASHINGTON, JAMES. 'The crisis in the sanctity of conscience in American jurisprudence', *DePaul Law Review*, 42 (1992).

WENZ, PETER. *Abortion Rights as Religious Freedom* (Philadelphia, PA: Temple University Press, 1992).

WILLS, GARRY. *Under God: Religion and American Politics* (New York, NY: Simon and Schuster, 1990).

WILSON, BRYAN. *Religion in Secular Society* (London: Watts, 1966).

——'The secularization debate', *Encounter*, 45 (1975).

——*Contemporary Transformations of Religion* (Oxford: Oxford University Press, 1976).

——'The Return of the Sacred', *Journal for the Scientific Study of Religion*, 18 (1979).

——*Religion in Sociological Perspective* (Oxford: Oxford University Press, 1982).

——'Secularization: The inherited model', in P .E. Hammond (ed.), *The Sacred in a Secular Age* (Berkeley and Los Angeles, CA: University of California Press, 1985).

——*The Social Dimensions of Sectarianism* (Oxford: Clarendon Press, 1990).

——and DOBBELAERE, KAREL. A *Time to Chant: The Soka Gakkai Buddhists in Britain* (Oxford: Oxford University Press, 1994).

WUTHNOW, ROBERT. 'Religious movements and the transition in world order', in J. Needleman and G. Baker (eds.), *Understanding the New Religions* (New York, NY: Seabury, 1978).

—— 'World order and religious movements', in A. Bergesen (ed.), *Studies of the Modern World System* (New York, NY: Academic Press, 1980).

——*Meaning and Moral Order* (Berkeley, CA: University of California Press, 1987).

——'America's legitimating myths: Continuity and crisis', in T. Boswell and A. Bergesen (eds.), *America's Changing Role in the World System* (New York, NY: Praeger, 1987).

—— *The Restructuring of American Religion* (Princeton, NY: Princeton University Press, 1988).

YINGER, J. MILTON. *The Scientific Study of Religion* (New York, NY: Macmillan, 1970).

——*Countercultures: The Promise and Peril of a World Turned Upside Down* (New York, NY: Free Press, 1982).

INDEX